CANADA *HAS* A FUTURE

S0-AXV-777

CANADA HAS A FUTURE

Prepared for the Hudson Institute of Canada
by Marie-Josée Drouin and B. Bruce-Briggs
Preface by Herman Kahn

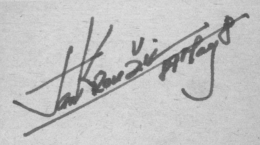

McClelland and Stewart

Copyright ©1978 by McClelland and Stewart Limited

Reprinted 1979

All Rights Reserved

The Canadian Publishers
McClelland and Stewart Limited
25 Hollinger Road
Toronto M4B 3G2

CANADIAN CATALOGUING IN PUBLICATION DATA

Drouin, Marie Josée.
  Canada has a future

Includes index.

ISBN 0-7710-2892-X bd.   ISBN 0-7710-2893-8 pa.

1. Canada.   2. Twentieth century — forecasts.
I. Bruce-Briggs, B.   II. Title.

FC600.D76   971.06'44   C78-001003-5
F1034.2.D76

Manufactured in Canada by Webcom Limited

It may be observed that provinces, amid the vicissitudes to which they are subject, pass from order into confusion, and afterward recur to a state of order again; for the nature of mundane affairs not allowing them to continue in an even course, when they have arrived at their greatest perfection, they soon begin to decline. In the same manner, having been reduced by disorder and sunk to their utmost state of depression, unable to descend lower, they, of necessity, reascend; and thus from good they gradually decline to evil, valour produces peace; peace, repose; repose, disorder; disorder, ruin; so from disorder order springs; from order virtue, and from this glory and good fortune.

Niccolò Machiavelli, *Florentine History.*

If some countries have too much history, we have too much geography.

William Lyon Mackenzie King

Contents

Acknowledgements

We would like first to express our gratitude to those who have contributed generously to the research that has made this book possible: L'Industrielle Compagnie d'Assurance sur la Vie, Nordair, Xerox of Canada Ltd., General Motors, Canadian National, Northern Telecom, Noranda Mines Ltd.

At the Institute, the authors have been most notably aided in their work by the research and analysis of John Kettle, William Brown, Colin Gray, Jane Newitt, and Michael Sherman. In addition, special thanks are owed to Harald Malmgren, Ralph Boston, Owen Anderson, and, of course, to our summer intern, Christina Caron.

This book has benefited from the insights of a number of Canadians throughout the country, who agreed to spend time with us discussing various issues. We will not attempt to list all of them, lest we inadvertently bypass someone; but we do want to thank all for their co-operation.

To the distinguished members of our Board of Directors, we would like to express our appreciation for their comments. We would like to express particular gratitude for written comments on chapter five by Douglas Fullerton and on chapter seven by Arnold Smith. We also want to acknowledge our debt to Antal Deutsch and Yvan Allaire for reading and commenting on earlier versions or portions of the manuscript.

We would like also to acknowledge the tireless efforts of Lynette Griffiths, who typed the manuscript, and Kathryn Savoy, who has drawn the graphics.

All the foregoing people contributed to making this book possible; but we, the authors, bear sole responsibility for facts, opinions, and views contained in the final text.

Introduction
by Arnold Cantwell Smith
Chairman of the Board

Given man's technological progress and consequent growing interdependence, it is not surprising that mankind faces challenges and problems on the global scale which are probably greater than any in our history. But it is ironic that Canada, one of the most affluent and freest countries on earth, should be facing domestic problems which many believe raise questions about its very cohesion. The resolution of these problems will require, above all, a sense of proportion.

This book is the result of over a year's research carried out by the Hudson Institute of Canada, an independent, non-profit-seeking, policy research organization with headquarters in Montreal. The Hudson Institute of Canada is an independent and self-financing affiliate of the Hudson Institute (U.S.A.) and is directed by its own board of directors.*

Formal liaison with the Hudson Institute (U.S.A.) is maintained through reciprocal board membership, the chairman of each organization sitting on the board of the other. In addition to the Canadian affiliate, Hudson Institute (U.S.A.) has affiliated organizations in Paris and Tokyo.

Ongoing contacts and exchange between these organizations make it possible for studies carried out by any of the Hudson affiliates to be set in a broad international context, a perspective too often lacking in studies of national development.

Canada Has a Future is the first of a series of reports being prepared by the Hudson Institute of Canada on the crucial issues of Canada's economic, social, and political future. The Institute should very soon complete a second study on the future of Quebec, and our 1978-79 research

* A list of the members of this Board appears at the end of the book.

program calls for a number of provincial studies with an emphasis on interactions between Canada's various regions.

The main purpose of this book therefore is to open up discussion, rather than to attempt to settle it. This report is not an exhaustive set of conjectures about every aspect of Canadian life, nor is it an attempt to predict any particular outcome. No one can pretend to predict with certainty those events or turning points that shape the future of nations. These are constrained by various considerations and contexts: of values, of will, of resources, of basic trends in the society, economy, and polity. This book is an effort to outline those constraints of social and political choice with which Canada may have to deal in the next decade. Hudson of Canada's hope is to provide concerned and interested Canadians with a framework for assessing alternative possible futures, and thus for intelligent planning and decision-making.

I would like to take this opportunity to express my deepest gratitude to those companies who have so generously contributed to this endeavour.

It should be emphasized that although the Board of Trustees commends the efforts of the research team that participated in preparing this report, the opinions expressed in the report are those of the authors and should not be construed as necessarily being the views of the Board of Trustees or the sponsors. Neither group pretends to unanimity. The Board of Trustees is happy to see the Institute contributing so actively to the debate on our national choices but final responsibility for the material contained in this book must rest on the individual authors.

Preface
by Herman Kahn

This report on Canada's prospects is the fourth book-length study of a national future by the affiliated Hudson organizations. The first, of Japan (published in 1970, but a similar report appeared in 1965), was characterized by many critics as blindly optimistic; nevertheless, almost all its favourable forecasts have been borne out by events, while only some of its negative ones proved faulty. Hudson Europe's study of the future of France was also optimistic, so much so that its authors were accused of being propagandists for the then-government; but its projections have also stood up well, including the suggestions that a number of problems might arise. The next Hudson Europe study, of Great Britain in 1974, painted a dismal picture of that country's prospects which, unfortunately, has been accurate.

This is the first published Hudson study of Canada's future. The study relies on a methodology and a perspective typical of many Hudson studies:

1. the extensive use of basic alternative future scenarios;
2. the systematic use of other scenarios, historical analogies, personal experiences, and other information from a variety of sources;
3. the inclusion in these scenarios of useful numerical data, scientifically established information, and acceptable theory; and
4. the setting of the whole study in a pervasive historical and international context.

Thus, not only is the study based on new and creative insights, but also new is the attempt to "put it all together," to synthesize and meld the literary, empirical, qualitative, and discursive with the analytical, theoretical, scientific, and quantitative.

The first, and perhaps most important comment to make on methodology is that although futures studies try to be as predictive as possible, in all cases the fundamental caveat, "other things being equal," must hold. In addition, Hudson's method of extrapolation necessarily involves much uncertainty, notably in the trends that we selected as important. Hudson therefore does not normally claim to be reliably predictive in its speculation. The major purpose of this study is in some ways less to predict accurately and in detail than to create reasonable and useful images of the future, images which will be helpful in the planning process.

However, one reason for concentrating on surprise-free contexts and scenarios is that surprising things can happen in an incredibly large number of ways. Thus, the analyst is faced with the almost impossible task of trying to decide which surprises deserve attention. A few surprises were therefore selected as an excursion to see what might happen or because they seemed particularly interesting. But in terms of taking things seriously, almost by definition, these excursions have to be "not unsurprising" or at least "not too surprising." Reasonable and prudent people, almost by definition, will not take surprising events and trends seriously, unless the surprises have a great significance if they nevertheless occur (and often not even then, if their probability seems very low).

Much use is made of context or canonical scenarios, i.e. hypothetical sequences of future events and future trends which supply either a context or framework for more detailed discussions or for comparison with other contexts. The term "canonical" indicates that the scenarios are standardized or normalized, and then named in a way which makes them stand for an explicit set of ideas or concepts that form a basic package or unit of analysis.

If I had to characterize Hudson Canada's forecast in a word, I might say, "so-so." The study team found Canada's future neither extraordinarily bright nor remarkably dim. Although many of the current popular doom-sayers and more pessimistic Canadians will doubtless consider a so-so future naively sanguine, my personal feeling is that it is unfortunate, indeed disgraceful, that Canada should not have an optimistic image of the future (with many benefits and pleasures that come from having such an image). Canadians are living in a veritable wonderland, and historically have been an energetic, resourceful, and noble-spirited people with rich and diverse cultural tradition. The emergence of the western provinces and Quebec as dynamic regions has clearly stimulated new problems, yet those could result in opportunities and a creative "challenge and response." But Canadians increasingly do not seem to believe in positive perspectives. Rather than having a high-morale, invigorating image of the future, they share, mostly with less reason, the general malaise which now characterizes the West and Japan.*

Let us consider this malaise issue further. The term has the connotation of general weakness, of not feeling well, of being run down (but not seriously so), and perhaps becoming seriously ill because the malaise may become chronic or lead to worse problems. Indeed, the general feeling of malaise is now pervasive enough and has been felt long enough to be widely perceived as a serious problem with its own self-generating momentum; it may increasingly become a self-fulfilling prophecy.

At a 1977 Hudson Institute conference held in London on the question, "Is There a European Malaise? If so, What and Why?" we found a surprising consensus that the following issues were plaguing much of Western Europe:

CLEARLY CENTRAL ISSUES
1. Continued stagflation: general feeling of helplessness, even hopelessness;
2. Annual OPEC price-setting drama and even greater feeling of helplessness, and sometimes of impotent fury (often, self-contempt at the weakness of the industrialized world);
3. Upper middle class (especially new class) malaise, alienation, and "decline"; subsequent "revolt against economic growth," e.g., Club of Rome and "Small Is Beautiful" movements;
4. Growing fear that science and technology are out of control and/or are increasingly hostile to a humane society;
5. Continued weakness and lack of creativity of European political leadership, including a loss of legitimacy and assurance; general public contempt for politicians; worse in some countries than others;
6. "Poverty of affluence": revolution of rising entitlements, excessive welfare state, excessive disputes about "priorities"; many bad choices by governments, much disillusionment, failed expectations, and morale-eroding disappointments;
7. Other limits to growth, including anti-industrialism, anti-technol-

---

* Some Canadians might well feel that a future which is neither remarkably bright nor dim is exactly what they are looking for. After all, there is a lot of wisdom in the Chinese and Italian curse, "May your children live in interesting times." And another aphorism holds, "Happy is the country whose annals are few," i.e., whose history is dull. At this point, barring a breakup which I still judge to be unlikely, Canada does not have such a bad future; but because of the low morale associated with this "so-so" future, I feel that Canada may also be trouble-prone, and perhaps even crisis-prone. This is particularly true if troubling issues are allowed, unnecessarily, to grow to high proportions.

13

ogy, and anti-GNP attitudes, along with the rise of the new issues of environment, ecology, and "quality of life" vs. standard of living (all of which usually emphasize how badly the country is doing and/or the basic corruptness or incompetence of the system).

OTHER GOVERNMENTAL ISSUES

1. No inspiring "image of the future"; in particular no shared concept of "European integration" or "European future," increasing lack of trust and confidence among various European countries with each other and with U.S.;
2. European sense of being a pawn between two superpowers and a passive actor on the international stage; seeming inability of "Europe" or EEC to respond effectively to "outside" events or initiatives;
3. Excessive power of most European unions combined with excessively restrictive and expensive labour legislation;
4. Heavy income taxation in upper brackets of Atlantic ex-Protestant countries.

OTHER ECONOMIC ISSUES

1. Balance-of-payments troubles caused by OPEC or structural reasons may soon lead to third world or other cutback in imports, and perhaps a wave of financial crises;
2. Apparent lack of profitability (or excessive risk) for much proposed new long-term investment;
3. Other "breakdown of world trade": the growth of protectionist sentiments; growing likelihood (or at least fear) of "beggar thy neighbour" policies; a failure of world trade to revive domestic growth.
4. Failure to recognize economic success, e.g., tendency to take achievements for granted and see inevitable costs as intolerable;
5. Guilt about economic success or even defining such success as failure (e.g., treating remaining injustices, inequities, and inequalities as intolerable or as a regression);
6. Finally the failure of economic success. This is in part the poverty of affluence and the "disillusionment" of the upper middle class, but even more an issue of meaning and purpose, of discontent and boredom, and of an absence of structure, constraints, and reality testing.

MISCELLANEOUS OR COMPLEX ISSUES

1. Increase, in many countries, of crime and drug use, particularly among the young;
2. Emerging race issues in U.K., and "guest worker" issues elsewhere;
3. An erosion of Communist morale and unity in Eastern Europe turns out to raise mostly unpleasant and potentially dangerous or humiliating issues;
4. Similarly, Euro-Communism, i.e., the current apparent movement of the left to the centre–appears to many as more menacing than beneficial;
5. Examples of U.K., Italy, Denmark as possible leading edge of general economic breakdown or eroding economy;
6. Possible additional examples of Belgium, Netherlands, and Sweden as excessive welfare states;
7. Continued (if decreasing) independence of NATO and of European science, technology, and business on U.S.; and loss of prestige by U.S. (partly regained in 1977); increase in Soviet military power and relatively slow erosion (as compared to similar phenomena in the West) of Soviet morale and unity;
8. And perhaps a moderate but general feeling of a decline in morality, traditional standards, and religion.

While these problems do not all apply to Canada, most Canadians will agree that most of them do, particularly if some obvious substitutions are made: e.g., the issue of Quebec separation could be thought of as a much more critical and intense version of European integration, and the discontent in the Western provinces is also comparable.

Thus, one of the most interesting things about this Canadian study is that so much of it is concerned with issues which are not specific to Canada, but are characteristic of almost all non-Communist industrialized nations, and many Communist nations as well. Many issues exist which are of course relatively specific to Canada: e.g., certain ethnic strains, regional tensions, federal-provincial relationships, linguistic conflicts, and the overwhelming presence of the United States. Concern over having a genuine national identity, which is taken for granted in most countries, is remarkably characteristic of Canada in the last generation. And, of course, the threat of Quebec separation has accelerated this concern. However, Canada does not have an overwhelming resource problem; Canadian cities operate well on the whole; the educational and welfare systems function not too badly; crime is not an intensely serious problem; and many other aspects of the society operate quite well.

Canada, as elsewhere, has a widespread lack of confidence in leadership—economic and intellectual, as well as political. Much of the current malaise is of course related to economic issues; thus much of the economic part of the malaise can be summed up in the term "stagflation."

Stagflation is basically a post-Second World War phenomenon, which was gradually created over the last ten to fifteen years by forces built into the system. These forces probably peaked in 1973 when Gross World Product grew by almost 7 per cent (about 40 per cent more than normal), and the oil shock occurred. This combination created an almost intolerable situation, though the oil shock was much less important than the slow growth of a variety of forces, trends, and accidental factors, the most important of which are listed below.

1. Excess creation of money and bad management of subsequent inflation:

   i. U.S. financial policies from 1969 to 1973 which increased U.S. dollar supply directly and also sent an unwanted $60 billion overseas (with corresponding increases in world liquidity);
   ii. Creation and growth of an uncontrolled Euro-dollar market (spurred by U.S. lending controls);
   iii. "Dumping" of U.S. dollars in 1972 and 1973 by the Japanese;
   iv. "Runaway" speculation and speculative practices by many banks and businesses;
   v. Decline of working capital in U.S. and U.K. because of taxation and dividends paid out of illusory inventory profits and understated depreciation allowances;
   vi. Other startling increase in world liquidity.

2. Pressure on capacity and resources:

   i. Growth in gross world product from mid/late 1972 to mid/late 1973 almost 50 per cent above normal;
   ii. But growing difficulties to investment in and other expansion of capacity, particularly of raw materials:
      a. Many aspects of the environmental movement (e.g. Alaska pipelines);
      b. Such irrational policies as U.S. keeping the price of natural gas very low;
      c. "Limits to growth" propaganda caused worldwide lack of confidence and strengthened "localism" and other opposition to growth;
      d. New class hostility to growth, particularly among upper middle

class elites and intellectuals in Japan and the Atlantic Protestant Culture;
  e. Surge of nationalism with regard to raw materials in Canada, Australia, and Third World.

3. Various pressures on food prices in 1973 including:
  i. A withdrawal in 1972 by U.S., Canada, and Australia of much land from food production in order to keep prices from dropping;
  ii. Bad weather in a number of places around the world causing bad crops;
  iii. A temporary decline in anchovy fishing off Peru;
  iv. A shift to meat by the Soviet Union and a willingness to buy foreign grain (actually this is more general than just the Soviet Union);
  v. An inadequate expansion of fertilizer industry due to a "backlash" from the overexpansion in the mid/late sixties;
  vi. A decision by the Indian government in 1969 to shift emphasis from food production to industrialization;
  vii. Relative short-term inelasticity of both supply and demand of food.

4. The energy crisis which contained a number of accidental elements, and the relative (only food and energy have these characteristics) short-term inelasticity of both supply and demand of energy.

5. Some other contributions came from:
  i.   A general fear of depression, a general willingness to accept inflationary policies, a general and increasing distrust in fiat currencies and a general acceptance and anticipation of inflation;
  ii. In the U.S. a combination of the Vietnamese War with great pressure to expand welfare and city programs;
  iii. The "poverty of affluence" in Western Europe;
  iv. The existence of extremely weak governments almost everywhere;
  v.   Structural changes in U.S., Canadian, and European economies which cause unemployment and excess capacity to have a lessened pressure on prices and wages.

In almost all countries a great deal of the blame for stagflation is placed on OPEC and oil. While the effect of the sharp increases in energy prices and of the huge flow of financial resources to OPEC has indeed been a very serious and continuing problem, it is often much exaggerated. Perhaps equally important in terms of producing malaise is the disconcerting, humiliating, and, for some, frightening and demoralizing experience of watching the OPEC nations meet periodically to decide the fate of the rest of the world (especially since outsiders seem unable to influence these deliberations in any serious way). But in reality, stagflation stems from much more basic causes than OPEC. Indeed, the rise in oil prices was probably responsible for less than a quarter of the inflation that took place from 1973-75.

The solution to current stagflation is probably the exact opposite of that normally recommended for a Keynesian depression. According to the Keynesian system, almost any money that anyone spent in a depression was helpful; in a stagflation, however, the problem is to make business profitable again by making institutions, both private and public, more efficient and less wasteful. Incentives must be restored to reduce the cost of production, rather than increasing consumption or improving distribution. The issue is less of restoring demand than of cutting costs and risks so as to restore profitability and stable favourable expectations. Doing so requires a different way of thinking from that usually associated with recovery. Various regulation issues are particularly important here. Uncertainty vis-à-vis government policy and legislation has created a climate in which investors are extraordinarily cautious and reluctant to commit themselves to long-term investments. As mentioned in the report, it is increasingly important for business to feel it knows and can predict the "rules of the game" and increasing emphasis on "planning the government" (as opposed to government planning of the economy) are a necessary prerequisite to a recovery in long-term investment.

I should also comment on another inflationary force which is quite strong in Canada as well as in many other countries. Consider the effect of moderately strong unions. If an economy is completely static, people's income can only change if they upgrade their status. As they get older they may earn more because they are more skilful, more experienced, or have more seniority. Any additional increases must come out of redistribution or increased productivity. Let us now, in a first approximation, think of the increased productivity as being distributed more or less in proportion to the share people are already getting. This would imply that, if the population of earners were fixed, every income would go up in proportion to the average increase in the nation's productivity (in addition to any increases through a change in status). For such countries as Canada, productivity increases have been averaging between 2 and 4 per cent a year recently. Therefore across-the-board raises should be limited to between 2 and 4 per cent a year. To the extent that any union gets more than this, its members will be getting a larger share of the gross national product. This is not necessarily wrong, but it cannot go on indefinitely. Indeed, many Canadians believe that the process of increasing one's share by bargaining power has gone about as far as it can. But most unions insist on obtaining at least the increase in productivity of their industry, and strong unions want more. In a modern service economy, increases in manufacturing productivity are usually substantially higher than the average increase in productivity. In many industries "excessively" large wage increases cannot be maintained because they put the industry's wages out of line, and competition will therefore mount from other industries whose workers have not been able to get such big raises. This is true even if unions in some exceptional industries can get and maintain increases without regard to the competitive wage situation. This has been particularly true of construction unions, strongly organized industrial unions, and, most important under modern democratic conditions, transportation, communications, municipal teachers, and other governmental unions. When unions cannot get such increases in their take-home pay they often are able to get them through fringe benefits, which sometimes have extraordinarily high costs to the employers (e.g., inability to lay off or reduce staff, or even fire undesirable workers), but are often of much less utility to most of the employees.*

This process of "excessive" gains in a minority – inordinate increases in some sectors and relatively large increases in other sectors – will cause problems if they are too much greater than the increase in *average* productivity. That is, under likely fiscal and monetary policies, the effect will spread through the economy and create inflationary pressures on other wages. And, when they do not spread, they result in serious economic distortions and increasing political animosities. In some countries, e.g. France, Italy, England, and Denmark, this process has gone so far as to threaten the political foundations of the state and the very existence of democratic procedures and institutions. While this prospect can be greatly exaggerated, and often is, it has become an extraordinarily important problem in many OECD countries, and threatens to become such a problem in Canada.

Democracy is not easy to practise because it requires that, at least part of the time, leaders be, by and large, responsible, self-disciplined, and prudent; furthermore the electorate should reinforce these qualities and possibilities or at least not destroy them either directly, by excessive pressures, or indirectly, by replacing responsible, self-disciplined and prudent leaders too often and for too long by the other kind.

Among the near-universal issues related to this are "poverty of

---

* E.g. Laid-off employees have lost the difference between their wages and unemployment insurance, but the employer who must keep redundant or incompetent or disruptive workers for years can suffer larger losses – and normally the employer cannot "tighten his belt" to make up for the loss.

affluence" and the "new class." By "poverty of affluence" we imply something like the following: imagine a relatively poor country where citizens demand more roads, more hospitals, more education, more money spent on protection of the environment, and so on. In almost all cases, the government's answer is straightforward and persuasive, "We do not have the money. There is no way to get the money. We can not afford it. No!" In most modern industrial countries this traditional response has simply not been credible, and correctly so, for the last decade or two–particularly if government was willing to "borrow now and pay later." Any claimant could then argue there was enough money to satisfy his urgent cause, indeed enough for almost all of the reasonable demands that were put forth with any force by almost any significant group. Of course, there is never enough money for immediate implementation of restricted to "reasonable levels" (however these are defined); and the government must argue, "Priorities must be set. Over the next decade or two we will do all these things that are being suggested or at least those that are reasonable. However, some claimants must wait their turn. Some programs will come early; some will come later."

Under modern political circumstances many groups get angrier at this "yes, but not now" answer than they would if simply rejected. Everybody understands when resources are very limited. It is quite different to be told, "You must wait in line behind other people," or that someone has set "arbitrary" limits (and all such limits appear arbitrary to the hostile) on the amount of borrowing. But someone must be in front just as someone must be in back. These issues of priorities are among the most intractable and difficult to analyse reasonably. It is even more difficult to get their analyses accepted, in part because they invariably contain arbitrary or dubious elements.

In many ways this issue of the poverty of affluence has become a dominating one. It interacts, of course, with the so-called "revolution of rising entitlements." People feel entitled to get more services, more subsidies, or even more direct transfer payments from the government. They not only feel morally entitled to these; proponents increasingly think of the expansion of such programs as almost an absolute good–indeed almost as a way of testing the moral worth and modernity of the country. But even though an affluent country can afford a high level of transfer payments, it cannot afford as much as is asked for, and in any case there will be growing objections from taxpayers and producers to this transfer of resources. (Actually, in the U.S. about 32 per cent of the GNP is spent or transferred by federal, state, and local governments, while in Canada the figure has reached 43 per cent. The U.S. figure will probably hold its own at least for the next four years; the Canadian proportion will probably grow.)

The situation is complicated by the excessively cautious (or even "puritanical") fiscal conservatives who have always argued (vehemently and unpersuasively) not only that almost any specific "luxury" is unnecessary, but also that the country or community is—or soon will be—living beyond its income and in dire danger of bankruptcy. These spokesmen usually only succeed in discrediting their cause and confusing the issue. Other observers are certain, again at almost any level of expenditure, to point out that income is not only ample, but will grow. They therefore argue that it is only reasonable and just to utilize these resources, at least for high-priority needs and perhaps to distribute the national income more fairly. In fact, in most countries Keynesian arguments will be cited to suggest that redistribution and/or spending are necessary for the economic and financial health of the economy. As argued earlier, I strongly feel that during a period of stagflation and anticipated inflation, this argument is most likely wrong.

It is quite difficult to prevent inflation in a "poverty of affluence" situation. Thus if a country has not been suffering from inflation—or at least most people are not anticipating an inflation—then the government is very tempted to increase the money supply and encourage a little inflation.

Governments gain in at least six ways from such an unanticipated inflation:

1. As recipient of seignieurage profits (can be considered as a debasement of currency or a tax on cash balances);
2. As a debtor and disburser of fixed payments (pensions, welfare, interest and principal on the national debt);
3. As a tax collector (brackets are moved upwards in real terms; understated depreciation allowances, and nominal inventory and capital gains result in taxable if illusory profits);
4. As an employer taking advantage of a lag in salaries and many other costs in keeping up with inflation;
5. As an advocate of full employment, high farm prices, etc.;
6. As a permissive umpire and bargainer and a supporter of satisfaction and contentment (e.g., can exploit money illusion), and a reluctant appeaser of squeaking wheels and strong or activist pressure groups.

The last five can reverse if the inflation is anticipated and this can create strong political pressure to control inflation.

Another important issue which weaves in and out of the Canada study involves what the authors call the "new class." As explained in the study,

21

the new class is a sub-group of what is generally thought of as the upper middle class. The group is basically intellectual, in that members of the new class often earn their living by the use of language skills, analytical skills, aesthetic skills, or the more academic professions, and are often removed from what can be thought of as direct contact with most mundane realities and pressures.

In most industrialized countries, many members of the "new class" have tended to have an increasingly ambivalent attitude towards further economic growth, i.e., to feel that such growth is as likely as not to lead to a decrease in their standard of living and quality of life. This perception can stem from relatively trivial, but still annoying trends such as overcrowding of recreational areas, too much traffic on roads, the absence of competent inexpensive services, or too many outsiders moving into their neighbourhoods; or the causes can be more serious, such as competition for the middle class for jobs or leadership, the distinction of neighbourhoods, the loss of perquisites or status and so on. In any case these people feel threatened by increased economic growth. They are usually ambivalent about the situation. While perfectly clear as to why they feel threatened and bothered, they are also aware of the many benefits they derive from economic growth, e.g., better jobs, more income, and increases in value of their property.

Many members of the new class generally do not understand that this fear more often reflects a class interest than the broader interests of much of society. Many tend to take the benefits of economic growth for granted or even claim to despise most these so-called "benefits," and thus often display very intense and actively hostile attitudes towards economic growth, a hostility which they feel arises solely out of having higher values, and moral sensitivity, and a greater degree of altruism and virtue than the rest of society. Many new class people thus believe that they are not "programmed" in the same way that the middle class and workers are. Indeed, they are usually convinced–as only a "true believer" can be–that their hostility to technology and growth reflects solely, and deeply, public spirit and public interest.

A very interesting recent book was *The Social Limits to Growth* written by Fred Hirsch, who might be characterized as a member of the new class. In my judgement, this study has considerable merit. However, it would be much better if the title were *Social Characteristics of Growth*, or *Why the Upper Middle Class Increasingly Dislikes Growth*, or even *Why the Upper Middle Class May Limit Growth Prematurely against the Wishes of the Rest of the Community.*

This book demonstrates, quite convincingly, how the upper middle class, and particularly the new class, can lose if economic growth continues. Professor Hirsch sometimes enormously exaggerates the intensity and importance of these losses; but he seldom overstates the irritation and frustration felt by many, at least among those in the new class. More important, he does not seem to realize that he is discussing a loss largely confined to a particular class, which is not characteristic of society as a whole. Thus, every new class loss is seen as a loss to the entire society. For example, he points out that having a good education no longer guarantees a good job; instead, one must now compete with children of the broad middle class who also are well educated. Obviously, this is good for the middle class, even if it is bad for the upper middle class.

Most important of all, Hirsch does not seem to understand that the person who climbs from middle class to upper middle class or from working class to middle class finds this to be an enormous improvement, even if he does not gain as much out of the transition as others did fifty years ago, and even if those who have already arrived lose a little as a result of lthe newcomers sharing in some of the spoils and in diluting the specialness of the status.

An anecdote illustrates this point. A couple who recently visited England were informed that a hundred years ago the average English middle class family had two or three live-in servants. The wife exclaimed, "That would be wonderful!" Her husband replied, "I don't think so. You would be one of the servants!" This crucial distinction is overlooked by almost all of the new literature on social limits to growth.

One aspect of these new emphases (typified by the new class) is reduced expectations about the future, a lack of confidence, morale, faith, vigour, and dynamism. This is of course in part a result of the limits-to-growth movement and the growing influence of the new class, and partly the result of the experiences of the last decade in general and the last few years in particular. As far as the first is concerned, the limits-to-growth movement is basically best thought of as a prophetic ideology which has generated expectations, on the one hand, of a doomsday or collapse of civilization and, on the other, of avoiding this event by policies which, at the extreme, come very close to demanding the perfectability of mankind. Having said this, the relatively extraordinarily rapid but incomplete replacement of the idea of progress with the idea of physical limits to growth is still one of the most remarkable phenomena of the twentieth century; it deserves discussion.

It is especially remarkable to find that this movement is so influential in a country, like Canada, with incredibly large open spaces, enormous resources, and a sparse population. It should be stressed that the Canadian limits-to-growth movement does not express fears that Canada may have to share its wealth with the rest of the world, but instead that the wealth of Canada is so limited that Canadians will have to live an ascetic life in the future.

One of the most remarkable things about the Canadian discussion of limits-to-growth is that it is conducted largely in the same terms as it is conducted in Japan and Europe, with little or no recognition of the fact that Canada should not, with reasonable management, have any serious limits-to-growth problems of a physical nature—at least not unless there is catastrophic bad luck or almost miserably bad management. But much of the discussion is dominated by people who are preoccupied with social, political, and cultural issues, and problems and interests of their own class rather than with the actual Canadian space and resource situations. As a psychoanalyst might put it, they mythify their own problems and then project them on the society as a whole. Since, however, the Canadian reality is quite different from that of the rest of the world, the discussion should, at least eventually, reflect these realities.

It used to be said, quite perceptively, that in some sense Canada's biggest problem was the lack of a big problem, or at least the absence of a clear dominating and dramatic challenge that created national unity, gave a shared meaning and purpose to the nation, and forced Canadians to focus attention and energy and to rise to the occasion. Indeed, many Canadian problems seem to arise as much from introspection as from objective difficulties. Thus, the phrases "national identity," "electronic rape," and "neo-colonialism" all have important, or dominating, neurotic elements as well as reflecting some objective reality.

The prospect that Quebec may attempt to secede will lead, I hope, to a creative challenge and response. It might also be very helpful to Canada if it could create a much more significant world role. This would be good for the Canadian ego, national identity, sense of worth, and otherwise help to create high morale, high confidence, and a positive self-consciousness. It is often said that Canada is a regional power, without a region. Thus in most parts of the world a country with Canada's GNP (almost 200 billion dollars) would be very important indeed. In fact Canada has the eighth largest GNP in the world. But Canada does not feel big and important because it is so dwarfed by the United States. But this should not prevent Canada from increasing its international prestige and influence, however; on the contrary Canada should seek a stronger international role as a counterweight to U.S. ties.

Canada could do this in a variety of ways which would serve both national and world interests. Probably the most obvious would be much greater activity in Canadian trans-national corporations. Worldwide, people often think of Canadians as being as rich and expert as the Americans, without any taint of great-power interests and activities typified by the C.I.A. And bilingualism confers a host of additional advantages. This makes Canadians extraordinarily acceptable in many regions and in a variety of roles. And if one compares Benelux or Scandinavia with Canada (all three have a little over 20,000,000 people and about $8,000 per capita income), one is struck by the fact that trans-national activity by indigenous corporations in the first two is ten times greater than in Canada. Of course, the former had pressures to do this because they lack Canada's resources; but this option could still be very advantageous for Canadians. They could do it by choice rather than by necessity, and find it very profitable.

Similarly, Canadians could be innovative in the international field generally. An innovation which would be terribly useful for the Third World and the First World alike, indeed perhaps the most useful single thing any advanced country could do, would be for Canada to innovate appropriate methods of alleviating a world problem which will become increasingly acute during the next two or three decades: an enormous and increasing labour surplus in the Third World and an almost equally dramatic labour shortage in the First World. There seem to be several practical ways to do this so that all parties benefit greatly (though there are some costs, of course), but all the suggestions raise so many related questions that I will content myself here with just raising the issues.

Canada has been complacent about its future. Internal difficulties are now forcing the country to reassess its image of the future, to rediscover its assets and opportunities. The result may be a very bright future and so the study team's forecast of a so-so future could prove insufficiently optimistic. If so all the better for Canada and the world, but given current attitudes, very surprising.

Has Canada a Future?

That question was often asked us when people learned we were studying Canada's future. Of course, what they meant was, Has Canada a favourable future? The frequency of the query reflected the pervasive pessimism in our country today. Certainly, given the widely perceived dismal outlook for our economy, society, and polity, that is a legitimate question, and we hope that this study will help to answer it.

Our commission was to examine the future prospects, potential, and problems of Canada over the next generation. The limit of the study period is the 1990s – the last decade of the twentieth century.

Futures studies are a formalized aspect of decision making. Every decision or action, great or small, is based on some assumption about the future environment. A heavy coat is bought on the assumption that the future winter may be severe. Good decision making is the art of the future – to try to respond to future events, and more important, to shape those events. At the time of writing we can see some excellent examples in this country: people are investing heavily in oil exploration on the projection that future energy prices will be high enough to justify the enormous expenses of development in the forbidding North. Similarly, expectations of inflation and government controls are leading some investors to put their money into the United States, where they consider that the short-term future economic environment will be more favourable. Perhaps most striking is the forecast of at least political uncertainty in Quebec, which is hindering investment in that province. A more positive projection leads to Canada controlling immigration: millions of people around the world project that their future lives here would be more satisfactory than in their native countries. Whether or not the above forecasts are accurate is in a sense less important than the fact that people act upon them; nevertheless, in most cases, it would be better if the forecasts were as correct as possible.

Who are we to say where Canada is going? Who are we to answer the question, Has Canada a future? Sneering at "crystal-ball gazers" is widespread, and this skepticism is certainly justified by the quality of much work in "futurology" (what sociologist Daniel Bell has called "future schlock"). We make no claim to predict the future. The reader will note that this study is filled with qualifiers such as "likely," "almost certainly," and "it seems to us that…" Discussions of the future must necessarily deal with possibilities and probabilities, not certainties. Nevertheless, some of these probabilities can be expected to be extremely likely. There is no guarantee that the sun will rise tomorrow morning; however, would you care to bet that it will not? The sun has an excellent and well documented track record, and there is a convincing and universally accepted theory of why it will rise tomorrow morning. The materials we will be dealing with here are somewhat less certain, but many of them have very high probability: would you care to bet that Halifax will be colder than Yellowknife next winter, or that *The Toronto Star* will be published in French? Obviously not, and it is upon these obviousnesses that we base many of our forecasts. Futures studies often rest upon some very simpleminded notions of continuity, that is, the study of what has happened–the past–in order to get a handle on what could and will happen–the future.

Throughout, we have relied heavily upon the methodology evolved over the last decade by Hudson Institute (U.S.A.), which makes no sweeping claims to predictive accuracy, but rather aims at making information available to assist in decision-making whenever possible with more or less subjective or objective judgements about relative probability. Some terminology may be useful:

A *prediction* is based on establishing high, perhaps overwhelming probabilities in favour of a specific event, as for example the probability that a tossed coin will turn up heads at least once in five tosses. The reader will find very few such stark predictions in this study.

A *forecast* tries to establish which events are possible, and then assigns at least rough probabilities to the various contentions, as for example, first finding out what horses are running in a race and then assigning odds to each of them. A good part of the study will be forecasts.

A *projection* is simply an extrapolation into the future. Sometimes the projection is done by a statistical extrapolation of past data; hence, the so-called *naive projection*. This often takes the form of a *straight-line projection*; but sometimes intuition, judgement, and speculation are used to modify the simple projection. In neither case is there necessarily an assertion of validity. A number of such projections will be developed.

A *scenario* is a hypothetical sequence of future events, not a predic-

27

tion, projection or plan. Its main purpose is to explore possibilities in the future by describing a hypothetical sequence of events consistent with available data, natural law, and human behaviour. Good scenario-writing is a synthesis of imagination* and plausibility. A set of scenarios will be a major organizing framework for this study.

Doubtless many people, especially those who disagree with our values or dislike our conclusions, will find a great deal to quarrel with in this study. While we have not tried to be all things to all people, we have attempted to be at least empathetic to most serious issues in Canadian opinion. Naturally, we have been more empathetic to our own than to others. This cannot be helped, but in many instances we have gone to a great deal of trouble to give full and fair treatment to other perspectives. We would be disappointed in our efforts if this study were judged of value only to those who agree with our various perspectives.

One particular problem could be that many of our projections and conclusions are at sharp variance with much of the conventional wisdom about what is happening and ought to be happening in enlightened circles in Canada, and at sharp variance with much of the conventional disagreement with the conventional wisdom. There are several reasons for this: First is that we have made a serious effort to avoid being "trendy." We are not journalists, so we are not concerned with "news." Sometimes, the most important statement is very dull or very obvious, but must be said because it has not been explicated or because many feel the opposite must be true. We particularly have avoided the fundamental error of most "future schlock" in assuming that what is new and attractive or frightening is necessarily a harbinger of the future. In fact, the opposite is usually true. What is news is usually transitory; only a tiny portion of new things are lasting or of lasting importance.

Similarly, the long-term projection of short-term trends has been avoided as much as possible. Long-term trends necessarily have many short-term fluctuations which, unfortunately, are often extrapolated by unsophisticated projectors. Taking a relatively long-term perspective has many advantages. It permits us to raise issues way down the pike which would be very highly sensitive and "political" if discussed in current terms. The long-term perspective has the more important function of

*Doubtless it will be reported that this study was the product of complex computer models. This is not true. Computers are very useful devices for data processing and making complex calculations of relatively simple formulae. Computer work has been used as an input to this study for some straightforward projections of demography and economics. The programs answered those arithmetical and data-processing questions that we asked. But the conclusions in this report are largely the product of the unprogrammed computer that sits on top of the neck. There is no substitute for human intelligence, intuition, and judgement. Whether ours have been adequate to the task is a question that is up to the reader's judgement.

giving us some sense of where the country is going.

While we cannot but be affected by current issues, if only because much of our audience is most closely interested in these, we have made a serious attempt to put them into perspective. For example, there were strong pressures on us to concentrate only on the issue of Quebec secession. We have given the subject a good deal more space than we would have five years ago, but certainly not as much as do current newspapers. We have not made the mistake of thinking of Quebec as the only issue although it is a key issue.* Conversely, five years ago this study would have placed as much emphasis on foreign, particularly American, ownership of our industry. This issue is now on the back burner, but we believe it will come up again and deserves a good deal more attention than the current level of discussion would suggest. Foreign economic influence may not be news or a political issue this year, but it is one of the endemic conditions that must be addressed in the long term.

Futures studies can be "descriptive" or "normative." The first attempts to be objectively scientific in describing the likely future so that people may adapt themselves to it. "Normative" is goal setting—it points to a future and tries to indicate how to get there. This distinction is partly an abstract one—in the real world it is impossible to separate the two completely, as what people think will happen will necessarily affect their decisions. Nevertheless, we have tried to make the distinction to the extent that it was possible and to emphasize the descriptive.

Today, most Canadian images of the future are pessimistic. Much futurology is dominated by the neo-Malthusian or limits-to-growth hypothesis which holds that the world is rapidly running out of natural resources, so economic growth will be forced to slow down and perhaps even stop. This is not an exclusively Canadian forecast though it is extraordinary that such a rich and prosperous country has espoused many of these views. One would not be surprised to hear that India's images of the future are pessimistic, but in fact the Indians seem to have a much more positive view of the future than Canadians have. We believe the neo-Malthusian theory to be almost completely wrong, and indeed some of the earlier proponents of limits-to-growth have modified and even reversed their position. (Surprisingly few of the limits-to-growth followers in the media and academia are aware of this reversal.) It is impossible to credibly demonstrate that the world is running out of energy and resources because of physical constraints.**

*The Hudson Institute of Canada is presently undertaking a study on the future of Quebec which will be available in the fall.

** In fact, almost the opposite can be demonstrated. See H. Kahn *et al*, *The Next Two Hundred Years* (Toronto, 1977).

We do, however, stand with the limits-to-growth proponents in our concern about the possibility of serious damage to the environment: as the scale of human activities increases the possibility of serious mistakes and bad luck also increases. However, the possibility of good luck also grows. For example, an affluent and technologically advanced society is more likely to be able to deal with major climatic changes and similar problems.

This point is so obvious, yet so important, that we must explicate it. Fifty years ago, it would not be necessary to mention that wealth can buy better medical care, better housing, better police protection, more margin against natural and national disasters, and so on. Today wealth and affluence are taken for granted, and many people do not seem to understand that they provide society with an important margin of safety. The major reason for economic development in the nineteenth century was not to increase the standard of living or quality of life, but to enhance national security against external or internal enemies or natural threats. This is probably still the overwhelming argument in favour of economic growth and technological advance; they give a society the ability to deal more efficiently with problems.

Another widespread pessimistic future is the "English scenario" – that Canada is merely a few steps behind the British, inexorably sliding towards economic stagnation, class conflict, bureaucratic tyranny, moral degeneration, and national collapse. Whether or not one takes the "English scenario" seriously, the prospect of permanent stagflation is also beginning to loom in many people's minds. Also, of course, the very dissolution of Canada is this year's favourite nightmare scenario.

It is of course important to have negative projections, if they are justified. Negative projections, by forcing a country to exert itself, to react to the challenge presented by the projection, may become a "self-defeating" prophecy. If a situation warrants a negative projection and people make a positive one, they develop false confidence and fail to do what they should do. It should also be clear that unwarranted negative projections can become "self-fulfilling prophecies," and that positive projections can be a source of high morale, dynamism, energy, efforts, and thus become "self-fulfilling prophecies." We have stayed away from such morale or propaganda issues, and have tried to be careful to include both negative and positive projections of the situations analysed.

Canada has not always had a dismal image of the future. Most of its images of the future in the past were reasonably favourable. Three hundred years ago, Canada's future was to be a valuable ornament in the crown of His Most Christian Majesty. Two centuries ago, Canada was to be a properly ordered British colony, insulated from the seditious views and near-anarchist local governments that engendered the revolutionary unpleasantness in the thirteen colonies to the south. A century ago Canada was to be a happy confederation, loyal to the Empire, with peace, order, and good government to prevent the brutal civil war which had just afflicted the American Union.

But, throughout most of our history, we have also had a pessimistic image of the future. In their hearts millions of Canadians believed that the American continentalists were correct, that Canada was a geographical, economic, and political anachronism destined eventually to be absorbed into the United States. But because of this forecast, much of our public and private policy has been designed to prevent this from occurring.

A less than favourable image of the future for a considerable part of our population was the widespread expectation among Anglophones, and even some Francophones, that as the French cultural presence was merely a fossil of former times, the French island would be eroded away by the inexorable lapping of the English tide. This was a "self-defeating prophecy," because Quebec heard it and dug in to resist.

From the late nineteenth to the mid-twentieth century, Canada had its most ambitious image of the future. The twentieth would be "the Canadian century" when we would have the population and economic base to make Canada a great world power providing a high standard of living to a burgeoning population that would flock to it from around the globe. Canada was to follow the path of the United States towards great power status. To our mind, one of the most important events in recent history was the abandonment of this Canadian dream of greatness. It went away for most decision-makers some time during the period after the Second World War. (If we had to pick a single event, we would choose the cancellation of the Arrow aircraft project; this was an indication that Canada was giving up on the big time.)

After the Second World War, Canada had a glorious world image. Its war record was heroic; its peace-keeping mission won it world-wide recognition; it had money, grain, and energy; the small aligned and non-aligned countries looked to Canada for leadership. In time, Canada let all of this pass, and we assumed a more "normal" status, viewed by many as a fall. Since that time Canada has been floundering. This is often expressed in terms of the search for "a national identity." Perhaps a better way to say it would be a search for "a meaningful Canadian future."

This is not to say that we as a nation have not been preoccupied with the future. In fact, despite our breast-beating, we have some rather clear-cut ideas about what the future should be. Almost all Canadians would agree with the following list, and a strong majority would agree with all of it. Indeed, these are clichés of public discourse and, like most clichés, they are such because they are so generally held and believed. Canadians generally support:

1. maintenance of our national territory and sovereignty;
2. continuation of liberal/democratic government;
3. harmonious coexistence of Francophones and Anglophones with a painless assimilation of other groups to one or the other;
4. maintenance of a high standard of living/quality of life;
5. benevolent useful participation in the world community.

While most of us would agree that these are desirable, they are no longer taken for granted. The governing political party of one of our largest provinces wishes to leave Confederation. Small groups in the West and the East also wish to opt out. Most striking is the widespread belief that a high standard of living/quality of life is no longer possible in Canada or indeed in the world, that we cannot live as well as our fathers lest we reduce our grandchildren to penury, and that we must look forward to a perpetual regime of austerity.

It is not the purpose of this study to provide Canada with a positive image of the future. We have provided a number of images of the future which many Canadians would empathize with. But we have also briefly described some "disaster" scenarios which most Canadians will want to avoid, though, of course, one person's disaster scenario may well be another's success scenario. We will make a strong case that a positive future is possible, that there is no necessity for things to go badly. It is possible, even likely, that Canada will have a positive future in its own terms. Certainly, a case can be made that much of the doom-saying in our country today is based upon incorrect analyses and downright illusions.

We conclude that a cool, dispassionate look at Canada's future results in a relatively optimistic view for the great majority of Canadian citizens and for the world in general. There are certain to be problems and challenges, yet we believe that, yes, Canada has a future, and potentially a fine one at that—but it won't be easy.

The Canadian Context

Let us begin our study of Canada's future with a general overview of the scene. This section organizes some central themes under three heads:

Conditions: forecasts (nearly predictions) of more or less fixed factors;

Long-term Trends: projections and forecasts of more or less continuously changing factors;

Base Scenarios: three plausible scenarios for the Canadian social, economic, cultural, and political environment of the next fifteen years.

This material serves as an organizing framework for the study and introduces themes developed in the following sections on population, economics, energy, politics, etc.

The Conditions of Canadian Life

A "condition" is something that is a part of life, like it or not. Conditions are not fixed by destiny, but it is very difficult to imagine a credible scenario for their going away. For each of these conditions we invite the reader to ask the same question we have: What could happen that could seriously change these? We think you will agree that it requires highly unlikely events to change any of these substantially, and then only under extremely strong pressures.

Often, conditions are described as "problems." We think this characterization is likely to be misleading and unproductive. A "problem" can be corrected or alleviated. A condition is something that must be endured; we can adapt to it or minimize its effects, but we cannot expect to eliminate it altogether. We believe that these conditions provide the framework within which the Canadian society, economy, and polity will continue to function, and place necessary limits on our national possibilities as well as offering us opportunities. On a technical level, these conditions also place limits on this study. They remind us not to permit our imagination to blind us to the obvious.

Adverse Climate

It has been said that the key to the Canadian experience is winter. We have one of the most demanding climates of any advanced industrial nation.* Our adverse weather injures us in many ways: The long and severe winters require artificial heat, which necessarily increases the cost of living and of industrial production of most goods. We are obliged to wear more, heavier, and more expensive clothing. The heavy snow loads require stronger and more expensive construction. Despite our remarkable advances in sub-zero construction, the building season is shorter and therefore more expensive. The great variation in activities between summer and winter pushes up seasonal unemployment. The snow increases transportation costs. Extremes of temperatures between summer and winter chew up our roads. Airports are shut down by snow and fog. Even automobile operation is more expensive because the cold starting increases engine wear, snow and salt corrode the chassis, and slippery roads increase the number of accidents.

Against this we must credit our climate with providing us and tourists with marvellous opportunities for outdoor winter recreation. The weather also provides us with our most popular sport–hockey. Because of the harsh climate, the population density of much of our country is trivial; this pays off in terms of great open spaces available for outdoor recreation during the few months of good weather. As the country is more affluent, Canadians are able to afford even more winter sports which makes it much easier to adapt to the cold weather. But these benefits must be balanced against the fact that our bitter winters drive millions of Canadians south to the United States and the Caribbean to the detriment of our balance of payments.

It was argued in the past that part of the reason for Canada having a lower GNP per capita than the U.S. was due as much to adverse climate as to any other reason. We are not sure of the validity of this assumption. After all, Sweden has one of the highest incomes per capita in Europe and lives under weather conditions very similar to Canada's.

Canada now has about the same income per capita as the United States, and we do not expect climate to be a dominant issue, except perhaps with regard to one important trend. Throughout most of human

*Margaret Atwood has even argued that a key characteristic of Canadians is their very "survival" and struggle against the weather.

34

history, the bulk of mankind lived in semi-tropical regions for the obvious reason that these had the most plentiful sun for the dominant human activity of agriculture. It is only within the last two hundred years, with the industrial revolution, that men moved north. In most industrial countries the resources were found in the northern part of the country. Perhaps there is some geological reason for this or perhaps it is a coincidence, but it happened that the coal and iron, and the transportation necessary to put them together, was located in the northern parts of industrial nations. Thus the population of England began to shift to the Midlands and the North; German population moved northwest to the Ruhr, the French population to Flanders, and the Chinese population to the north and Manchuria, with similar patterns in Sweden, Russia, Japan, and the U.S. It was the coal, iron, and transportation that created the prosperity and therefore the growth of Cape Breton, Hamilton, Windsor, Sault Ste. Marie, and even more forbidding places.

As the world moves into a post-industrial stage (by which we mean a situation in which now-traditional production industries become relatively less important and people-related service industries become more important), relatively fewer numbers of people provide our resources and manufactured goods, and they certainly are not the leading edge of the economy.

Canadians have read about the move to the "sun belt" of the south and south-western U.S. to the detriment of the traditional industrial areas of the north-east and mid-west. One can overestimate the issue of the "sun belt" because part of the shift is attributable to the persistence of old values in the south, and to a catching-up phenomenon. Nevertheless, the force of the "sun belt" seems very strong, and a similar pattern has been developing in the south of England; the same process is continuing in Sweden, France, and Germany. This is a powerful urge, as evidenced by the Soviet Union: Despite a tough internal passport system supporting the national policy to populate Siberia, Russian authorities are tearing their hair out at the migration of Soviet citizens towards the south: Turkestan, the Crimea, the southern Ukraine, and the Caucasus.

This does not bode well for Canada. We are seeing evidence of the same trend here in that there is a tendency for the population to increase in the warmest parts of our country. Climate is not the only locational factor and traditional economic factors are still relevant. So long as we are a major producer of resources, there will be economic activity and therefore population growth in those places where the resources are. Nevertheless, to the degree that people become more important than goods, those "footloose" industries which can locate anywhere will tend to gravitate towards the parts of the country which have the kind of total environment in which an increasingly educated, cosmopolitan, and even hedonistic population wishes to live; and a major part of this environment is good climate. In our country, these are principally coastal B.C. and southern Ontario, and to a lesser extent southern Alberta and the coastal Maritimes.

Since Canada does not have a sun belt, most of the population hugs the southern border. A serious sun belt shift would likely imply high levels of emigration. One of the reasons that Canada should want to maintain high morale and dynamism in the country is to counter such a potential shift–brain drain, investment drain, etc. Equally important, given the climatic variations in the world and on this continent, we do not have a comparative advantage.*

Abundant Resources

Reference to our vast potential of abundant natural resources has long been a cliché of discussions about Canada. In the last few years that cliché has been challenged in a way best exemplified by the phrase "non-renewable resources." "Abundant" implies inexhaustible, while "non-renewable" implies exhaustible. Both terms are essentially accurate, but it seems to us that the most useful way to consider our resources is still by the traditional characterization of "abundant." It is true that in some abstract sense our and the world's resources will be eventually used up or converted into some other form. But the real issues are the size of the reservoir which is being exploited and the rate of exploitation. Imagine a mother warning a child taking water out of the ocean with a pail, "Careful, Johnny, you'll drain the ocean." Of course, the mother is right: if Johnny continued, the ocean would be empty at some calculable time in the future. But it is not a very useful statement without consideration of the size of the ocean and Johnny's ability to empty it.

We are doing a little better (or worse, according to your point of view) than Johnny with his pail, but not much. Our resources have barely been scratched; indeed, the country has barely been explored. Let us make this point clear by reference to the characteristic neo-Malthusian or limits-to-growth projection: Take reports of X known reserves of some resource, divide that by current usage, and find only some thirty years remaining. A more sophisticated calculation is that because we are accelerating our usage only perhaps twenty years of that resource remain. Those calculations are specious. The estimates of reserves come from those companies, pub-

*Recent increases in energy prices merely slow, not halt or reverse this trend. Despite the rapid price hikes, energy is still cheaper than it was a generation ago, and much less expensive than at the beginning of the century.

lic or private, who are in the business of extracting and selling resource products. They are *not* in the business of searching for resources. Exploration is a tedious and expensive process; companies only take the trouble to find sufficient reserves to guarantee production over the planned lifespan of their capital investment. It would be wasteful and foolish to look for more reserves. In fact, as we shall discuss in the energy and materials section of this study, our resources can be considered for all practical purposes to be nearly unlimited in their abundance.

Today, Canada is spotted with former mines, abandoned because more economical sources of the same material became available. Enormous amounts of material remain in these places. Furthermore, there are numerous locations of materials that were not exploited for the same reason – cheaper resources were found elsewhere. This applies to metals, hydro power, and energy.

It is true that the exploitation of some of these resources has been delayed or halted by political considerations, that is, a question of politics, which ultimately rests upon our national values, but does not affect the basic fact of abundance. The richness of our raw materials must continue to be considered a Canadian condition during this century and the next. Fundamental questions on what to do with these resources will also continue to be one of the fixed factors of Canadian life.

Excellent (but not the best) Health

As a nation we have excellent health, and that health is getting better; but we will always rank low on a list of relative health indicators of the advanced industrial nations. This is a condition because of our severe climate, which provokes and complicates many disorders, particularly of a bronchial nature, and because the scattering of our population makes the provision of health services, especially emergency services, less efficient.

Political Democracy

Very few Canadians can even conceive of any system other than political democracy as suitable for us. We find it impossible to imagine a credible scenario for the destruction of democracy in Canada as a whole. (And only in an extreme "nightmare" scenario for a Quebec break-away is dictatorship in an independent Quebec conceivable.)

Parliamentary Government

Ditto. But, as we shall see, Monarchy and the existing two-party system are not so perfectly assured.

Continuation of Liberal Values

By "liberal," we mean those ideals of the sanctity of the individual, and the equality of men, and the views that society should be so ordered to achieve goals of social justice, human development, and general well-being. In terms of human history these are new ideas, and are strongly held only in Western civilization, but they go deep here and will not go away in our lifetime.

Survival of Other Traditional Values

These values of dedication, loyalty, responsibility, order, organization, tradition, justice, self-sacrifice, freedom, prudence, moderation, honesty, together with traditional religious values, family values, and patriotic values have been challenged over the last decade or two. While we expect some erosion, they will continue to be dominant in our society.

The new or "changing values" of freedom, creativity, perception, spontaneity, self-actualization, participation, and hedonism, are to some degree present in most of us, but despite some enthusiastic predictions, are dominant only among a small minority of our population which is likely to grow slowly at best during the rest of this century, and will certainly not dominate the society (although it will have more influence on the more privileged and ruling orders than on the rank and file of Canadians).

Also we must expect the continuation of many of what both our traditional and new value systems consider the least attractive values–greed, lust, selfishness, materialism, snobbery, authoritarianism, hypocrisy, jealousy, and hatred.

Survival of the Traditional Family

Most of the talk about new types of family structures is just that–talk. Almost all Canadians will either live in, look forward to, or look back upon more or less traditional nuclear family arrangements of husband-wife-children. This pattern will survive at least till the end of the century.

The much publicized deviations from this ideal–increased divorce, separation, arrangements, even homosexual marriage–are marginal phenomena. Divorce is a serious problem in our country, and in our view will continue to be so, especially when the evidence of effects of single-parent raising on children becomes better documented and more widely publicized. However, we must not forget that most divorced people remarry, so we are experiencing "serial" marriage, not the dissolution of marriage altogether. Young people are not turning away from marriage altogether but postponing it, returning to earlier patterns of marriage in their mid- or later twenties.

For many years people have thought that they noticed a spread of promiscuity among young people, but we would argue that until recently this was probably more due to a decrease in reticence than a decrease in restraint.

Continued Dominance (but some erosion) of the Upper Middle Class

It can be said that Canada is the most upper-middle-class country in the world.* In no country is the UMC threatened so little. Our UMC has had no hereditary aristocracy to deal with. Except in Quebec, there was no over-weening church hierarchy to thwart its aims. Compared with Europe, the working classes are spread thin and poorly organized. The CCF/NDP has been a poor imitation of the great European socialist parties, and compared to most industrialized countries, Canadian unions are scattered. On the other hand, we have had little of the fierce democratic-populist sentiment of the U.S., where the lower middle classes are mobilized against upper-middle-class objectives. Much social policy desired by the upper middle class in the United States and considered so difficult there is taken for granted here–metro governments, green belts, high civil service salaries, aid to private education, government health insurance.

As we shall discuss in the "values" section of this report, this upper-middle-class dominance has had important effects on our national history during the last generation. Before roughly 1960, the upper middle classes were the most stable and respectable element in the industrial democracies. About 1960 they began to become progressive; largely because of UMC domination of our society and culture, in ten years Canada went from being the squarest to the hippest country in the Western world. For example, in no country this side of Israel would officials appear in public in sports clothes without neckties. In no other country could the wife of the leader of the *conservative* party keep her "maiden" name–imagine what Mrs. Thatcher would say. A good part of our internal malaise is due to the fact that much of this was trendy, and we are now undergoing a reaction to it.

We forecast that there will be some erosion of this UMC dominance, but that it will still remain. The sources of the erosion will come from external challenges and internal divisions. The most obvious external challenge is the attempt to mobilize the "working class" of Canada along the European model by the unions and the NDP. The major political parties have been trying to fight off this threat by the same policy that the English Liberal party attempted in the early part of this century–by grant-

*By upper middle class (UMC), we mean that part of the population which makes from 2 to 10 times the median family income, which is characterized by property ownership, status occupations, and university education.

ing major concessions and hoping to provide for the claims of labour through government, rather than by collective bargaining through unions.

A less obvious, but probably increasingly important challenge is the ethnic changes within the country. In Anglophone Canada, the upper middle classes have been almost exclusively Anglo-Saxon. As what used to be called New Canadians are assimilated into the system and begin to move up, the leaders are no longer as eager to submit to Anglo-Saxon dominance. Some will be assimilated to the existing UMC, but others may attempt to organize their lower-middle-class and even working-class compatriots against the existing establishment. The attempt to mobilize an ethnic awareness is a symptom of this movement. In a considerable sense, recent developments in Quebec have been a version of the same phenomenon: there the Anglophone UMC has dominated the economy, and the Francophone agitation, whether by federalists or separatists, can be interpreted as an attempt by the upwardly mobile Francophones to use their compatriots as a battering ram to break the existing UMC dominance.

But, in Quebec as elsewhere in the country, the principal threat to UMC domination is divisions within the upper middle class itself. This reflects fundamental structural changes in the economy. The historical upper middle class was primarily composed of property-owning proprietors and rentiers—true bourgeois. In recent years, this group has been augmented and is now probably outnumbered by the salariat of the private sector—corporate managers, engineers, and other highly skilled technicians. However, in recent years we have seen the rise of what is coming to be called "the new class" of civil servants, academics, journalists, and others, who define themselves not in terms of family background, property, entrepreneurial or managerial skills, but knowledge, i.e., literary and analytical skills as endorsed through formal education. A good deal of the turmoil in our country, as elsewhere in the industrial west, can be seen in terms of conflict between these two upper-middle-class groups and their interplay with other elements of the society.

Again, we believe that these forces will challenge the predominance of the upper middle class and will probably reduce it somewhat, but we cannot imagine a situation in which the existing upper middle class would suffer serious cuts in its power, standard of living, or its domination of the tone and values of the whole society.

Continued Dominance (but relative decline) of TOM

By TOM we mean Toronto-Ottawa-Montreal, which has really run Canada for the past century. By the end of the next generation TOM will still run Canada, but, we project, not quite as powerfully as today. The West has

40

always kicked at dominance by the East, i.e., TOM, and will have more economic and voting power to kick more effectively. TOM will have to gradually give way point by point, complaining all the time. Still, though the relative power will have shifted somewhat, TOM will still be on top.

It is common to all contemporary societies that the state has enormous power. It is possible that the federal system could be modified to transfer substantial power to the provinces and weaken Ottawa, and it is not clear that this will not happen. All provinces are asking for it. But we would guess that even substantial amounts of devolution to the provinces would not greatly diminish Ottawa's power in economic and foreign policy. In economics and culture, the country will probably appear to be dominated by Toronto, and to a lesser degree, for obvious political reasons, by Montreal.

In actual fact, the dominance could become more social and cultural than economic, especially if Western Canada emphasizes rapid growth. The mere fact that a head office is located in TOM does not mean much if competition is strong. The ability of the West to seek financing on Wall Street, to enter into multi-national joint ventures, to achieve more status both within and outside Canada could reduce much of TOM's current power. Of course, appearances are very important here, and to the extent that TOM continues to appear dominant, this may well be a self-fulfilling prophecy.

French-English Conflict

This condition is a hundred years old in Canada, two hundred years old in the British American colonies, three hundred years old in North America, and can be traced back at least six centuries to the Hundred Years War. Does anyone believe it will be eliminated altogether by sending mandarins to language school or bilingual labelling of soap boxes? Of course, no one does. The issue is not the existence of conflict, but the level and the costs. As we shall see, these are among the major variables in this study. The current Quebec-Canada tensions will drive Canadians to seek more basic solutions to the French-English conflict, and will encourage more compromise; but as with any "living arrangement" some tensions remain.

Federal-Provincial Conflict

Canada has always had federal-provincial conflicts, and we see no reason to believe that it will not continue to do so. Even if there is enormous devolution of power to the provinces, and Ottawa has severely restricted sovereignty, conflicts will continue. In fact, the weaker the central government, the more likely the federal-provincial conflicts because the areas of conflict increase. The questions are whether or not the level of conflict will increase or decrease, and what will be fought over. Most people today believe that the short-run projection is for an increase in federal-provincial conflict, due to the weakening of TOM and the effects of accommodating the demands of Quebec. These are true, but an even stronger factor is at work: as government becomes more and more involved in the economy, decisions are increasingly made at a government rather than individual level. What were once economic conflicts between individuals become political conflicts between groups, and differing interests are represented in different strengths in different parts of the country. Thus the old fight between the farmer and the railroad, and between the manufacturing and consuming interests, becomes subsumed into struggles between the West and Ottawa, and everybody versus Ontario.

In the short and medium run, there probably is very little that can be done about this. At the present time, many people believe that the federal government has taken too much upon itself and there is a push towards decentralization. This will only partially alleviate the problem because, judging from our experience and that of other industrial countries, decentralization schemes rarely remove much power, much less many bureaucrats, from the central government, but merely build up larger subnational bureaucracies with more resources and with more powers to fight it out with the national government. In the short run this situation is likely to get worse; in the long run it will probably turn the other way, if only from exhaustion.

Reliance on Foreign Trade in a Competitive World

We must continue to be competitive in the economic sphere for the very simple reason that we must export in order to import what we need from abroad. While we are a large economy by the standard of the whole world, we are only medium size by that of the industrial world. Much high-technology equipment we must import. We must also import tropical produce of all sorts. Perhaps most obvious, we must "import" our tourism abroad. If ten percent of our population goes to Florida every year, we need to earn American dollars to pay that back.

The U.S. will remain our largest trading partner. Even a successful diversification policy will not incur changes significant enough to substantially decrease the American share of Canadian imports and exports and vice versa.

Continued U.S.–U.S.S.R. Economic, Cultural, and Political World Dominance and Rivalry

The end of this century will see the United States in approximately the same position relative to the rest of the world as it is today. It will be Number One, although probably (unless there is some sort of ferocious nationalist revival) less predominant than it is today. Not that the U.S. will be any less rich and powerful, nor that other countries will not have come up; but none of them individually will be able to rival the U.S.

It would seem that by the end of the century, as military capability becomes more and more reliant upon advanced technology and less upon such "old fashioned" criteria as infantry divisions, tanks, and fighter aircraft, the American military lead over Russia may also have lengthened. This is by no means a certain result; but in any event, the U.S.S.R. cannot successfully challenge the U.S. in the economic and cultural spheres, because the Soviets have lost a great deal of their status as leaders of the left. The growth of independent communist parties, the Sino-Soviet split, the "greening of America," which gives the Soviets the appearance of being square and rigid, and finally the Soviet record of territorial expansion and domestic failures have taken much of the charisma out of the Soviet image. However, at least in the next decade, we cannot see the Chinese as replacing the Soviets in terms of political and cultural domination.

Continued Comparisons with U.S. Standard of Living

In the last twenty years, Canada has grown more rapidly than the U.S., but part of this was a catching-up phenomenon. Certain factors make it difficult for Canada to be as prosperous as the U.S.:

1. the climate;
2. the smaller internal market;
3. the "unnatural" east-west trading pattern;
4. the cost of maintaining the Canadian government and other national institutions.

In other words we must pay for being Canada. However, other factors contribute to more rapid growth:

1. availability of resources;
2. fewer minority enclaves;
3. more efficient cities;
4. fewer educational disparities.

This is not to say that every group must have the same percentage of equivalent U.S. income. Historically, the privileged classes have had approximately a U.S. income, while workers and farmers had lower incomes, which was a major impetus to the massive emigration to the U.S. Over the past generation this has changed – the middling Canadians have achieved near parity with their peers in the U.S., so the prosperous (except high civil servants) have suffered and are getting restless.

Continued American Economic and Cultural Influence on Canada

American influence on Canada will not change appreciably in the next generation. The disparity in size and power between the two nations will continue essentially unchanged. The similarity of the cultures and values and near-identity of language of the U.S. and Anglophone Canada leaves us open for continuous penetration. (Quebec is more insulated by language, but popular culture is also influenced by the U.S.)

We feel that the principal reason for the continuation of the American economic dominance is that Canadians do not want to do without U.S. markets, capital, technology, management skills, and entertainment. After all, the U.S. dominates the Western economy. Canadians would not be willing to pay the price in prosperity and liberty of cutting economic ties with the U.S. Similarly, we cannot break the cultural domination, short of attempting to put up an iron curtain along the forty-ninth parallel complete with a massive investment in jamming of U.S. commercial broadcasts and preventing travel to and from the U.S. It should be noted that it is not only geographical proximity that makes us vulnerable to American influence. Worldwide, American television programs, for example, are immensely popular. "Bonanza" is one of Bulgaria's favourite shows. Again, we do not wish to pay the price.

We want to make the point very strongly that even though some poll data might indicate that Canadians would accept a drop in their standard of living to reduce foreign influence on the country, in actual fact when it comes to paying the price, there is little support for such a policy. Basically, it is the upper middle class and the intellectuals who feel the strongest about this issue.

This does not mean that we are helpless, but there is relatively little that we can do except what is symbolic. Much of this we are already doing by subsidizing our own television network, taxing foreign publications and, of course, the recent attempts to limit U.S. cable television transmissions. Cynics might say that these policies merely levy on the citizenry to support second-rate entertainers, writers, and promoters who lack the ability to make it in New York or Hollywood; but it is not without effect. There is a market in Canada for Canadian productions. It may not be a very large market, but it does exist and we should not ignore it. In our view, that market will grow slowly and the quality of productions will continue to improve. To invent a number, let us say that ninety per cent of our cultural products are now imported from the U.S. Perhaps in the 1990s, that number will be down to eighty per cent. That *is* a difference: it doubles Canadian content, and probably most Canadians think it is worth the investment.

In economics, this same factor is true. Again, it is easy to be cynical about our "feeble" attempts at economic nationalism, seeing them as the result of lobbying by inefficient Canadian industries to protect themselves and their profits against the more efficient operations of American multinational firms who, among their other employees, have engaged the cream of Canadians. Nevertheless, many Canadians believe it is worth some cost to keep at least the essentials of an independent economy not controlled by the decisions of anonymous corporate bureaucrats in New York, Detroit, and Chicago who are answerable only to anonymous financiers in Wall Street and anonymous officials in Washington.

At the time of writing, the emergence of other issues has pushed that of economic nationalism to the background. But it will continue to be a major concern, whose emphasis will ebb and flow over the years. On the whole, it is our analysis that economic nationalism can be a modest success if pushed prudently with modest aims and no grandiose expectations.

In fact, it can be argued that the principal effect of the Canadian nationalist movement of the last decade has been to teach American businessmen that Canada is not part of the United States—it is a foreign country, and as in all foreign countries, expatriate businessmen must play according to the local rules. If Americans must be more sensitive to the odd "prejudices" of Canadians in order to make money, they are accustomed to doing the same in other countries.

Continued American Psychological Domination

This is more subtle, but perhaps more annoying. We too often appear to have a national "inferiority complex" vis-à-vis the Americans, a feeling that who we are and what we have is second rate compared with that of the U.S. This is most obviously evidenced by the fact that we will not recognize talent among our own people until it has the imprimatur of American authority. John Kenneth Galbraith, Marshall McLuhan, Gordon Lightfoot and Mordecai Richler are the most obvious recent examples. In fact, as we shall argue, Canadians have a great deal to be proud of, and in many aspects of individual and public life it can be argued that we are superior to the United States. Again, we know that, but have difficulty convincing ourselves.

This psychological dominance places strict restraints on our public policy. So long as we measure ourselves by U.S. standards, no Canadian government can survive which seriously cuts the standard of living or the individual liberties of any group in our society noticeably below equivalent U.S. levels.

Continued Anti-Americanism

Anti-Americanism is the corollary of American predominance and our inferiority complex. It is not going to go away, nor should it go away. Canada exists in opposition to the United States. Each for its own reasons, our two great cultural blocs did not wish to be Americans. Just as Switzerland exists by virtue of its people not wishing to be Germans, French or Italians, and Belgium exists by virtue of its people not wishing to be French or Dutch, Canada's existence presumes the desire not to be American.

Anti-Americanism is to some degree a substitute for true national feeling, and that is unfortunate because the healthiest nationalism is that which presumes that what is good for the nation benefits humanity, but in the real world such sentiments are often mixed in with hostility. There may be nations who are proud of themselves and do not despise some other country, but we cannot think of any offhand.

So long as our nationalism takes the form of our believing that we are more civilized and just than the Americans, that is a healthy condition. So long as we take symbolic steps to stick it in the Yankee ear, that too is harmless. But if we take the symbolic or even real actions principally to gain satisfaction from annoying the Americans, that is childish and potentially dangerous. To the average American, Canada is a place inhabited by people who are very much like Americans and should behave in the same way. Americans have a real difficulty in seeing that there are genuine differences.

Let us try to make this point clear by reference to what seems to be a favourite national nightmare scenario. Judging from the enthusiastic reception given to Mr. Rohmer's novels, it would seem that plenty of Canadians find the notion of an American take-over plausible. Perhaps somewhere in the United States is some person who would like to grab Canada; but he is certainly not in a position of power. The Americans have no interest whatever in seizing our country or taking us in even if petitioned. They have no contingency plans of what to do if, say, Alberta or New Brunswick or Quebec applied for admission to their union.

The idea of Americans plotting to seize us is not only paranoid, but egomaniacal. It is not that the Americans do not want us, rather they do not worry about us. This should not be interpreted as utter lack of interest in Canada, but rather that the Americans think Canada-U.S. relations are healthy and, consequently, they take us for granted. As long as there are no real problems, they do not worry about Canada.

When Americans need foreign comparisons for government programs, they look to Europe, to England, to France, to Sweden, and even Italy – but rarely to Canada where the similarities would seem to make a comparison more relevant. One reason is that Americans often assume that Canada is just like the U.S. Another reason is based on this theory: the Americans are a proud people. They "know" they are the greatest people in the world and have the most benevolent institutions. They also "know" that Canadians (except for perhaps the French-speaking people in Quebec) are just like them. So there are "Americans" who do not wish to be part of the American nation. That is a paradox and working out the problem raises some fundamentally difficult questions about the nature of the great American people and their wonderful republic. So it is understandable that they would prefer not to think about it at all.

In our view, the United States has completely abandoned all interest in territorial expansion, and would pay attention to Canada in any serious way only if something terrible happened here. This is not to say that the U.S. attitude towards us is utterly beneficent. Since it would like to ignore our presence, if in clumsily pursuing its own policies it happens to injure us, that is a matter of little or no consequence to the U.S.; but there is generally no malicious intent.

Of course there are examples of "crazy" standards of the extent to which we want Americans to listen to us. During the Cuban Missile Crisis, Canada took offence at being "told" and not "consulted" about U.S. policy. Every other country in the world, every other leader that President Kennedy had briefed on the subject accepted that this was no time for consultation. Only the Canadian Prime Minister complained at being pushed around by the U.S.

There are cases of U.S. retaliation towards Canada, but not nearly as many as could be the case. When we are hurt, that may not be much solace – indeed, it makes the hurt worse.

Continuation of the Canadian National Character(s)

We find it a little odd that many of our commentators are concerned about our presumed lack of national character. There is unquestionably a Canadian national character which has been well established for many years. For example, the following quotation is from a book by a Canadian writer for an American audience published nearly forty years ago.* Today, it is still largely applicable:

*John MacCormac, *Canada: America's Problem* (New York: Viking, 1940) pp. 153-156.

...Canadians take their work more calmly and their pleasures more sadly. High-pressure salesmanship never threatened to blow off the cylinder heads in Canada. High-pressure radio announcing is not favoured...Canadian theatre audiences are among the world's coldest. A political convention in the United States bears the same relation to a political convention in Canada as bedlam bears to a cemetery.

Canada...is less thoroughly democratic than the United States. There is more reverence in the Dominion for authority and for the great.

Canadians are less impulsive than Americans and far less given to violence. The gun on the hip has never been part of the Canadian tradition, nor the cure of colour blindness by auto-da-fé. Canada has hanged rebels but no "radicals"...Gangsterism is only sporadic in Canada and organized racketeering unknown. No hooded figures have ever dominated the Canadian night scene. The law tolerates fewer technicalities and is far swifter. Relatively fewer Canadians murder each other and many more are hanged when they do.

Justice, if more efficient in Canada, is also more dignified and aloof. Trial by newspaper is not tolerated and he would be a bold man who took a camera and a flashlight bulb into a courtroom. The law of slander is more strictly enforced...

Although Canada has had many stars in Hollywood none of them went there as "Miss Canada," for the female form, though admired, is not apotheosized.

Canada, like the United States, is Puritanical at heart, but it is at the same time more tolerant...there is less fundamentalism in Canadian Protestantism than in American. Catholicism in Canada, although far more important in point of relative numbers than in the United States, is less of a political power than it would be if its adherents all spoke the same tongue.

The differences that have been cited between Canadians and Americans are differences of tempo rather than of character and reveal themselves in the mass rather than in the individual. The gap that divides the Canadian from the Englishman is far wider...

Of course, we do not have *a* national character, but two national characters properly reflecting the two peoples who co-exist in the Canadian nation, or if you prefer, the two nations that co-exist in the Canadian state.

Like all national characters ours has been evolved by the influences of history: in this case, Bourbon France transmitted to the wilderness, cut off from French development, and subjected to two hundred years of British and Anglo-American pressure. Francophones have no problem with national character; it is of concern principally to Anglo-Canadians. Nevertheless, we have been fretting about our presumed lack of national character for a century, and there seems to be no particular reason to doubt that we will not continue to do so. It may be that the search for a national character is the characteristic aspect of the Canadian national character.

Long Term Trends

This class of variables represents those aspects of life which have been continuing for a long time, often centuries. The trends have by no means been continuous–there have been shorter-term counter-trends–but on the whole, the change (or "progress," if you like) has been in the direction indicated. We believe it reasonable to project these trends to the end of the century, but with some local and short-term reversals.

These trends represent a constraint within which our projections must operate. Most of them are not specifically Canadian, so there is very little that can be done in a purely Canadian context to control them.

Increasing Secularization

Religion, once the centre of the life of the culture, has been in decline for many centuries, and further decline must be expected. Although Canadians are still one of the most religious peoples in the Western world, the influence of institutional religion on everyday life will almost certainly continue to slip. "The Quiet Revolution" in Quebec is merely the most striking example of this movement, but it is certainly not absent in Anglophone Canada either.

The Rise of Meritocratic Elites

By this we mean that the positions of privilege and power in the country are more and more determined by individual attributes than by family connections. This process is slow, by no means even, and certainly far from completion, but it inevitably continues.

This implies the decline of "Roserockmount," an acronym for that class of people who live in such places as Toronto's Rosedale, Ottawa's Rockcliffe, and Montreal's Westmount–the rich and near rich rentiers, entrepreneurs, managers, financiers, lawyers, and "mandarins." While ours is among the most democratic countries in the world, it is not completely so. Economic and political power is not perfectly distributed, and access to such power is not entirely independent of family connections. Certainly, these people have done well for themselves and their descendants. Roserockmount has led the country from its beginning and, on the whole, can be said to have run it very well. Indeed, privately, many claim that they have made the country. Without a strong will among the old elites, Canada would likely have slipped under American rule. And without the strong interest of the elites of TOM, the country would not have been developed.

Be that as it may, history is not known for gratitude. Throughout the world, established elites are losing their power, status, and income. We project that Canada will not be immune from this tendency and that Roserockmount will continue to slip in relative power and position. A good many of the complaints about what is wrong with our national life will be the universalizaton of the social and economic perceptions of this class of people. It is somewhat of a delusion to imagine that economic and social democracy is always good for the privileged.

Again, while we project that this group will lose some of its power, it will not lose it all. There will still be a "Canadian establishment" in 1991 which will certainly continue to live in Rosedale and Rockcliffe (and almost certainly in Westmount, or at least Outremont), that will live well and will have more than its share of leadership positions. Many members of the establishment will have names that are familiar today; in some cases they will be the same people and in others their children. In no society and especially in socialist countries is it a disadvantage to be the offspring of a powerful man. But there will continue to be "new people" coming up through the system who have the good sense or the good fortune to marry children of the former people or make their way in the world on their own. There will certainly continue to be many "new people" coming up, especially in Western Canada, to mitigate the influence of Roserockmount. There will probably be more new people in Canada than in the past, if only because there will likely be considerably less emigration of talented and ambitious people to Britain and the United States.

However attractive this prospect may be to those who see it as progress toward achieving "social justice," we must remark that the decline of the traditional establishment in a sense weakens our prospects for a distinctive national character. Outside of French Quebec, it is the establishment that has created the most distinctively Canadian style. Our upper-class lifestyle, evolved during imperial days, is not British, not American, but distinctively Canadian. The weakening of this class implies a different Canadian style evolving in the future. In this respect, bilingualism confers distinctive attributes to Canadian culture.

Increasing Education, Growth of the "Knowledge Industry," and the Rise of the New Class

Here we are clearly a "blip" in this trend today. The vast educational expanse in the 1960s is being accompanied by retrenchment, not entirely caused by mere demographics. However, in the long run we must expect that the growth of education goes hand in hand with the general tendency of our society towards "meritocracy."

Throughout the industrial world, we are witnessing a gradual rise in the power of a new class to challenge the existing dominant class of rentiers/entrepreneurs/managers. This new class of bureaucrats, academics, and journalists derives its income, status, and power from the possession of knowledge, especially formal education, analytical skills, and literary talents. This class has been with us for a good long time, but in relatively small numbers, and was not taken particularly seriously by the whole society.* But in recent years the proliferation of formal education, of the media, and of staff people of all types, mostly in government and other non-profit organizations, but in business and commerce as well, has led to a huge burgeoning in the numbers of these people. Unlike the old classes, they do not derive their position from privileged family or the possession of capital, or even from entrepreneurial and managerial skills, but from their education and literary skills. These groups are moving towards power in every country in the Western world.

The characteristic political vehicles of the New Class in Europe are the various social-democratic parties, such as England's Labour Party, which have been alliances of the organized working class with the "intellectuals." By most indicators, European social democracy has been a great success in seeing that the working class gained the major part of economic growth in this century and in seriously reducing the costs of class distinction. Part of the reason for this success was that workers and trade union leaders on the whole tended to be practical and sensible people who were able to control and harness the New Class to their purposes. But in recent years, most especially in England and Sweden, the balance has shifted; the New Class has become more dominant in these parties, and they seem to be moving a bit towards the deep end.

This suggests that the rise of the New Class is not necessarily an unmitigated blessing for Western society or for Canada. This may be a temporary phenomenon but it suggests that the rise of the New Class will not be without conflict and difficulty.

Of course, Canadian examples of social-democratic political organiza-

*Those people have been called "intellectuals"—a word Canadians dislike, because it implies being out of touch with everyday reality.

tions are the Parti Québecois and the NDP. Because of the relatively weak organization and class consciousness of Canadian working men and their continued attachment to the two major political parties, the PQ and NDP tend to be dominated by the New Class and therefore their leadership of professors, journalists, and miscellaneous bureaucrats.

The policies of the Liberal Party during the past decade can be interpreted as an attempt to compete for the allegiance of the New Class and of the working people of the country.

No matter what else happens in Canada, this group is going to continue to be important. Even if it is a minority, it will have power far outstripping its numbers because of its effective control of the media which will form our images of ourselves and each other. Of course, there are also strong possibilities for backlash against it.

While most members of the Canadian New Class consider themselves "nationalist," the rise of the New Class is a threat to the potential development of a distinctive Canadian nationality. It is the professors, journalists, and publicists of all kinds who throughout the world are the most cosmopolitan and least parochial. Of all the elements in Canada, it is the New Class who are most like their equivalents in the United States. Their "anti-Americanism" is in itself American, because the same elements in the United States are also anti-American. While Canadian anti-Americanism is ancient, its contemporary manifestations and style are themselves imports from the United States. The current wave of world anti-Americanism originated in Berkeley, California around 1964, and was rapidly disseminated through American universities and media until it was imitated by the New Class worldwide. Most of the conventional contemporary Canadian complaints about American materialism, racism, exploitation, vulgarity, et al. are the stock in trade of the Harvard faculty or the staff of *The Washington Post*. *The Toronto Star* is not as hard on Americans as is the *Boston Globe*.

Today, it is looking like the American intelligentsia is making a turnabout in its opinions of the American character and institutions. It is beginning to move towards the "neo-conservative" position we will discuss later on. *The New York Times* has recently changed its editorial policy in that direction; it will be interesting to see if the *Globe and Mail* follows the new line as faithfully as the old. We expect that our New Class is on the verge of a rediscovery that traditional North American values and institutions are not so bad after all.

Levelling

A fundamental trend in all modern societies is a tendency towards "levelling" or a more equal (or less unequal) distribution of access to the

52

desired things of society. While inequalities remain substantial, the history of the last two centuries is one of uneven movement towards the reducing of those disparities in all industrial societies, whether they be capitalist, mixed, or socialist. Compared with an ideal communist utopia, of course, all societies are heavily differentiated; however, compared with a pre-capitalist, feudal, society we are remarkably egalitarian. For example, in the late seventeenth century, the Lord Chancellor of England could count on an income from his job of five thousand pounds, while a labourer made fifteen pounds a year–the ratio was more than three hundred to one. The present-day ratio is about five to one (after tax).

This levelling takes many forms: to begin with, a significant part of our economy distributes services freely on demand, presumably equally, to all citizens–defence, police protection, parks, public education, sidewalks. In addition, an increasing amount of the wealth in our society is collectivized in one form or another through government and other non-profit organizations. Published figures which indicate vast disparities in the wealth of Canadians refer only to *individually* held assets, and do not count the growing part of wealth which is held by or in trust for masses of people–endowments of schools and hospitals and the growing employees' pension funds, not to mention crown corporations and other government property.

Moreover, there is a levelling of money incomes. Published data which indicate disparities in income typically do not adequately display income after taxes and after government transfers. Governments chop off large amounts of income from the relatively high earners and deliver it down in terms of welfare payments, unemployment insurance, and any other number of goods and services which are rarely "monetized" in calculations of income distribution. The family assistance grants are perhaps the most obvious examples of this phenomenon.

Perhaps most important is a levelling of lifestyles. It used to be that there were glaring differences in the living and consumption patterns of the economic classes. In particular, the privileged urban classes were almost a separate nation from the working classes and the farmers. The last several generations have closed this gap through mass affluence, universal education, and improved communications. In previous times, only the very prosperous had vehicles, the rest took mass transportation, walked, or went nowhere at all. Today the difference between the upper-middle and working class possession is a foreign car instead of a Chevrolet. In almost all consumer goods, the difference between the top and the bottom is now one of modest degree and amount, rather than the sharp differentials of quality in the past.

Levelling by mass prosperity also gives the lower classes the means to physically penetrate places once reserved for the rich. Cars of workers fill the roads; tract development spreads into upper-middle-class suburbs; secretaries go skiing on slopes once a preserve of the privileged.

Levelling shows up in many ways. A striking manifestation is the decline in domestic labour. When there were huge income disparities, the rich could afford battalions of "help." Even an ordinary middle-class household had one or two live-in servants. Today only the very rich can afford a few full-time domestics, and the middle classes are pleased if they can obtain a part-time day maid. Levelling of incomes is reflected in the erosion of all manner of the services. The performing arts (operas, ballets, orchestras) historically relied on the large disparity of income between the producers and the consumers.

Another adjustment to levelling is to substitute government for private privilege. Since the prosperous cannot afford the performing arts as easily as in the past, the arts are increasingly supported indirectly by everybody through government grants. Conversely, live entertainment is "mass produced" through television and phonograph records.

Public privilege substitutes for private privilege in another way through the provision of "perquisites." Expensive cars, aircraft, fancy restaurants, and foreign travel are all increasingly supported on expense accounts for corporations and government. More and more, access to privileged goods and services is a reward for holding a job in a large organization rather than a return for owning property.

Needless to say, this prospect has not been entirely attractive to those on top of the society. But several historical phenomena have made this situation tolerable up until the present time. First, the process has been very slow, giving people time to adjust. Second, the process has been masked in the "circulation of elites." Unless a society is locked into a rigid caste system, there is bound to be considerable turnover at the top. Most established families will inevitably decay. The workings of our system have permitted (indeed encouraged through inheritance taxes) decline, and have hindered new families from rising to the old heights. Also, the costs to the rich in our system look rather trivial compared with what has happened to the privileged classes in many of the countries abroad which have undergone revolutions. The prosperous have adapted in another more fundamental way—people have given up trying to accumulate great fortunes, but have concentrated on achieving a decent standard of living and gaining great power. The sort of people who once wanted to be millionaires now wish to become managers or mandarins.

But, the process is unsettling to the middle classes as well. There is a real sense that their "quality of life" is eroding. This perception of decay, we believe, is fundamental to the understanding of the widespread malaise among the privileged/educated classes in Canada, as elsewhere in the industrial West. It is also, we think, largely at the root of the abandonment of laissez-faire ideology and the acceptance of government intervention as natural and desirable. The privileged classes may now be looking to government to achieve their social ends–to halt or at least slow levelling.

Continuation of a Conserver and Consumer Society

During the last few years a dichotomy between "conserver" and "consumer" economy/society has been presented. We believe that this is a false opposition. Every society is both a conserver and a consumer society. What differs is what is conserved/consumed and the rate at which things are conserved/consumed, which are largely functions of the society's technological capability, its relative prosperity, and value system.

Let us consider the Indian economy which preceded ours. On the whole, we could describe it as a "conserver" society because the Indians lacked the means to consume most of the natural environment around them–yet they were rapacious consumers because they lived by hunting and slash-and-burn agriculture with utter disregard for the conservation of nature. They lived to the limit of their capacity. However, so much effort was invested in hunting and farming that they conserved every bit of what they had exploited from nature as long as they possibly could. Thus, every bit of an animal was consumed in one way or another and conserved as long as possible.

Contemporary society has the technological ability to consume much more of the environment. However, its consuming-conserving patterns vary considerably. The largest variable appears to be the amount of labour input. Ours is a rich society. In a rich society labour is expensive and things are cheap. Things are less cheap when they are relatively valuable, so we conserve them by maintenance and replacing of parts. Of course, this "conservation" is really a form of consumption because the maintenance requires the consumption of labour and materials. As a car gets older, its value decreases and it becomes less and less economic to conserve it so it is eventually junked–consumed. However, to some degree it is conserved, because it is stripped for parts for other cars and the residue is scrapped to make new iron and alloy products. A very few classic cars are so valuable that they are conserved at any cost–and that cost is considerable because it requires hand labour to restore the machine and even to custom-make individual parts.

Note our emphasis on labour. This, we think, is a principal weakness in previous formulations of the conserver-consumer issue–it concentrates on materials and not on labour. In a very considerable sense, labour cannot be conserved. It must be used now or it will forever be lost. Yet our society and economy are fundamentally based upon the conservation of labour because labour is the most expensive input to most goods and services. For this reason, our society is organized around the principle of substituting capital-intensive mass-produced goods for labour-intensive services. In the past, when things were expensive and men cheap, we made use of services, we repaired, we "conserved." Today it is often more economic to throw away and make a new item.

If, for whatever reason, our society should become poorer, we will move to conserve more. We see this in the everyday fluctuations of the economy. During times of recession, new car sales decline and the auto parts business booms. Unemployed workers value their labour cheaply and have the time to keep their cars running longer. Most advocates of a "conserver" society can be said to be forecasting, and sometimes advocating, a state of permanent depression. But even such a society will be a "consumer" society. It will merely consume less materials and more labour. We know a great deal about how such societies operate–we need only look at our history or at contemporary India or China. To most Canadians, these would not appear to be attractive models. Of course, the quality of products can be improved and consumers can exercise more discipline without drastic changes in their lifestyles, so we forecast the continuation of a consumer society–which will continue to conserve.

Increased Affluence

The rate of increase in the growth of affluence is one of the central variables in our three base scenarios, and we shall discuss at considerable length what these different growth rates mean for the whole country. But it must not be forgotten that all of them are *growth* rates, even the slowest. Under the most adverse credible conditions, Canada remains one of the richest countries in the world and continues to become richer.

Population Growth

The same point is true here of population growth. In this century, even under slow growth, there still will be population increase, the rate depending on social values.

Urbanization

This too is a fundamental trend of modern civilization; yet, as will be developed in the urban section of this report, we will argue that this trend will "top out" because we will have achieved almost one hundred per cent urbanization, though of a type barely recognizable to most contemporary experts.

56

Decreasing Importance of Primary and (recently) Secondary Occupations; Increasing Importance of Tertiary and (recently) Quaternary Occupations

Even though we expect that Canada will continue to have a larger primary (resources and agriculture) sectors than most other advanced industrial nations, the percentage of the labour force directly involved in these activities will relatively decline. Our somewhat anemic secondary (manufacturing) sector will also decline relatively. Job growth will be in the service sector–not so much in tertiary industries, which are services to primary and secondary industries, as in "quaternary" industries, which are services done for their own sake, or services to such services, or oriented towards ultimate consumption rather than towards production.

Expanding Technology

Of course, we believe that new technology will appear. How can anyone doubt it? History will not stop, nor will the human mind turn off.

A practical reason for downplaying technology in this study is purely to avoid misunderstanding. We are expressly challenging the limits-to-growth notion that further economic growth will lead to disaster. If we brought in issues of new technology, our neo-Malthusian critics would say, "Hudson has *faith* that new technology will bail us out of our problems." We do not believe that. Our studies indicate that *existing* technology is sufficient to provide a high standard of living for tens of billions of people worldwide, though of course technological advancement increases the margins of safety. This is the main reason for wanting technological progress.

Centralization and Concentration of Economic and Political Power

This means a shift from individual to corporate power of various forms; this, too, has been going on for centuries. This should not be interpreted to necessarily mean centralization at the national level. Sub-national government and private corporate powers are as vital.

Westernization, Modernization, and Industrialization

For Canada, this has long been achieved for most of the population. But the next generation will likely see the trend towards levelling of lifestyles and standard of living continue to influence what remains of the traditional societies of the native peoples.

Erosion of Authority and Deference

Throughout the Western World the habit of obedience is being forgotten.

The instruments and rituals of reinforcement of authority are being abandoned. It is hoped that these can be replaced by "rational" appeals to self-interest and/or benevolence; less sanguine cassandras see the world of the future ruled by fraud and force. Be that as it may, the process is very slow. Fortunately, Canada lags far behind the U.K. and U.S., but we seem to be on the same road–ask any politician or policeman.

Increasing Universality of all the Above

Not only are these trends occurring in the Western world, but increasingly in the entire world; and everywhere they are feeding back on one another. We are affected in many different ways, from the important to the trivial, by these trends and movements everywhere. This is not McLuhan's "global village" but a "global city." In a village, everyone knows each other; in a city everyone interacts with strangers. Villages are supportive; cities alien.

Increasing Ethnicity

While our historic Anglophone-Francophone difficulties have long been a Canadian problem, we ought not to think of this issue as uniquely Canadian. Throughout the world, ethnic difficulties are coming to the fore. The prediction of liberals and Marxists that the world would evolve from a primitive tribal level to a higher plane of "rational" economic conflict is coming to naught; indeed, the opposite is true.

The withdrawal of Western power from the Third World has produced a cauldron of ancient and some new ethnic conflicts. It is impossible to understand the politics of any new nation without knowing the "tribal" or ethnic background of the players. This was to be expected, but what is even more interesting is the revival of ancient ethnic hostilities in the most advanced countries. Except for a very few nations which are homogeneous in population (e.g., Denmark and Iceland), nearly every country in the advanced Western world is having trouble with "minority groups." The Dutch have Indonesians, the French have resident Algerians, the English have their newly arrived "Coloureds," and Japanese their Koreans and untouchables.

Ethnic conflict is most exaggerated when the minority ethnic group has a firm territorial base. Here ethnic awareness slides off into nationalism and separatism, so we have the rise of Scottish, Welsh, Flemish, Basque, and Breton nationalism, as well as like movements among smaller groups in Switzerland, Austria, and Italy. Regional awareness builds up in Germany, the United States, and Canada.

There are two ways to look at these phenomena: the first is as a short-

58

term fashion. However, there is an alternative theory, circulated most persuasively by the American social scientists Nathan Glazer and Daniel Patrick Moynihan, that ethnicity plays a vital role in modern society. One of the great complaints about modern life is its homogenization and levelling. Ethnicity is a form of self-identification, counteracting both the perceived loss of individuality and community.

Furthermore, there is a cynical view of this phenomenon. If modern high status, power, and income depend on formal education, that is, possession of literary skills, it is extremely important what language those skills are expressed in. Language is a means of obtaining entry and also of excluding competitors. The relevance of this factor to Canada is too obvious to elaborate upon.

The (Relative) Natural Waning of French

One long-term trend which is having a direct impact upon present day decision-making is the gradual decline of the percentage of Canadians who are Francophone. Very slowly, but inevitably, it becomes more and more difficult to maintain that Canada is a truly bilingual nation. As the proportion of French Canadians shrinks towards one quarter, the political courage to "sell" bilingualism may weaken.

If present trends continue, the percentage of Canadians who speak French will drop below 25 per cent before the early 1990s—French outnumbered more than three to one. Unless provincial governments push bilingualism especially in the field of education, and unless federal efforts to achieve bilingualism achieve more success than they have in the past, Canada could become an Anglophone country with a large, localized French-speaking minority.

Of course, this relative shrinkage of French is a by-product of the "Quiet Revolution" which led to the secularization of Quebec. Historically, the French fact has been maintained in spite of massive immigration to Anglophone areas, by the high birth rate in Quebec. With secularization and the related sharp decline in that birth rate, Quebec's demographic weapon has been blunted. Understandably, this is making Francophone leaders nervous, and this projection is at the root of the emphasis on teaching French to immigrant children in Quebec.

However, the relative waning of French *nationally* does not mean that French is declining in Quebec; quite the contrary.

The Rise of the West

In any reasonable scenario, Canada must expect a continuation of the long and gradual rise of the Western provinces relative to the rest of the country. From Manitoba west, but particularly in Alberta and British Columbia, growth will be the most rapid—how rapid will depend upon other variables treated in our scenarios.

The Unravelling of the Connection with British Symbols

Strand by strand, the ties that connect Canada to British symbols are being undone. National policy has been to do this slowly, almost imperceptively, because these represent ancient loyalties and there is no wish to disturb unnecessarily these historic sentiments. Nonetheless, the situation of the United Kingdom and the so-slow evolution of the Canadian nation imply that these ties be cut, one by one. Today, few are left. Some time during the next generation, we can reasonably expect such things as the Ministry of External Affairs becoming the Ministry of Foreign Affairs, our High Commissioners in Commonwealth countries becoming Ambassadors, the obliteration of "Royal" in the few places where it still remains, and the removal of the Monarch's profile from Canadian coins and bank notes. We can also expect the patriation of the British North America Act. We are not prepared to forecast the termination of the Monarchy, although we cannot deny that it is a serious possibility.

The Rise of France

During the next generation, we project that France will be the leader of Europe. Many of our readers will perhaps be startled to learn that France, not West Germany, has had the fastest growth rates during the past generation. So long somnolent, during the post-Second World War period, France has led in advanced technology and economic growth. As pointed out by the studies of Hudson Europe, it invests more in education, especially technical education, than does West Germany. Germany's traditional skill at producing heavy steel goods, machine tools, and automobiles has left it behind; these are no longer "leading edge" industries. With considerable government urging and support, France is the European leader in such high-technology areas as aircraft, electronics, and computers. This is expected to continue, although the nation is not without its internal political problems.

This is bound to have important repercussions on Quebec. Indeed, it already has. The long established Anglo-Saxon view that French Canadians are backward, emotional, and immoral is hard to swallow given the relative situations of contemporary France and Britain.

The recent developments in Quebec are very similar to the French experience—too similar to be entirely coincidental. Most obvious on the cultural front is the Quiet Revolution whereby Quebec in a generation has caught up with French secularization. In the economic area, the dominant force in Quebec is the same sort of government induced high-technology industries (James Bay) with dynamic, brash technicians and managers–new men who are a little contemptuous of the old bourgeois and the products of the classical "humanistic" educational system. (The same weaknesses also occur in France and Quebec–perhaps too much confidence in "rational" modes of thought, of "systems.")

If France looks rather well and Britain looks like the sick man of Europe, this is bound to boost the morale of Quebec and also affect the views of Anglophone Canada. The achievement of France and the upgrading of France's image is bound to reflect favourably on Quebec.

The Rise of Japan

This has been well publicized in recent years, not the least by Hudson Institute (U.S.A.) studies. If recent growth rates continue, and there is every reason to expect that they will in the longer term, one of the most important world conditions is going to be an extremely prosperous Japan. It will be a major manufacturing power, and if not the largest, certainly the most aggressive trading power and a huge potential market for Canadian resources and a potential source of foreign investment.

The Rise of the Pacific Rim

The principal motor of expansion of the Pacific Basin has been the rise of Japan, but growth is rapidly picking up in the "little Sinic" areas of South Korea, Taiwan, Thailand, Singapore, and Malaysia, where ethnic Chinese or other peoples of Chinese culture are showing a remarkable talent for industrialization and economic growth. Australia and New Zealand, Indonesia, the west coast of the United States, the western part of Latin America (and perhaps eventually Mainland China) are being drawn into this orbit. By the end of the century we project that the total volume of trade in the Pacific will be equal to that in the Atlantic.

This move to the Pacific Rim portends a shift in the centre of gravity in the world. For Canada it has crucial importance. We will increasingly be distracted from our traditional ties towards England and France. The St. Lawrence will decline relatively in importance compared with the Fraser. Railroads will haul relatively more over the Rockies and relatively less over the Laurentians. The West will become more than ever the boom area. Our hotels and airports increasingly will find their clientele to be Orientals. The pull to the West, of course, will affect the regional balances within the country. Western consumers and producers will find it increasingly difficult to endure paying super-prices for eastern Canadian manufactured goods.

All this is happening already. We expect that it will accelerate. To some degree, Canadian involvement in the Pacific rim is inevitable; how great this involvement or how much we gain from it is not inevitable. The industrializing nations of the Orient have need of raw materials, but they do not necessarily need Canadian raw materials. Australia, Indonesia, Latin America, Africa, perhaps even Mainland China and Siberia offer strong competitors to our produce. Furthermore, the remarkable ingenuity and skill of oriental craftsmen and manufacturers are formidable competitors. It will be extremely difficult to compete with Oriental manufactured goods in world markets, and Western resentment against paying for Eastern protected and subsidized goods will be very strong.

Keep in mind that we are not here projecting any apocalyptic developments. These shifts are already in progress and will continue to go on at a reasonable pace that we will find not too difficult to adjust to. But the tendencies are there, the pressures will build, and we must adapt to the changing world order.

Three Core Scenarios

Throughout this study we will refer to three "scenarios" for Canadian life. Please keep in mind our caution that these are not meant to be predictions, but hypothetical constructions which are intended to be plausible and internally consistent, and to reflect the explicit or implicit expectations of large numbers of informed Canadians. They are not exhaustive. We could have considered many more.

The three scenarios represent a reasonable range of national development over the next generation, because they take for granted the previous conditions and assume the long-term trends, but at different rates of change. For this reason, the scenarios are alike in many ways, differing mainly in their emphases. They should be seen as different, not in kind, but only in degree, reflecting alternative national priorities. For example, economic growth and environmental protection are major national concerns in each scenario, but are of differing relative weight in each.

All three scenarios are moderate in their expectations. We have deliberately eschewed extremist scenarios – such as Canada being taken over by people who would rather accept a sharp reduction in living standards than damage the environment, or others who would advocate the pursuit of growth at any cost to the environment and amenities.

The core scenarios are also intended to be "surprise-free," that is, they deliberately disregard all those "surprises" or low probability events. The reader may reasonably ask what good is a view of the future which does not include such matters. All of us know that life is full of surprises, but we know that we cannot anticipate most of them, so we make our individual plans on the basis of expectations without surprises. In fact the biggest surprise would be if there were no surprises, but the selection process is so arbitrary that we have not attempted to guess the likelihood of a host of possible surprises.*

Some events which would be surprising and which would make a difference to Canada and which are of low probability, but still plausible, will be dealt with in alternative scenarios elsewhere in the study. Today, the most obvious of these is the secession of Quebec from Confederation, and the scenarios for the outcome of this event are described in some detail.

But, our concentration will be on our three core scenarios which together probably describe the least *un*likely outlooks for Canada:

Standard Canadian Scenario

This is the central scenario. It consists for the most part of "straight line" projections of trends from the recent past. This is a "business-as-usual" world. However, it is not a naive extrapolation of all recent trends. (For example a mindless extrapolation of recent unemployment rates would lead to one hundred percent unemployment by 1990. The real trend here is probably a regular fluctuation around 6%.) The scenario assumes the constant and long term trends in Canadian life.

Almost by definition, the standard scenario should be familiar and not very exciting because it assumes either a continuation of what we have long been experiencing or very natural evolutions. It will be surprising to those who believe either that we are in the throes of radical change or that the continuation of business-as-usual leads to disaster. In our view, business-as-usual works and will continue to work in most areas. This does

*Just for the record, here is a list of extreme surprises which could seriously affect the future:

1. Major or minor nuclear war;
2. Nuclear terrorism;
3. Intense revival of cold war;
4. World depression or continued stagflation;
5. Major climatic changes;
6. Major man-induced ecological damage;
7. Bizarre technological breakthrough;
8. Concurrent failure of major food producing regions with consequent world famine;
9. Dictatorship (of right or left) in major industrial democracy and the subsequent wave of the future ideology;
10. Successful revolution in a major Communist nation;
11. Accession to power of a fanatical regime in the U.S.S.R. or in China;
12. Dissolution of NATO or withdrawal of U.S. garrison from Germany;
13. Revival of U.S. territorial continentalism;
14. Appearance of second Communist regime in Latin America, and creation of dynamic Communist movement.

not mean that this projection assumes a stagnant Canada; in fact, the business-as-usual world is a fairly progressive and dynamic world, and the continuation of most current trends, if only by accumulation or compound interest, produces some rather interesting variations on the present scene. But as we shall see, the continuation of some other trends leads to some serious difficulties.

Accelerated Growth Scenario

This assumes that the social and economic conditions of Canada favour a more rapid growth of economic base and population than the standard scenario. In this scenario we have not attempted to produce the highest growth possible, but one that is reasonable even given many of the existing political and other constraints. The principal variable is a commitment by the country as a whole to more rapid growth. There is a sense of dynamism and excitement attached to this scenario with less concern for the environment, for the preservation of wilderness areas, etc., though there is much more concern than there has been traditionally—this is not a "rape nature" scenario. It is, we believe, less likely to occur than the standard scenario at least until the early eighties.

The Constrained Growth Scenario

This scenario exists practically in opposition to the accelerated growth scenario. This is a Canada in which there is slow economic and population growth, because the country, or at least those who "matter" in the country, are less interested in the benefits growth realizes, preferring to concentrate on its costs. The constrained growth scenario is *not* in any way restricted by a running out of raw materials or an increase in pollution (the limits-to-growth scenario would not even be a surprise, because it is incredible). Rather, growth slows because groups in Canada do not wish to grow as much. In this scenario, concerns about the environment increase at the same time as environmental degradation is being decreased. The constrained growth scenario posits not a radical shift in values, but a change in emphasis in directions heralded during the past decade.

The three scenarios are outlined on the following pages. The points will be developed in the topical sections.

STANDARD SCENARIO
1. Short-term "neo-conservative" shift; later reversion to "new values" trend;
2. Continued low birthrate, slow population growth, modest cut-back of immigration;

3. Moderate GNP growth: GNP/capita:

    1976-1980: 4-4.5%   1976-1980: 2.5-3.0%
    1980-1985: 3.5-4.0%   1980-1985: 2.0-3.0%
    1985-1990: 2.0-3.0%   1985-1990: 1.0-2.0%

4. GNP deflator initially follows U.S. pattern but downward trend lags;
5. Permanent high levels of unemployment: 7-10%. Unemployment insurance increasingly part of regular stream of income;
6. Balance of payments deficit: erosion of Canadian dollar;
7. "Wait and see attitude" in early years: what worries foreign investors is the same as what worries Canadian investors (e.g., "new society" issues, FIRA, government attitudes towards business);
8. Nationalists continue to search for a "grand design": try to achieve an emphasis on national unity, values of stability, order;
9. New approaches to federalism: emphasis on flexibility;
10. Growing government: rising pressure for government reforms, rationalization, financial control and cost cutting (at all levels);
11. Mild improvement in environment for business—"can hardly get worse";
12. As Canada increases its dependence and vulnerability (trade and external borrowings), the more pressures for "responsible" behaviour;
13. Some improvements in labour relations;
14. More attention, but not necessarily action, given to long-run issues: new energy developments, food policy, inflation, labour relations;
15. While actual secession will probably not occur, the possibility has become conceptually real. Some Canadians are even considering this without any real apprehension, but they represent a minority.

ACCELERATED GROWTH SCENARIO
1. Growth-oriented long-run policies: e.g., forward resource policy, active export policy, land use, inflation correction and/or management;
2. A counter-reformation and "square" synthesis: some partial return to and grudging respect for traditional values;
3. More rapid population growth: higher birthrate, higher immigration rate, lower emigration;
4. Rapid growth in GNP:

    1976-1980: 4.5-5.0%
    1980-1985: 4.0-4.5%
    1985-1990: 2.5-3.5%

5. Halting and selective turnaround of growth of government;
6. Industrial policy with emphasis on specialization vs. diversification with active government promotion of leading-edge growth industries;

7. Major improvement in labour situation: lower unemployment;
8. "Grand design," e.g., major resource developments;
9. More rapid western and northern development;
10. More rapid suburbanization;
11. Simmering of Quebec problems;
12. More emphasis on more active international role;
13. Greater willingness to cooperate with U.S. on selected issues;
14. If successful the resulting affluence lends itself to a re-emergence in mid-1980s of new class and various new class issues.

CONSTRAINED GROWTH SCENARIO

1. Further and faster movement to the left with emphasis on "new values";
2. Slower population growth: very low birthrate; controlled immigration; growing emigration.
3. A "limits to growth" emphasis:

   1976-1980: 3.5-4.0%
   1980-1985: 2.0-3.0%
   1895-1990: 2.0-2.5%

4. Emphasis on distribution rather than production of wealth;
5. More government involvement: high tax, high "service" state;
6. Conservation emphasis;
7. "Small is beautiful," i.e., no great interest in defence, rapid economic development, or in becoming international power;
8. Tough environment for business: slow increase in the rate of growth of investment;
9. Selected nationalization and provincialization of enterprise;
10. Restraints on foreign and Canadian multi-nationals;
11. Possibility of intensified federal-provincial conflicts;
12. Forced decentralization;
13. Counter-reformation backlash in mid-1980s.

Population

The treatment of population possibilities in great detail is always one of the central features of comprehensive future studies, largely a result of convention and of the availability of copious data on the subject. However, let us warn the reader that this exegesis is not as significant as some might believe. Demography is not destiny.* Despite the apparent ease of population projection, the record of past forecasts is dismally poor. Conventionally, statistical agencies will produce a range of projections from high to low, and the realized population will either turn out higher than the high or lower than the low. This is due to the tendency to make long-term projections on the basis of short-term trends. So we would not be the least bit surprised if someone picked up this report in the 1990s and laughed that we have done exactly what we warned against.

More important, the expected variation in population growth is of less consequence than is often assumed. Whether it goes up two million or four million by 1991 has little effect on decision-making, because increases or decreases in the birth or migration rates normally occur incrementally and turnaround points can be identified. Births are counted accurately every year, so public and private policy can adjust itself to most changes. For example, elementary schools have at least five years lead time and secondary schools a twelve year lead time. For services and

---

*As a warning to those who make too much of population trends, we offer the following from an interview in *Time* (Canada) May 11, 1970:

"...the economic problems will be less serious in four or five years...We will have lower social expenditures because the birthrate is going down. We will have lower unemployment, because the pyramid of age will ease that problem...If we can pass these years, the problems of '75 and '76 will be less serious, demographically, because we will have a smaller number of children, will need less to invest in schools, and will have more money to invest in the economy."

The speaker was then-Premier Robert Bourassa of Quebec.

products for young couples, we have more than a generation lead, and for older people nearly more than a half a century, provided that we take the time to study the data.

Thus, for completeness we must discuss population further. And more important, while the discussion of population is not likely to produce accurate projections, it gives us a considerable sense of what is happening in the country.*

Future population depends upon four factors: births, deaths, immigration, and emigration. As the record shows, it is incredibly difficult to forecast births; but actuarial calculations or death projections have been highly accurate, so those parts of the population who are alive today can be predicted with a great deal of assurity.

Immigration is a function of the desirability of the nation for immigrants (which we expect to remain high), the ability of immigrants to get to Canada (which with cheap international air travel will remain easy), and public policy towards immigration (which, we believe, has a strong chance of being revised significantly in the immediate future). Emigration is a function of the relative desirability of Canada versus other nations and of their immigration policies. Historically, most of our emigration has been to the United States.

*First, we must reject the notion that Canada has or will have a "population problem" in terms of overcrowding or overstrain on resources. Just compare Canada with other northern nations, none of which is overcrowded.

If Canada's provinces† were occupied at the density of:	Canada's population would be:
U.S.S.R.	68 million
Norway	72 million
Finland	84 million
Sweden	110 million
Iceland	267 million

†i.e., excluding the territories

Perhaps more striking is the comparison of Canada with other advanced nations which have a high standard of living and quality of life.

If 10% of Canada were occupied at the density of	Canada's population would be:
Ireland	44 million
Austria	90 million
France	96 million
Denmark	117 million
Switzerland	156 million
United Kingdom	230 million
West Germany	250 million
Belgium	320 million
Netherlands	332 million

68

Sub-national populations (regions, provinces, metropolitan areas, and cities) rely on the same factors, except that internal migration, which is not directly controlled by government in a free society, is a relatively more important factor.

Let us take up at some length the tough variables of births and immigration.

Births

A reasonable forecast of social trends would suggest that the remainder of this century will be a period of relatively low birth rates for Canada. In addition to the rapid decline in the birth rate during the past decade, a large number of elements would encourage low fertility among Canadian families for the remaining twenty years of this century. Two groups of phenomena should have a cumulative effect of retarding population growth:

1. The "topping out" of trends towards increased longevity and increased likelihood of successful birth;
2. Elements promoting low birth rates.

Topping Out of Trends Towards Population Growth

Certain factors which have contributed substantially towards increased population have nearly achieved their peak and cannot in the future be expected to continue to add substantial numbers to the population:

1. *Earlier marriage:* In this century the age of marriage was dropping, thus increasing the opportunity to bear children. Earlier marriage can be credited to the affluence that permitted young couples to have sufficient income to set up housekeeping at an earlier age. However, this long-term trend has run up against another trend, that of young people staying in school longer, and thus having less earned income. In the 1960s the trend towards earlier marriage reversed. We can anticipate that demand for extended schooling will continue to delay marriages.
2. *Improved fertility:* A long-term trend towards more births during this century has been the improved fertility of women. Health advances have reduced the number of women who would have been childless under natural conditions. This percentage is now so low that one cannot expect a significant increase in the birth rate from reducing the percentage further.
3. *Lower maternal mortality:* Death in childbirth, once a major killer of

69

women, has become a negligible factor. Further improvements will have only trivial effects on total population.

4. *Lower infant and child mortality:* In traditional society, death of small children was commonplace. Of one hundred births, a third would be dead by age six and only 40% would survive to age sixteen. Today, less than 3% die before age six and only 1% more by age sixteen. The major gains in this area have already been achieved and only slight improvements can be expected.

Elements Promoting Low Birth Rates

More important will be the social changes and pressures which make people no longer desire many children, and which offer them the opportunities to avoid having them:

1. *Children are no longer economically beneficial:* In an agrarian economy, children represent cheap and loyal workers. Except in a few family-owned shops, a declining economic form, children have very little economic value to the family today. This trend has gone on since the Industrial Revolution, and we may doubt that any Canadian today considers economic productivity in his family planning. (The group for whom economic conditions are now least unfavourable to childbearing are welfare families, who have relatively high birth rates.)

2. *The erosion of family property and occupations:* Our rigid meritocratic standards and competitive society erode the importance of the family business or profession. Since heirs can rarely be expected to carry on the family enterprise, this reason for childbearing is eliminated.

3. *"Social Security":* Historically, the children provided for their parents in old age. Today, this "family security" has been largely supplanted by "social security" through various government and private pension programs.

4. *Children are expensive:* The costs of childbearing are increasing, and are probably increasing faster than family income because children require large amounts of services, such as medical and dental care, recreation and education, for which productivity is not gaining as fast as in the production of goods. Many parents have come to believe that by having many children they are short-changing each of them. Within the middle classes in particular, the costs of higher education are burdensome.

5. *The erosion of the family:* The breakdown of social disapproval of divorce is obvious, as is the increase in divorce, separation, and informal sexual "arrangements," all of which tend to discourage

family formation. A similar factor is the reduction of societal disapproval of remaining single and of overt homosexual activity.

6. *Women's "liberation":* More women are questioning their traditional orientation towards kitchen and children and seek work in the general economy. Currently, upper-class women can hire housekeepers and nurses; but with the general levelling of incomes, obtaining "help" becomes more difficult.

7. *The rebellion of youth:* This phenomenon has been doubtlessly exaggerated by the popular media and may well be a transitory phase; but, still, the vision of ungrateful children turning against their parents' values and standards must give some persons pause in considering having more children.

8. *Improved technology:* Controlled conception made great advances in the last decade. Considerable scientific and medical capital is being invested in this field. In the next decade we can expect further advances in the prevention of conception and termination of pregnancy, making "planned parenthood" more and more a reality.

9. *Decay of religious and legal sanctions against conception control:* As part of the general secularization of society, the traditional religious opposition to contraception has already decayed to almost nothing among the Protestant denominations. Although widespread expectations that the Roman Catholic Church will follow suit may be ill-founded, nevertheless, individual Catholic couples appear to be increasingly ignoring their Church's teaching on this issue, particularly because the curtailment of Roman Catholic education will probably decrease the laity's awareness of the rationale behind the prohibition against artificial birth control.

Once the legal sanction against abortion has been removed, an enormous number of artificially terminated pregnancies can be expected. To most older Canadians, the idea is distasteful; but people coming of age today are more sympathetic to the view that the individual has an absolute right to deal as he/she pleases with his/her body (the "body" is defined as including the potential life within). However, we can expect continued social conflict on this moral issue.

10. *Prolonged education:* It has long been known that there is an inverse relationship between education and urbanization, and fertility. As education levels increase, a corresponding decrease in births may be expected; although it may be that as education becomes more a mass phenomenon it will not continue to be associated with the same behavioural characteristics.

11. *Higher occupational status:* There has long been a negative correla-

tion between occupational status and fertility. During the 1960s birth rates for the higher economic groups dropped faster than for the lower groups. However, this was not a new phenomenon, but rather a return to a previous trend. During the 1950s, the higher economic group had an unusually high birth rate, at least partially caused by glorification of family life and maternity among upper middle-class women. Now this group has reverted to the small family pattern typical of the early part of this century.

12. *The closing of ethnic gaps:* Traditionally there has been a higher birth rate among Quebeckers, native peoples, and New Canadians, than among other Canadians. Most of these differences in birth rates can be attributed to social and economic discrepancies. Generally, as economic levels are upgraded, we can expect a levelling of birth rates.

13. *"Materialism":* Children are no longer "producer goods" but "consumer goods," and are especially costly because they reduce the earning power of one member of the family. The characteristic just-married Canadian couple quickly adjusts its expectations to a life-style supported by two incomes. Withdrawing one earner for child-bearing and child-raising means abandoning many accustomed luxuries which have appeared to be necessities.

14. *The ideology and ethic of "zero population growth":* For many young people, having large families now seems immoral. Public concern with pollution, ecological imbalances, imperilled wild-life, and depleted natural resources reinforces this attitude. The argument that Canada is far from being overcrowded may be countered by arguments for a global perspective which emphasizes the disproportionate share of world resources consumed by the U.S. The value of motherhood is diminished.

15. *Economic stagnation:* This, we hope, is a temporary phenomenon, but to the degree that it persists, the birth rate will be depressed. Few women (like few men) work for "self-actualization" or "fun," but for money. To the degree that their husband's wages do not adequately support their expected standard of living, married women are driven into the labour force.

16. *Pessimism:* A family in a society with a dim view of the future has little incentive to produce children subject to that future.

Factors Keeping Birth Rates Up

Even today it is not clear that we have really dropped to the replacement population level. Young women are having fewer children, partially as a result of later marriage, but it is not certain that they will not have more children later. Even young women expect more children than the average of 2.1 necessary to replace themselves; and despite contraception and abortion, production will surely exceed the number planned.

It has been suggested that a reason for birth forecasts being higher than the birth rate is that many young women are postponing childbirth. There is also a trend towards spacing births further apart. So at least part of the present depressed birth rate is postponement; however, the principal factor is the tendency towards smaller families described earlier.

Nevertheless, against the impressive list of birth-depressing factors we must balance some reasons why we expect the continuation of a substantial birth rate:

1. *Canadians like children:* In fact, one major reason for having few children is that the parents can devote more attention and resources to each individual child. But this tendency must bottom out at some level: probably mostly at one, two, or three children, depending on the parents.

2. *Women want to have children:* The great majority of Canadian women believe the bearing and rearing of children to be their most important activity. Except on the issue of job discrimination and equal pay, the so-called women's liberation movement has hardly touched their attitudes. And most liberationists emphasize their rejection of male domination and sex-determined roles, not child-bearing itself.

3. *The desire for children of both sexes:* Obviously a family that wants boys and girls has a minimum of two children. The statistical odds will provide half the couples with children of both sexes in two births, another quarter in three births, another eighth in four births, and so forth. However, early sex identification of fetuses and legal abortion could reduce the number of extra children produced while trying for the second sex.

4. *Great affluence:* Today, the very rich tend to have large families. Why not? They can afford them. If Canada continues to gain in affluence, more Canadian families are going to be very rich and might continue this pattern.

5. *Public take-over of many child-bearing costs:* Today the cost of universities is an important constraint to the size of middle-class families. Free (i.e., entirely tax supported) higher education would erode this factor. The same effect is possible from free day-care centers.

6. *Fashion:* Small families were fashionable in the twenties and

73

thirties; large families in the forties and fifties; small families in the sixties and seventies. Fashion could change again.

7. *"New Values":* There is an internal contradiction among "progressive" women: many of them simultaneously espouse anti-capitalist values, yet seek to enter the competitive "rat-race." A possible pro-natalist outcome to this tension is suggested by the following scenario.*

"Return of the Three-Child Family," Maclean's, *July 17, 1987*

With kindergarten enrollment up thirteen per cent in the past five years, Canada's schools are beginning to face a new baby boom, unprecedented since the decade following the Second World War. What ever happened to the goal of zero population growth? And what happened to the liberated women of the sixties and seventies?

The answers are various. According to Dr. Alma Fitzpatrick, professor of sociology at McGill University, what has happened, more than anything else, has been the liberation of both men and women from the constraints of the industrial era. Dr. Fitzpatrick sees the larger family as a logical product of value and attitude changes dating back twenty years or more:

"Once significant numbers of young people began to value co-operation over competition, pleasurable experiences over career status symbols, it became inevitable that social value would recentre on the family. Today, with nearly a quarter of the work force enjoying a four-day week, the unpaid employment sector has become the centre of life for many; and men as well as women increasingly esteem its varied tasks, its homey satisfactions, its opportunities for warm personal relationships and for being one's own boss, far above the arid routines and specializations of the paid job."

Harriet Linz, a student at McGill, offers a different perspective: "The first thing I remember was having to be quiet so my mother could study. She was getting her Ph.D., and everybody thought that was so great. Maybe it was great, for then; but, you know, women have proved all those things. She's earning as much as my father. So what? I could do that, too. She used to talk about how narrow *her* mother was. My God, what could be more narrow than a research chemist for a soap company! I'm not going to be like that. Raising children seems to me like the greatest thing there is–for the father, too. It's producing *people.* I'm convinced we can make people better, if we try, and no generation really tried before."

*By Jane Newitt.

74

While a sampling of male undergraduates yields opinions about desirable lifestyles similar to Harriet's, recent statistics on educational attainment tell a somewhat different story. "It's simple economics," says a university dean who requested anonymity. "While the number of kids of both sexes attending university has increased enormously since the Second World War, the percentage of girls has been declining. The feminists turned this around for a while, but they were basically anachronistic. They were boosting career commitments for women at a time when the rest of the country was turning anti-intellectual, anti-technology, anti-success, anti-rat race. As soon as the girls and their parents and the high school guidance counsellors started listening more to that, economics took over, because it is still true—you can't slice it any other way—that boys can expect to have to earn a living while most girls can get out of it if they want. Unless the girls are really pressing for equal education, they're going to slide backwards, just because it's so damned expensive, and that, in fact, is what has been happening.

What does this have to do with the birthrate? "If women don't have as good academic credentials as their husbands, they can't benefit from non-discriminatory practices in hiring and promotion," says Henri Lemieux of Statistics Canada. "When they see the kinds of jobs they're qualified for, raising kids looks like more fun, and their husbands encourage that. Maximizing income matters little now. People want a real home with an acre of land. The population is spreading itself out much thinner and this means that job opportunities for women are also spread thinner. Mainly there's marginal self-employment—crafts, shops, tutoring, interior decorating, taxi-driving, other services and some clerical work—and of course jobs are now starting to pick up. But all this can be done as a sideline to raising kids. Also, when it's all that's available, it's an incentive to have a big family.

A four-day work week, an acre of land, three or four children: this is the ideal for the eighties, but is it good for the country? Expert opinion appears unanimous that it is not good if it lasts. On the other hand, much of the increase in the crude birthrate has reflected an unusually large number of women in the prime age group for childbearing, and also a phenomenon which demographers call "deferred births": that is, the most dramatic rise in fertility in the past five years has been among women ages 30-34, the group which caught the statisticians by surprise in the early seventies by having the lowest birthrate in the nation's history.

Thus many population experts are adopting a wait-and-see attitude, and some are predicting an imminent resumption of the birthrate decline. "This is not the beginning but the end of an era," said one. "We're seeing the last hurrah of the post-war baby boom generation."

Even among those who disagree with this analysis, the need to reach and sustain "zero population growth" seems to have less immediacy than it did a decade ago. Probably the most influential theorist who expects larger families in the next ten or fifteen years is Dr. F.P. Ober, who describes himself as a "non-alarmist."

Dr. Ober contends that the economic factors which cause declining birth rates in industrializing societies cease to apply above a given level of family income which, he says, was reached in this country during the 1940s. What happens thereafter, Dr. Ober says, is an intergenerational birthrate cycle governed by fashion rather than economics. "Oversimply, a girl coming of age in 1950 wanted a big family because her mother had a small one. A girl coming of age in 1970 wanted the reverse. Family income was much lower in 1950 than in 1970 and suitable housing for young families was scarcer, so these decisions weren't based on rational economic calculations; and this is equally true today. People aren't having and wanting more children because it's new and different. A whole cultural philosophy builds up to support it."

Dr. Ober's theory of population growth, which accurately forecasted the current baby boom, indicates that population growth characterized by an intergenerational fertility cycle can probably be sustained for a century or more without creating serious problems for the society. We'll see. In the meantime, babies are in.

Immigration

In very few countries has international migration been as important to the population and national life as in Canada. We expect this to continue, but at a less intense level. Immigration and emigration will continue to be considerable, but a good deal less important than in the earlier part of the century.

Currently, the country is undergoing a national debate regarding the future of the immigration policy. This debate has concentrated almost exclusively on what is good for Canada, not for prospective immigrants. We may presume that over the next generation, whatever happens to Canada, however adverse it may appear to us, our country will continue to be considered one of the most prosperous, free, and desirable places in which to live. With cheap long-range immigration capability made possible by low-cost mass air travel, we would likely be overwhelmed by people from all over the world without some sort of restrictions on immigration.

But these immigrants would originate less in the traditional sources in northwestern Europe than elsewhere, particularly the Caribbean, Latin America, and Asia. Let us be candid in recognizing that the present debate over immigration largely derives from this change in its character. Our immigration will no longer be white, presumably easily assimilated Europeans, but mostly Third World people of darker skin and presumed difficulties in being absorbed. In considering the possibility of large numbers of non-white Canadians, we of course are being reminded of the long history of racial strife in the United States and especially of what has happened in the United Kingdom during the past fifteen years. The English, like us, used to be very sanctimonious about U.S. racism; now the Americans are snickering at the discomforture of the English with their "coloured" population.

Of course, Canada does not wish to publicly recognize this factor. Our anti-racist sentiments bar us from looking at this explicitly as a racial question. But based upon the past experience of other "Anglo-Saxon" nations, we are faced with a peculiar paradox—Canada can be relatively non-racist if it has no large racial minority. This paradox necessarily, and quite properly, leads us to hypocrisy. Because of this, Canada will certainly put forward a policy over the next several years which will not explicitly, but will *de facto*, have the effect of making it more difficult for non-white immigrants to enter the country. We expect that the next generation will see this issue worked out subtly, without explicit national quotas such as was the U.S. immigration policy of 1924, but with a tightening of the existing system of controlling immigration by screening and queueing. People from the United Kingdom, France, and western-European countries will find it very easy to get through the screen, but East Indians, Jamaicans, Colombians, etc., will find it difficult. Except for a few clergy and civil-rights activists, almost all Canadians will support such a policy, including the already arrived non-white immigrants who fear that a further build-up of their numbers will incite more backlash and make their lives and their children's lives less pleasant.

The concerns about the character of immigration are particularly poignant today because of the low birth rate. With native Canadians breeding at historically unprecedented low levels, a major portion of whatever population growth we have will result from immigration. At current levels of 180,000 a year net in-migration and 340,000 births, more than a third of our new population comes from immigration. If this should continue unchecked for half a century at something resembling these rates, the permanent balance of the population would change substantially.

A particularly interesting possibility for Canada is that we will suffer some side effects of recent changes in the U.S. immigration law which, as we shall see, will make it more difficult for Mexicans and other Latin Americans to enter the United States; therefore some of them will surely have more incentive to try to make it into Canada.

The racial aspect is at the root of the current immigration debate. Nevertheless, the traditional arguments for and against immigration still are relevant: It is good for the country to have a larger internal market, to have a larger population from which to draw talent and leadership, to have people who are eager and willing to take low-skilled and entry-level jobs which longer-established Canadians are no longer willing to perform. This last point is obvious, but perhaps needs some expansion. Being a ditch digger or a bus boy is not a very attractive job for most Canadians. We tend to look at them as "dead end" jobs and a good part of those Canadians ineligible for more skilled positions would rather go on the dole than take them. However, being a ditch digger or a bus boy in Canada is a very desirable job for most of the people in the world. The immigration of people to do low-level jobs serves to benefit the host country (us), the immigrant, and the home country as well because the immigrant often ships some part of his income back to his family. Without immigration, Canada will have a serious shortage of labour at low-skilled jobs, denying us many services, and having a general effect of pushing up costs and injuring our national competitiveness.

On the other side, the old costs of immigration remain. Immigrants will crowd certain areas of our cities, put an additional load on our school systems to integrate and assimilate foreigners, and create more chips in our national mosaic. Immigration will have substantial regional and local effects as well. Immigrants on the whole go to those places which are booming and this will accelerate whatever disparities of regional economic growth are evident.

Emigration

Immigration cannot be discussed without looking at emigration. The emigration numbers have long been the hidden Canadian statistic, partially because a free country keeps track of who enters but not who leaves its borders, but also because it is somewhat embarrassing. Canada has suffered a long loss of national blood to the States. It has been estimated that half the descendants of a Canadian couple married in 1900 are U.S. residents. More persons of Canadian birth live in the United States than in all but four of our provinces. In addition, there has been a continuing re-emigration of immigrants. To a large degree our historical open immigration policy has been a means of replacing the losses to the U.S. Can we expect this to continue, especially given the very low level of recorded Canadian emigration to the United States during the last decade, as well as the increased interest in Canada by American immigrants (only a few of which have been the well-publicized "draft dodgers")?

Mere numbers do not properly measure the emigration issue. The quality of the emigration is vital, especially if we are experiencing a "brain drain" of talent. American data regarding U.S. residents of Canadian birth indicate that they are an extremely prosperous group, even more prosperous than would be expected on the basis of formal education alone. This suggests that Canadian Americans tend to be go-getters who lack the educational background and probably the family and social status which is generally agreed to be more useful for economic success in Canada than in the United States.*

Recent changes in the U.S. immigration law might affect the attractiveness of the States to Canadians. Everything we have said about the desirability of Canada to immigrants throughout the world applies to the United States. As U.S. immigration patterns have shifted towards the "Third World," things have been tightened up. The most recent (1975) revisions to the U.S. immigration laws dropped the policy of treating the Western Hemisphere as a single block and established individual national quotas. What this means is that Canadians no longer have to wait in line with Mexicans, Bolivians, etc., but have their own line. This will make it more difficult for Central and South Americans to enter the United States, and easier for Canadians.

Our analysis indicates that emigration to the United States is no longer a serious factor and may indeed be counterbalanced by immigration from the United States. Nevertheless, it is unreasonable to expect that emigration will disappear altogether, and it is certainly possible that the relative attractiveness of Canada and the United States might again be revised. If the Canadian standard of living should drop appreciably below that of the U.S., emigration, particularly by ambitious individuals, would pick up again. Also, political changes in Canada which provoke a lesser degree of personal liberty or economic opportunity might also shift the balance. Independence by Quebec could also provoke a major emigration to the United States. Some French Canadians who would not wish to live under a separate Quebec government might prefer the United States.

But in any event, no matter how favourable is the Canadian quality of

*Analysis of U.S. data also indicates that much more recently arrived Canadian residents in the United States are much less likely to take up U.S. citizenship than their predecessors. This suggests either a higher level of national sentiment today or an intent eventually to return here.

life, some leakage to the States must inevitably continue. The larger U.S. economy and society must necessarily provide a wider range of personal opportunities. Individual Canadians who seek a highly specialized occupation or environment (particularly those who require more temperate climate) will move south. Also, the vast size of the U.S. economy and the fact that it is the capital of the world economy and culture means that ambitious Canadians who wish to make a name for themselves sometimes feel that they must necessarily go to New York or Los Angeles for the centre of activity. This leakage, particularly of the very bright and ambitious, for the centre of activity is the price that smaller countries often pay to big neighbours.

Three Scenarios*

Following are three scenarios for Canadian population change. These are linked to the overall economic growth scenarios to be described in the next section. Population growth has been associated with economic growth for several reasons: We believe that, within the social framework of a mature industrial society, high growth indicates optimistic national attitudes which provide the morale and the money for a higher birth rate and a higher demand for labour, which attracts and permits higher immigration. Lower economic growth suggests low morale, the prevalence of limits-to-growth policies, a lower level of immigration, and higher emigration.

The population pyramids and charts shown in the appendix illustrate the range of our three scenarios. The chart that follows shows the outlines of the assumptions going into the projections. In 1977, it seems reasonable to believe that the high and low projection are the upper and lower limits to growth. However, as we caution above, such projections normally have a dismal record. In any event, note that there is not that much difference in the total population by 1991 caused by three rather widely varying assumptions. Even high birth and immigration projections do not have substantial effects on the total population.

These are the assumptions of fertility and immigration in the three scenarios:

A. Accelerated Growth:
1. Fertility: total fertility rate (*roughly* the equivalent of intended family size) moves from 1.835 per woman actual in 1975-6 to 2.5 in 1986-7, and stays there thereafter;
2. Immigration: climbs to 295,000 in 1992-3 and continues to climb

*The population projections presented here were calculated by John Kettle.

80

at same rate thereafter;

3. Emigration: 42% of gross immigration (therefore *net* immigration is 58% of gross immigration).

B. Standard:

1. Fertility: total fertility rate drops to 1.8 in 1978-9 and 1979-80, climbs back to 2.0 in 1989, and stays there;

2. Immigration: cut to 150,000 in 1981-2, at which point it is 0.625% of population at start of year; thereafter it is that same percentage of the population: 159,000 in 1986-7, 168,000 in 1991-2, and 177,000 in 1996-7;

3. Emigration: same as in A (42% of gross immigration).

C. Constrained Growth:

1. Fertility: declines in flattening curve to 1.5 in 1993-4, and continues at same rate of decline thereafter;

2. Immigration: declines in flattening curve to zero in 1985-6, partially because Canada is a less attractive place, but mostly because of a restrictive immigration policy provoked by racial and neo-Malthusian values;

3. Emigration: increases from 42% of gross immigration in 1975-6 to 100% in 1985-6; thereafter increases by 5,000 a year, resulting in 75,000 net emigration at end of century.

Most important, because of the assumption of death rates improving at historical rates, the numbers of adult Canadians do not vary very much during the study period.

In all scenarios, the most striking feature is the effect of the post-Second World War "baby boom" during which there was a remarkably high birth rate compared with that of 1920-1945. As this group came into its adolescence during the 1960s, the centre of the culture focused on "youth." By 1991 this baby-boom generation will be entering its early forties. Unless the birth rate goes up again as projected in the accelerated growth scenario, for the first time in history population pyramids will no longer be literal pyramids: wide at the base and narrow at the top. Actually, as indicated most clearly on the constrained growth chart, the population pattern will resemble a truncated diamond; we will have an older and more mature society. There is no historical precedent for this, so we can only conjecture about its social aspects. Most people feel that an older society will be conservative, interested in security more than freedom, less prone to risks, and skeptical of political demagogy and appeals to grandiose visions.

If this perception is true, the range of variables in our scenarios will not be affected very much. Although the standard and accelerated growth scenarios project increases in the birth rate over the current low level, this will not initially have major impact because infants do not have a direct effect on the society. In fact, the accelerated growth scenario might be the most conservative of all because the dominant element of the Canadian population will be mature couples with children. Thus, Canada would be an extremely family-oriented country. As such, central values would likely be concerns for "what is good for the kids," special interest in the future. Almost by definition, the constrained growth would seem to be conservative yet hedonistic, in that couples would be more involved in themselves and the present and less in the future as represented in children.

The three scenarios also have important regional implications. The high growth scenario assumes rapid development of resource industries, which promotes the growth rates of resource parts of the country. High growth also implies high prosperity, which means rapid exurbanization (to be discussed in the urban development chapter). This implies much growth outside but adjacent to existing metropolitan areas. High growth also means trickle down to the less prosperous parts of the country, giving them relatively more growth than they would under the business-as-usual world. Low growth, however, means powerful social attitudes towards "localism" or local limits-to-growth, which will bar penetration of new people into existing desirable areas. These variations are developed in more detail in the regional development section of this report (See population charts 1-4 and Tables 1-7.)

Economics

In 1978, the economic issue of widest concern is "stagflation," which caught the entire world by surprise after a prolonged period of prosperity. Yet, as recently as five years ago, a futures-oriented discussion of the economy would have concentrated on issues related to the potentials (and problems) of world affluence. Perhaps the most remarkable economic event in our century was the world-wide boom from 1950 to 1973. While industrial nations have grown an average two or three per cent per year through most of modern economic history, gross world product (GWP) climbed at an average annual rate of five per cent, more than tripling in the twenty-three years after the Second World War. The world, or at least the industrialized world, was enjoying what seemed to be an endless boom, and even as recently as five years ago, had every reasonable expectation of more of the same.

Canada was among those countries with the most impressive economic performance. In fact, during that post-Second World War period Canada had one of the highest growth rates of all industrialized countries–excluding Japan–and experienced an unprecedented increase in national prosperity, both absolutely and relative to the U.S. The gap in standard of living between Canada and the U.S. narrowed markedly. We had a golden age–yet how many Canadians were aware of it?

Today we do notice economics. World stagflation was *the* surprise of the post-war period. Along with slow or no growth and high unemployment came double-digit inflation, and it became obvious that our economic system was not operating efficiently. Earlier inflation rates of up to three per cent were associated with strong economic activity. But today, the anticipation or fear or high inflation has crippling effects on economic activity. As faith in the value of currency is lost, the system cannot function effectively. If people expect inflation, they hesitate to tie themselves into long term commitments–whether supply contracts, wage contracts, construction contracts; prices tend to be adjusted more rapidly to all increases in future costs, the duration of collective agreements is shortened, and various measures for indexing wages and pensions are built into the system. In addition, the anticipation of inflation is reflected in high interest rates—the lender not only requires "rent" for his money, but also enough interest to cover the expected decline in the value of money during the loan period.

The economy cannot be expected to pick up significantly unless investors and consumers stop anticipating inflation and/or feel protected against its effects. For example, though nominal rates of interest are high, the real rates are actually low, i.e., if inflation is seven per cent and interest rates are ten per cent, the borrower is getting a three-per-cent rate for his money, the rest being a hedge against anticipated inflation. The borrower feels exploited, while the lender feels short-changed. House buying becomes less and less available, and housing no longer acts as an economic stabilizer.

Canada cannot solve its inflation problem alone. As pointed out in the preface, the causes of the current inflation are multi-faceted. Commodity prices, oil prices, too rapid simultaneous growth in industrialized countries, speculative stock-building worldwide, are issues Canada can do relatively little about. However carefully we deal with domestic inflation, the volume of our trade means that we will necessarily import other nations' inflation.

On the domestic side, a number of factors point to a possible resurgence of high inflation. As controls are phased out, prices will probably increase more rapidly to make up for "losses" incurred during the control period. When concealed inflation becomes revealed, there may be overshooting. Also, the fear of reimposition of controls may lead business to jack up prices, just in case.

Furthermore, prices may also be increased to generate profits for purposes of financing corporate investment (to make up for slow investment in the last few years), unless there are major changes in tax laws.*

In recent years, the economists' theory of a dichotomy between inflation and unemployment, the "Phillips curve," has virtually disappeared. Inducing inflation to stimulate the economy and reduce unemployment no longer works: As inflation increases, the stock market drops, investor confidence falls, investment collapses, and jobs are not created.

*Ironically, while businessmen stress the importance of permitting market forces to operate naturally, they often advocate the need to establish prices sufficient to produce rates of return adequate to attract investment—in other words, a "just price" for capital.

In anticipation of further inflation, investors run to liquidity which translates into higher, short-term interest rates reducing the availability of long-term capital for expansion. Capital expenditures are discouraged by the fear of being caught between rising costs and policy restraints or worse, price control. In fact, much of the inflation/unemployment discussion overlooks the impact of rigid labour markets and physical capacity shortages on prices. The inflation/unemployment tactic appears to have been spent in the pre-stagflation period, in those years of unprecedented growth when the world forgot about the importance and value of the business cycle, and believed that we could simply "fine-tune."

Occasional recessions, painful and costly as they may be, perform important social and economic functions: they "teach lessons" in prudence and sound management; they facilitate the squeezing and elimination of marginal activities; they allow adjustments in lagging sectors, a slowing down of excessive growth sectors, a liquidation of excessive inventory; they put pressures on increased costs, waste, and inflationary trends; and finally, they provide a kind of pause and motivation for other necessary adjustments.

During the post-war period of unprecedented prosperity the world seemed to forget about the value of the business cycle (even though there were minor recessions during that period) and downside risk. Canadians, particularly younger Canadians who cannot remember the Great Depression, assumed that a constantly increasing standard of living was a part of the natural order, and took economic growth for granted. This almost smug acceptance of current high standards and even richer future was seen as a national right, indeed almost a natural law. Other industrial nations, especially Scandinavia, Holland, the United Kingdom, the United States, and Australia, have shown similar tendencies. Certainly, our economic situation cannot be compared with that of Great Britain; yet we are, as one foreign observer remarked, "the sick man of North America." Today, the economic future of the country is an issue of wide concern (Quebec is seen as a major problem principally in Central Canada). This is a new and unsettling development. What has happened?

Like the other liberal democracies, Canada has pursued the political economy of "the welfare state." The reasoning behind it was exquisitely practical: while laissez-faire capitalism was making the nation rich, it produced certain unpleasant costs, particularly in poverty for those who could not compete successfully. Moreover the market did not provide for all the goals that citizens of different classes found desirable: national goals, social goals, and environmental goals. Recognizing that any serious revisions to the system would require income redistribution impossible to achieve in a liberal capitalist system, the "social" adjustments have been

85

made from impending growth. Welfare claims have been paid out of the additional national income provided by economic expansion, thus reducing the trauma of redistribution and preventing counter-attacks by the established wealth holders.

Conservative cassandras have long said that such policy would lead to tyranny and/or disaster. Yet, on the historical record, the welfare state has worked well. In Canada, as in the other liberal democracies, the combination of a growing economy with the diversion of part of the growth through the public sector has led to a political economy of unprecedented prosperity, security, and individual freedom. The welfare state has been a great success. Unfortunately, some elements in our society lately have only considered the redistribution aspects of the welfare state, and have forgotten about the restraint, responsibility, discipline, and economic growth that made it practical. This we feel is largely at the root of our present difficulties. The contemporary manifestations of economic unrest–growing foreign debt, a growing tax burden, inflation, the outflow of capital, high unemployment, and increasing labour militancy–all can be laid ultimately at the door of a failure to recognize the need for continued discipline and responsibility to preserve the present system.*

Welfare economies may be more difficult to operate than laissez-faire or command economies. A welfare economy requires a high degree of discipline, and a greater sense of responsibility on the part of all economic agents.

The "poverty of affluence"–a rich country cannot blithely tell people that some benefit cannot be afforded–means that everything becomes a question of priority and timing. This constraint becomes all-important. One of the problems, worldwide, was failing to impose these constraints of priority and timing, until it was nearly too late.

All of our scenarios assume the continuation of the welfare economy for the next generation at least. Canada, like almost all industrial nations, will be characterized by these fundamental elements:

1. Continuation of the ideal or rhetoric of private/free enterprise;
2. Most economic decision-making in fact by private individuals and organizations;
3. Some selective pragmatic government ownership of means of production, transportation, and communication;
4. Special statutory provisions for organizations that sell labour collectively, i.e., trade unions;

*Economic growth per se is not the only issue here. What is important is economic growth in relation to consumption or vice versa. The problem we face is not that of consumption per se but rather of too much, too soon.

86

5. Some state-supported private monopolies;
6. Direct government regulation of all the above to varying degrees;
7. Government intervention through taxation and social services to redirect parts of the national income.

We seriously doubt that any observer of the Canadian scene could make a credible case for a demand for a real alternative political economy by any substantial group of Canadians. Except for a tiny radical fringe, our socialists advocate moving along the lines of northern-European social democracy, that is to say, with more government intervention but the private sector left essentially intact. Nor do we believe that there can be a plausible scenario for economic disaster sufficient to force the country to reorganize its economy in any significant way. As discussed elsewhere, a no- or a trivial-growth economy almost demands increased government activity, yet it does not necessarily require, in our view, a command economy. Conversely, the restoration of independent small enterprises, whether individual entrepreneurships or communes, seems inconsistent with contemporary Canadians' desires for economic security.

Three Economic Scenarios

Our three base scenarios are reasonable variations of projections of existing conditions. They vary in the emphasis that the country will put on relative material benefits as reflected in fundamental social values. We have used "growth rates" as the key indicator. This should not be interpreted as some sort of GNP determinism; in fact, the growth rates in GNP are merely used as what they were intended to be–an indicator. They reflect, in total, natural resources, investment opportunities, inflation, labour force skills and attitudes, and fundamental national values.

All of the economic scenarios assume an initial short-term catching-up period as Canada climbs out of the recession, and a slowdown of growth towards the early 1990s. They vary in the rapidity of the recovery, and how soon the slowdown hits the economy. Again, while we present the standard scenario as the least unlikely, we cannot disregard the possibilities of the accelerated or constrained growth scenarios; but obviously we think of them as less likely to be realized, and therefore somewhat less suitable for prudent planning.

These scenarios will not be merely the function of impersonal forces and Canadian attitudes, but of deliberate policy by government, business, and organized labour. There is a great deal of leeway in outcomes derived from intelligent decision making. But Canada must continue to operate in the world economy, and its rate of growth and general prosperity will also depend upon the movement of the other industrialized (OECD) countries. Our view is that GNP growth for the OECD countries will likely run at an average annual rate in the neighbourhood of 4.0 to 4.5 per cent in the next decade, probably slowing slightly towards the end of the decade and after that. The developing countries should average 5 to 6 per cent, with some remaining relatively stagnant and others continuing to grow much faster. World trade should grow at a rate of 7 to 8 per cent.

In the shorter term, the challenge of the next few years is dealing with relatively slow growth, sluggish capital investment, high unemployment, and inflation. There appears to be no underlying fundamental confidence in the economic outlook worldwide as evidenced by the virtual absence of net long-term investment in most industrialized countries. Capital expenditures are weak because of inadequate profitability, the high costs of equity financing, inflation, uncertainty over capacity utilization, uncertainties about energy, environmental regulation, consumer protection regulations, labour relations, stimulation or anti-inflationary policies, and politics in general. A significant portion of new capital investment tends to be of special nature, e.g., energy and/or short term. Rates of return on capital remain low according to historical standards. In Canada for example the average post tax rate of return in the mid sixties was 8.0 per cent; it fell to 3.5 per cent in 1974 and was only 4.5 per cent in 1976. Looking to the years ahead, it is not likely that business investment will pick up unless the expected profitability of new investment increases significantly. The fragility of the world economy is further compounded by the issues of increasing overseas borrowing not only by LDCs, eastern European countries, and the sick economies of Europe; but also by relatively stronger economies like Canada. The markets are jittery. Exchange rates are unsteady and flexible rates inject an additional element of price and market uncertainty. Economic nationalism and pressures for increased protectionism are intensifying, and the lack of political stability breeds increased caution towards new investment. We therefore forecast a quite bumpy recovery to the end of the decade and the likelihood of a recession in 1979 or 1980 is indeed serious.

The impact on Canada is all too obvious. We, too, are experiencing high inflation; removal of controls as well as currency devaluations will only exacerbate world inflationary pressures. Our competitiveness on world markets has largely deteriorated (currency devaluation is only a short term, artificial mechanism for increasing competitiveness). Further investment will be required to increase our effectiveness and efficiency. The prospect of curtailed energy exports in the late seventies does not bode well for our balance of payments situation; likewise our track record on services and invisibles is bleak. And political uncertainty is clouding economic prospects. Big projects such as Northern gas pipelines will likely contribute about 1 per cent to GNP growth rates but their full impact will only begin to be felt towards the end of the decade. The next four years will be difficult.

Our standard scenario does not however assume that the economic movements of the last few years will continue over the long term. A continuation of trends of 1971-1977 would not be "business-as-usual" but a nightmare scenario. Continuation of those trends quickly leads to disaster. And such a scenario would, in a considerable sense, not be a Canadian scenario, because it is doubtful if Confederation could survive under conditions of accelerating inflation, massive unemployment, and the inevitable regional conflicts. A continuation of 1971-1977 is the English scenario. Even in the United Kingdom, which has been a unitary country for nearly four hundred years, there have been regional strains, as evidenced by the rise of Welsh and Scottish nationalism. Our national unity is much more recent, fragile, and much more easily dissolved.

Like the United Kingdom, what can hurt Canada's economy the most is excesses, most likely excesses in the areas of social welfare, government misregulation, and trade-union militancy. But, the comparison with Britain is not a very good one. Canada and Britain do not have the same resource base, class structure, industrial mix, and morale. The British economic malaise is the result of failure—the failure to keep up. Although Britain maintained a steady 2 to 3 per cent growth for the past twenty years, it fell behind the other industrial countries which grew faster. It did not really participate in the remarkable boom of the last twenty years, but tried to live as if it had. Canada has caught up and even grew faster than many other countries, the U.S. for example. This is a result of success, not of failure, and in no way do Canada's problems approach Britain's. But Canada now has to learn to cope with the poverty of affluence. The danger is that Canada will try to continue to increase its consumption without corresponding increases in production.

The Standard Scenario

The standard scenario assumes that the economy continues to recover from the recession and moves back towards the long-term trend lines. The recovery may be bumpy, but on the average the economy grows about 4-4.5 per cent per year from 1976 to 1980, which places the national unemployment rate in the range of 7 to 8 per cent during the period. This will fall short of "full employment" by about 1.5 to 2 percentage points.

During that period, inflation, as measured by the GNP deflator, will average between 6 and 7 per cent per year. It will be prevented from dropping lower by the effects of economic recovery, likely price and wage increases following removal of price and wage controls, price increases necessary to generate profits for purposes of financing corporate investment, high energy costs, and a high, though perhaps more controlled, level of government expenditures.

Government efforts to stimulate the economy will be cautious and moderate. The tone will be one of gradualism as evidenced by recent pronouncements focussing on "medium-term policies." Primary reliance will continue to be placed on monetary policy. Existing wage and price controls will be phased out and some combination of tax cuts and investment tax credits may be implemented without, however, major changes in the tax structure. There will be few major economic initiatives. Investment in energy-related developments will continue to be a driving economic force.

There will be a few new initiatives in social welfare, but costs of current programs continue to swell because of present commitments, despite selective reforms and administrative tightening. Regional disparities follow the current pattern, with Alberta, Southern Ontario, and British Columbia registering the highest growth. Quebec continues to lag. Because of this unevenness and because of political circumstances in Quebec, increased attention is paid to the regional effects of federal programs.

Of course many uncertainties continue to hang over the economic outlook—the future of Confederation, the increase in energy costs, government regulations, etc.—and investor confidence may well be the major factor whether the Canadian economy gets moving more strongly and retains vigour of growth. Nevertheless as Canada increases its dependencies and vulnerability, e.g., trade and external borrowing, pressures will build for "responsible" behaviour, for moderation of certain "anti-business" attitudes, for government reform, financial control and cost cutting at all levels, for improved labour relations, and for a more positive attitude towards investment, both of domestic and foreign origin.

The years 1980-85 should see GNP growth rates of about 3.5 to 4 per cent. More attention will be given to long-run issues such as energy development, technological development, rationalization of industry, and food policy. The environment for business will have mildly improved (but business feels things can hardly get worse).

Growth rates should begin to decline in the mid-eighties with GNP growth averaging about 2 to 3 per cent per year to the end of the century. (See Table 22.)

*This scenario might be labelled as too optimistic by those who see Canada going the route of the British or the limits-to-growth proponents. In fact this scenario is not at all overly optimistic. If we were to define a standard scenario for the U.S., we would show growth rates slightly higher than the Canadian growth rate, at least during the next three to four years.

The Accelerated Growth Scenario

The accelerated growth scenario assumes stronger reactions against current limits-to-growth psychologies as a basis for revival of industrial-era values and aims and for a commitment to more rapid growth. Average growth rates for the 1976-1980 period are estimated at 4.5 to 5 per cent. Emphasis is on growth-oriented long-run policies, e.g., more effective inflation management, a forward resource policy, an aggressive export policy, along with an emphasis on a more active international role and a greater willingness to co-operate with the U.S. on selected issues. A halting and selective turnaround of growth of government and a major improvement in the labour situation are achieved. The accelerated growth scenario also reaches the slower growth rates of the standard scenario but at a later date. The 1980-85 growth rates are of the order of 4 per cent slowing to 2.5-3.5 after that. Although this scenario appears feasible in the sense that sufficient labour would be available and adequate supplies of capital should be forthcoming if the right policies are followed, it is less likely to be realized than the standard scenario at least in the short term. However we believe it is plausible in the longer term.

This scenario does not imply achieving the highest rate of growth possible, but rather a growth rate that is both feasible and probably desirable from the point of view of those who like growth, i.e., at least the majority of the Canadian population. To achieve the economic prospects of the standard or accelerated growth scenarios, however, it will be necessary to restore the idea of legitimacy and desirability of economic growth, and to curb the common current mental attitude that encourages low morale or hostility to growth. This is not incompatible with continued concern with social and environmental issues. On the contrary, economic and technological growth and the ensuing prosperity they confer may well be the only way to solve these.

The Constrained Growth Scenario

This scenario emphasizes slower population and economic growth, conservation, and increased government involvement. In this scenario the slower growth rates of the standard scenario are felt in the early 1980s rather than in the early 1990s. The growth in GNP over the 1976-80 period averages about 3.5-4 per cent, slowing to 2-3 per cent in the early 1980s and down to 2-2.25 per cent beyond 1985. Canada is a high tax, high service state that emphasizes redistribution of wealth. Selected nationalizations and "provincializations" are combined with restraints on foreign and Canadian business. Governments are increasingly involved in almost every aspect of the economy to achieve ends which have not been traditionally thought of as the government's business or at least not within the government's capability.

There are social tensions latent in Canadian society and polity that might intensify and cause a serious setback to economic "progress"; currently the most obvious tensions relate to political uncertainty vis-à-vis Confederation, labour militancy, and the stability of economic policy. But the constrained growth scenario is not the result of exhaustion of resources or over-population or pollution, but the result of deliberate policies to slow growth which reflect the decreasing value attached to economic growth as the country comes to believe that present affluence is adequate. In this case, the pressures for slower growth in the long term would result from the very success of our economy and the resulting desire for no hassle and more leisure.

Eventually, the Canadian economy will probably tend towards slower growth, irrespective of whichever scenario occurs. But it is doubtful that slower growth will be seen as desirable in the 1970s and early 1980s–this would seem just a little too early. But it may well become the policy of the 1990s.

This is not a transient phenomenon. Examination of poll data indicates that the emphasis on limits-to-growth appears to have peaked in 1974. Nevertheless, as will be discussed in the values chapter, new values and priorities will continue to dominate thinking after the next decade. Although there will be more pressure on nationalists and/or doomsayers to consider the economic implications of their actions, pressures will remain for more emphasis on the costs of growth. The more manic aspects of the environmental movement will tone down, but the basic pressures and concepts will increase. The most important trend, which will dominate the subsequent decade, is that the world economy will gradually revert to historical growth rates. This occurs in all three scenarios, though at different times.

Investment and Capital Formation

Some very concrete economic issues also point to slower growth rates. One such issue has to do with investment and capital formation. This issue is important not only in terms of long-term growth but is vital to the current recovery. The next few years will likely show that there is less slack in the economy than common estimates of unused capacity would suggest. The index of capacity utilization stood at about 95-96 per cent in 1973 at the height of the recent boom. Current estimates range between 83-87 per cent. (See Chart 5.) However, investment growth has been slow since 1973, energy and environmental considerations have increased, and the changing age-sex composition of labour seems to have reduced the growth of labour productivity—none of which is adequately reflected in capacity utilization figures. Since 1973, in a few sectors—energy, utilities, and chemicals—investment showed a great deal of strength; but in most others, it was virtually stagnant or even declined from high levels.

Government ventures accounted for a disproportionate share of new investment, and real capital spending by non-financial private corporations changed very little. Canada reached bottlenecks very quickly in 1973; the situation seems to have worsened. Without significant increases in capacity in the immediate future, 1979 should be the year when tight capacity and the corresponding inflationary effects increase. Nineteen eighty could well be a repetition of 1975.

Even if excess demand is limited to a few sectors of the economy and is balanced by deficient demand in other sectors, this points to another bout of inflation. The price rise in markets with excess demand will not be balanced by falling prices in other sectors, and the tendency is for wage changes in rapidly expanding industries to influence wages across the board.*

Our economy is inherently capital intensive. This, combined with inadequate levels of investment in the past fifteen years, the special requirements of the energy sector, the increase in the cost of energy, the need for anti-pollution investment in the order of about 2.0-2.5 per cent of GNP by 1990, the heavy demand for food and minerals, and the increasingly capital-using nature of production as wages rise and labour force growth slows, contribute to a higher and probably increasing capital-output ratio which also points to the likelihood of slower growth rates in the long term.

It is a popular pastime to discuss the upcoming shortage of capital. The idea of a capital shortage implies that the flow of money through the capital markets will be inadequate to finance the investment required to meet demands for goods and services, or that the cost of capital will be much too high. This we would claim is almost completely wrong. Capital is available—if investors want to invest. Given inflation, interest rates are low, not high. The high growth regions of our country, Alberta for example, could attract significant amounts of capital; there is no reason why Canada would refuse to attract OPEC capital especially since OPEC investments are shifting from short- to long-term investment.

*This view is not inconsistent with the monetarist theory that inflation cannot occur while the money supply is fixed. Monetarist theory states that the percentage change in money supply should be the same as the percentage change in real income, so that the price level is fixed. However, we do not believe that the money supply will be managed in this way, because governments will want to avoid hardship and bankruptcies.

Our standard scenario estimates new capital spending to the year 1990 in the order of 600 billion 1975 dollars.

If we take energy for example, according to the Department of Energy, Mines and Resources*, a very substantial part of this represents energy investment requirements—about 170 to 180 billion 1975 dollars.

Historically energy capital spending has accounted for about 17 to 22 per cent of total non-residential capital spending. As Table 23 indicates, even with the projections for very large requirements, required energy financing should rise only to a peak of about 31 per cent of total non-residential capital spending in the early 1980s.

As the table further indicates, in 1975 dollars, the average compound growth of the total non-residential investment including projected energy demands will peak at about 6.3 per cent in the early 1980s. This compares with a rate of 4.1 per cent since 1970. Thus, it is obvious that a substantial shift into investment will be required to meet future demands. This is not impossible, and the idea that Canada cannot achieve 6.3 per cent average compound growth in non-residential investment does not hold. In the late sixties, the average compound growth rate was 6.7 per cent. Note that the accelerated growth scenario would require growth rates in non-residential investment closer to those of the 1966-1970 period. This can be attained if sufficient incentives exist.

Nevertheless, we do not expect capital investment to be strong enough to maintain our economy's growth rates in potential output in the range of 5-5.5 per cent per year as in the sixties, much past the 1980s. The problem is not lack of capital. Structural changes, including the sharp rise in the price of energy, changes in the composition of the labour force, and alterations in the international environment (e.g., competition from LDCs) have tended to reduce the growth rate of potential output or productive capacity. These forces will continue to operate during the next decade, albeit relatively slowly.

Another important factor influencing growth rates and investment is, of course, the general environment for business and the whole confidence issue. It is terribly important that confidence be restored to both consumers and businessmen. A modern economy depends upon confidence to a degree that is not adequately recognized. For example, since almost every consumer has a closet full of clothing, he could "make do" by repairing clothes for a number of years. Similarly, the average consumer does not have to buy furniture or a new house; he can repair the old and double up. He does not have to buy a new car; he can fix the old one. And so on down the line. If really frightened, most consumers

---

*Ministry of Energy, Mines and Resources, *A Strategy for the 1980's.* (Ottawa, Information Canada, 1976.)

could economize severely by cutting back their purchases and not suffer great hardships or even seriously change their standard of living.

Similar remarks can be made about capital spending. When the question of investing in new plant and equipment comes up today, almost any corporate finance committee says something like: "The future is very uncertain, the calculations are dubious (particularly because they have to count the high nominal interest rate as a genuine cost), and, for the time being, we would be better off to patch up existing capacity to increase its output. Rather than making expensive, long-term, irreversible commitments for new plants, let us wait a year, and then reassess the situation." This willingness and ability to defer such decisions for a year or more can play havoc with capital expansion.

It is clear that many people have been a little spoiled in their view of what is normal; this in turn affects their expectations and morale. As mentioned earlier, almost everyone now takes the post-Second World War economic performance for granted. But the confidence issue is not only one of expectations, attitudes, and psychology. The problem is an objective one. As Chart 6 indicates, operating profits as a percentage of GNP have declined steadily since 1960 and inflation has eroded working capital, profits, etc. Business has lost confidence not only because of uncertainties vis-à-vis government and labour, but because of very real economic factors.

The Depressing Effect on Capital Formation and Business Expectations of Economic and Political Uncertainty

How business perceives the general environment will be one of the most important factors determining the growth path of our economy over the next ten to fifteen years. If we had to describe quickly the trend in government business relations over the last decade we would say that politics seem to have become more liberal, economics more conservative.

Our standard scenario forecasts that as growth progresses, government's share in GNP should be in the area of 45-48 per cent. The issue of course is broader than the level of government expenditures. It has to do with the concept that government must, to paraphrase Prime Minister Trudeau, increase its role in our economic system unless major changes in private sector behaviour are brought about. For one thing, we believe it most unlikely that behaviour can be altered significantly by "jawboning." It is increasingly recognized both within and outside that government is just as prone to diseconomies of large-scale activity as huge business complexes (The standard comment is something like the following: "If you like our post office, wait until you see nationalized oil.") Increasingly, pressures will increase for *planning the government for economy rather than government planning of the economy.* We do not believe that the sectoral approach, proposed recently, will provide miracle solutions either. A sectoral approach would require an effective competition policy based on our need to compete internationally. Canada has yet to agree on such a policy. The mood right now is for an improvement in government-business relations. The period of unthinking optimism about the future seems to have ended. Closer scrutiny of business will continue; but, at least in the short term, the climate is right for the "less-intrusive" economic policy of our standard scenario.

As important as the stability and direction of government policy for the business climate, is the trend in labour relations and costs. This will be discussed in our section on labour. Briefly, our feeling is that labour relations will continue to be a function of economic growth. This does not suggest that labour problems disappear with hard times. On the contrary, as unemployment increases and prosperity increases are slower, we can expect more severe social tensions. But the pressure on labour to behave in a more disciplined fashion would be likely to intensify. The main factor determining the future of labour relations may well be the need to compete internationally to preserve jobs.

Many of these issues, of course, are policy issues and not conditions of Canadian economic life. The investment or capital formation issue—once one accepts the trend towards higher capital output ratios—can be dealt with by deliberate policy decisions.

Historically, Canada has been a high-investment and a high-savings country, but not quite high enough to meet domestic needs. Foreign investment has had to fill the gap, giving rise to much discontent, mostly in central Canada. We would expect the level of personal savings to increase from 6 per cent in the late 1960s to about 9.5-10 per cent of GNP in the late 1990s as a result of increased affluence, demographic factors, government tax incentives for savings in registered retirement savings plans and registered home ownership plans, contributions to the Canada and Quebec pension plans, etc. (See Table 24.)

The key to corporate investment lies in allowing corporations to maintain an adequate level of internal cash generation. The share of corporate profits in GNP has increased much less rapidly than the share of labour income. In this context the "corporate rip-off" theme current in Canadian politics and the questioning of the market system are highly inimical to the necessity of achieving higher corporate savings for investment. A number of opportunities to increase corporate savings and to raise the incentives to invest might be made available through changes in tax policy and financial instruments—for example, if present tax laws were changed so that both equity income and debt were treated equitably or if non-productive capital spending, e.g., for environmental or safety purposes, could be deducted as current expenses.

An important point with regard to financing is the growth in government security issues relative to the growth of corporate issues. Table 25 highlights the relative shift of the importance of borrowers, with governments now accounting for 66-75% of the total net new issues in recent years.

The vulnerability of Canada to its dependence on external borrowing is also great. At year end 1976, net indebtedness in all forms stood at about $50 billion, up $21.5 billion from the 1970 level. Eighty per cent of the increase occurred since 1974, and Canada now has the highest ratio of net indebtedness to GNP of any OECD country. In 1976, Canada was the single largest borrower on the international market, with provincial and municipal governments doing an increasing part of their financing abroad. (See Table 26.) A quick look at provincial and local government expenditures over the last few years indicates a significant increase in social welfare spending and salaries, and increases in budget deficits which in some provinces are larger than amounts earmarked for capital expenditures, suggest that part of the provincial debt has financed operating deficits.

The ratio of foreign indebtedness to GNP has always been high in Canada. But rapid increases in borrowing, especially by government, indicate a loss of manoeuvring room. Canada becomes more exposed, and consequently more vulnerable, to the pressures of its creditors. Excesses could lead to serious trouble or to the "British scenario," if borrowing is increasingly used for maintaining consumption. In this respect, the examples of Britain and New York City have provided a very useful lesson on what happens to those who seek to live beyond their means.

Canada is also vulnerable to American enterprises attracting our savings. Net direct foreign investment in Canada has plummeted from an average of 13 per cent of all external financing in the late sixties to 2 per cent in the last five years. In fact, recently these flows have become negative. Canadians now invest more abroad than foreigners do in Canada. In itself, this trend could be beneficial; it is good for business to seek opportunities, to expand overseas. However, business is not investing abroad for positive reasons, but because of concern with anti-business attitudes in Canada, political uncertainty, and exorbitant increases in unit costs. The trend is a symptom of the country's economic malaise. Likewise, the weakening of net capital inflows indicates a declining willingness of foreigners to invest in Canadian operations for much the same reasons that Canadian investors are reluctant to invest. Of course, it also reflects the growing confidence in the American economy.

97

The build-up of American investment in Canada and consequent "control" of Canadian industry still preoccupies Canada. Although the future of Confederation is currently the dominant Canadian concern, articles continue to be written and speeches made about the "truncated" production apparatus of Canada and the "miniature replica effect" of foreign enterprises operating in Canada. As and if the constitutional problems are resolved, and as the country prospers, we can expect a resurgence of discussions of economic nationalism.

Yet, since the writings of A.A. Berle and Gardner Means in the 1930s it has been recognized that legal "ownership" of big industry had very little to do with control or decisions on management of large enterprises. Rates of return, based on "profit centres" domestically and internationally, increasingly dictate the pattern of production and investment of trans-national enterprises. National laws, regulations, and administrative practices, together with "social responsibilities" imposed on business, determine the context, and "control" in financial terms has less and less meaning. The separation of ownership and control is a reality that has been recognized in business schools and economics circles for several decades. Even France, once so fearful of "le défi Americain," today is concerned more with the national implications of business operations than with their ownership.

The large multi-national or trans-national enterprises are increasingly recognizing that times have changed, and that ownership is less and less a vital question. The multi-nationals are likely to move to non-equity relationships based on long-term supply understandings or to special types of joint ventures, to acquire the resources they will need in the next generation. In manufacturing control will continue to be vital, but usually more in connection with technology exploitation, quality control, productivity, and maintenance of profits.

Slower Productivity Growth Rates

Nearly half of Canada's rapid economic growth since 1960 is attributable to the increase in jobs; we had the highest rate of all industrialized nations. In comparison, our productivity record has been quite bleak. Canada's future can no longer be discussed in terms of natural increase in the labour force. Because of the decline of the birth rate, 4% economic growth during the next decade would require much higher levels of immigration and/or increases in female and youth labour-force participation rates (despite high levels of official unemployment). Female participation rates in Canada are lower than in many European countries, and will almost certainly continue to increase.

But in the recent past, young people and women have tended to be less productive, mainly because of their occupational and industrial distribution, their lower level of experience, and the fact that they work fewer hours a week. Many women have entered the labour force only recently or have worked less regularly than men, and have less experience than men of the same age. Gains in their experience will increase their productivity, as should become increasingly apparent in the later 1980s. However, at the same time, female labour force improvements will likely be offset by the declining labour force participation of men, and by losses as the age distribution shifts towards groups in which aging and obsolescence of skills can reduce the level of the labour force. (See Tables 27-30.)

During the last decade the educational performance of students has declined markedly. Other things being equal, the students entering the labour force in the 1980s can be expected to be less well prepared than those who entered earlier with the same, and in many cases fewer, years of school completed. The pattern may reverse its effects in the 1990s. The existence of a high level of education may even be conducive to a more rapid growth of learning on the job. The ability to gain from exposure to knowledge which is constantly being generated and more widely disseminated may be enhanced, and the ability to deal with growing complexity may be increased.

The possibility of an upturn in student performance could also be a positive factor, as could be an improvement in school curricula. But the issue of what will happen to learning, both off and on the job, for those who have completed their formal education is one of the most uncertain questions. A highly educated labour force with unprecedented access to communications systems may increase its skill level rapidly without corresponding increases in the length of the formal schooling period. On the other hand, part of any effect of increased affluence on the level of effort may take the form of reduced willingness to take advantage of learning opportunities.

What about increased immigration? As discussed in the population section, Canada will have no difficulty attracting all the immigrants we desire. One of the major issues of the next century will be severe unemployment in the developing countries coupled with underemployment or labour shortages in the developed world, despite high official levels of unemployment—that is, individuals in developed countries may simply refuse unattractive jobs. Canada may want to mitigate this problem by importing workers for specific periods or in specific jobs, thus providing the worker with additional income and training, and us with construction and services. Many European countries are now moving in this direction as they are trying to cut back on near-permanent "guest labourers."

The U.S. has unwittingly dealt with this problem through illegal immigration. Canada would probably not want to involve itself in any such program out of sheer altruism, but it may find such a solution very useful for Canada: jobs Canadians would not do, except perhaps at an inflated price, get done. In this sense, the idea is both in the national and in the world interest.

From a regional standpoint, those provinces that have relied more on immigration and continue to attract a relatively higher proportion of immigrants – namely Ontario and British Columbia – will be least affected by all of the above-mentioned factors. They should register increases of about 2-2.5% in their labour force. Likewise, if resource development continues at a rapid pace, Alberta will register a similar increase in its labour force. In the other regions, however, growth in the working-age population could be close to zero as the natural growth rate declines, and as immigrants are attracted to higher growth regions. Immigration adds a useful degree of mobility which will not be available if immigration is restricted.

The Changing Industrial Mix

As important to productivity growth as labour supply will be changes in the economic importance of certain industries. What is most important here is, of course, the shift away from agriculture and manufacturing towards private services and the public sector. At the same time some jobs become less and less attractive, at least to relatively affluent Canadians: maids, bell boys, waitresses, unskilled labourers, etc. The shift is both in the industrial mix itself and in the attraction of certain jobs. (See Table 31.)

White-collar occupations will continue to increase their share of employment, and will account for about 60% of jobs in 1980 and 66% in the late 1980s. Thus, 66-75% of the growth in employment in the next fifteen years would come from white-collar jobs. The growth will continue to be concentrated in professional and technical employment for both men and women. Historically, of course, these sectors show lower productivity growth, though not necessarily lower average productivity. To the extent that female productivity growth rates may improve, and as increases in female labour-force participation raise the white-collar share, the decline in productivity growth in some white-collar jobs may not be as severe as is usually anticipated. This would tend however to slow employment growth.

The next decade will provide opportunities for productivity improvements in our economy, namely: further technological improvements, more sophisticated management techniques, improved services, better education, etc. Technological change, for example, has certainly not yet shown significant signs of abating. While it is not clear whether technological change in manufacturing will continue to be as rapid as in the past, there are increasing signs of innovation and technological changes in the service industries at far faster rates than in the past. The most pervasive change is part of the computer revolution just beginning to make itself felt in many industries. Another basis for optimism is that the length of time between the period in which a new technology is conceived and the time it is widely used appears to have been shrinking rapidly unless delayed by politics.

Technological improvements will help mitigate the pressures for slower productivity growth, changing industrial mix, and changing age-sex composition of labour, as well as new attitudes to work; but technological improvements are not expected to wipe out these trends.

The regulation issue is here particularly serious. Not only are regulations affecting environment, energy, land use, and an endless array of other areas proliferating and making it difficult for some ventures to succeed; but we also fear a growing set of regulations over the development of technology itself. Thus, though an exogenous technological slowdown does not appear to be immediately threatening, other forces could reduce the flow of innovation. In the constrained growth scenario, anti-technology, anti-bigness and anti-growth attitudes arising out of a fear of running out of resources or excessive concern for job security or environmental concerns would further reduce the incentives to innovate.

Smaller countries than Canada have been capable of developing high technology products and remain in the forefront of world markets. Very interesting examples are the Norwegian Tanberg recorders, and the Swiss Uher. Northern Telecom is an example of a Canadian company that is a leader in its field. But the examples are few. We have been preoccupied with regional job creation and preservation, with "buying back" Canada, with defending low-wage industries, with protecting fledgling industries long after protection was desirable. Where government assistance is provided, the purpose is *adjustment resistance rather than adjustment assistance.* In Canada, a strategic sector is a troubled sector, an industry of the past: in most other nations industries of the future are thought of as strategic.Canada's spending on research and development, especially industrial research and development, is obviously much too weak.

New developments in technology transfers are occurring rapidly. New generations of technology are increasingly being transferred to noncontrolled foreign enterprises from U.S. companies.* Transfers are even being made for manufacturing known to be aimed at traditional markets of the companies providing the technology. The nature and extent of transfers is increasingly related to the bargaining sophistication of the enterprises involved and the governments assisting them or participating in them. Canada has not been geared to these changes.

Continued Unsatisfactory Levels of Unemployment

We must project that unemployment will continue to be a major economic/social/political issue in Canada over the next generation. However, we forecast that the issue will wane slightly, not so much because unemployment will decline, as because the reality of the phenomenon will come to be better understood. Our image of unemployment is flavoured by the experience of the Great Depression, remembered personally or transmitted through our parents—of people desperate for work, of bread lines, of malnutrition, and despair. Contemporary unemployment is quite a different matter. Largely because of the unfortunate consequences of the Depression, we have built into our system palliatives to reduce the cost of not working. This has been done for individual, and national, but also regional benefit. In effect, we have said that people have the right to remain in their home communities even if there are no jobs. They are not entitled to be supported at an income level of working people, but yet have a right to a lesser "wage."

In effect, Canada is now paying some people to be unemployed. We are not implying that unemployment is not serious, nor maintaining that nothing should be done about it, nor are we advocating that unemployment benefits be curtailed. Rather we are making the simple economic point that the more you pay people to be unemployed the more people will be unemployed. Unemployment is not particularly rewarding, but its duties are extremely light: it requires no investment in education, clothing, tools or transportation, and offers a large amount of leisure time. Therefore, we should not be surprised that a small percentage of the population at any given time has taken up this economic "activity."

Unemployment insurance is particularly attractive for younger people who have few economic responsibilities, and can work for a while and take some time off on unemployment. Similarly, it permits people to select their jobs more carefully by offering a cushion while searching for what they consider to be a job appropriate to their status, standard of living, and career prospects. In this sense, unemployment represents a

*Jack Baranson, "Technology Exports Can Hurt Us," *Foreign Policy*, No. 25, Winter 1976-77.

higher standard of living and quality of life. However, this should only be so interpreted insofar as unemployment is of a voluntary character. Despite all of the rhetoric about changing values, work is a central organizing aspect of life to the bulk of Canadians, offering pride, responsibility, and the satisfaction of making one's own way and supporting one's own family. This is particularly true of male manual labourers, to whom supporting their families through honest work is a central definition of manhood–and, as such, unemployment remains a serious problem in our country.

The unemployment rates of the next decade should be in the 7-10% range. The problem is nothing like the unemployment problem of the Great Depression. Our unemployment can be attributed as much to structural as to cyclical phenomena. It does not arise only from a scarcity of jobs, as was the case in the Depression years. Enough jobs are available to reduce the rate of unemployment significantly.

Historically, Canada exhibits a higher unemployment rate than most if not all Western nations. Why? Its climate, its geography, the rapid growth in participation rates, more lenient or lack of "dismissals" legislation, and a very generous unemployment insurance scheme. More recently, the changing age-sex composition of the labour force, regional and job mismatches, new attitudes towards work, increased demand for leisure, significant improvements in unemployment benefits, wider availability of consumer credit, the increased labour force, and participation of other family members have further contributed to blocking the flow of people to jobs.

Over the years there has been a downward shift in the degree of labour market tightness which can be associated with any given overall unemployment rate. An indication of such a shift is the failure of the unemployment rate to fall below 5% in the 1973 boom: unemployment held at 5.3% with an inflation rate of 11.9% and a real GNP growth rate of 5.5%.

If we examine the relationship between unemployment and job vacancy rates, Chart 7 shows that from 1962 to 1970 movements in this relationship were roughly along the same downward sloping curve, but that after 1970 there was a clear shift in the job vacancy-unemployment rate curve; this suggests that forces other than demand are pushing up the unemployment rate.

Probably not so coincidentally, this shift coincided with the liberalization of the unemployment insurance program which has had the effect of increasing voluntary quits, layoffs, and job turnover because of the reduction of the cost to individuals of periodic bouts of unemployment. Job seekers are more selective and have less incentive to search vigorously for work until benefits come to an end. From 1968 to 1975, the percentage of those moving off benefits in less than five weeks dropped from 36% to 22% for women and from 46% to 21% for men. In 1974, a year of strong employment growth, 33% of male and 25% of female beneficiaries had worked less than twenty weeks before receiving benefits.

Unemployment benefits are also an inducement for others outside the labour market to seek work, knowing that they could qualify for benefits after twelve weeks of employment. Again, in 1974, nearly 50% of those drawing benefits had been employed less than six months, and 66% had been employed less than one year. Unemployment insurance has been a factor in the acceleration of the entry of women and youth into the market. For example, some who are not heads of households voluntarily combine temporary employment with unemployment insurance. This has tended to raise the degree of slack associated with any level of the unemployment rate.

The Changing Age-Sex Composition of Labour

Women and youth often tend to have less "interesting" or "rewarding" jobs. The jobs they hold are often easier to find, but also easier to leave. If they have no previous experience, they may also want to experiment more and try out a few different jobs with bouts of unemployment in between. Youth already account for close to 50% of the unemployed, even though they make up only 30% of the labour force.

Weighting the low 1960s' unemployment rates for the projected age-sex composition of the labour force in the next decade gives an unemployment rate of about 5.5% in 1986.

The entry into the market of young and female workers who generally have less or no previous work experience could further increase unemployment rates by intensifying skill mismatches, unless changes in the pattern of qualifications demanded by the economy are matched by sufficient retraining. The trend, already obvious today, will be towards underemployment of skilled technical and highly trained workers, and high unemployment in the unskilled and semi-skilled categories. Canadians will likely turn down the lower-skilled, lower-paying jobs.

Youth unemployment especially can be expected to improve only very slowly. There are even some forces that may work in the opposite direction. The deterioration in educational performance over the last decade could make all youth more susceptible to unemployment in the future. Income maintenance programs may have serious consequences by adversely affecting work incentives, particularly for youth who have the lowest paying alternatives.

Early experiences of youth may be of special importance, because they affect the way their lives are shaped. Youth unemployment may produce particularly serious consequences, and these consequences are likely to be more serious as youth unemployment is most out of line with unemployment of other groups.

Particular attention will likely be given to means of reducing the causes of these types of unemployment. A variety of programs has evolved including various combinations of consulting, referral, manpower training, and public and private creation. Policies regarding minimum wage laws are also likely to be reviewed.

The effects of the minimum wage laws on the hiring of young people are quite clear: many youth have been priced out of the labour market. Those regions–especially Quebec and British Columbia–with high minimum wages and relatively high unemployment might want to revise their policies. Most solutions have stressed public sector employment. Another, probably more efficient, solution could be policies that reduce the cost to employers of employing youth, which could reopen private sector opportunities. Two suggestions that could make sense for Canada are (i) a lower minimum wage for youth; and (ii) wage subsidies for youth to pay for the difference between productivity and the socially acceptable wage; this would also provide on-the-job training for these young people. However, the effectiveness of the latter depends on the ability to target subsidies to those youth who would otherwise remain unemployed. If available for all youth, the costs become prohibitive.

Regional Unemployment

The unemployment picture is complicated even further when one tries to take into account regional unemployment. The lack of an adequate manufacturing base in the Prairie Provinces and in the Maritimes means that many of the usual stimulative effects of new investment on local supply industries flow back to the central provinces.

Given the slower growth rates in certain regions–the eastern Prairies, Maritimes and Quebec–there is bound to be a continued leakage of employment to the stronger provinces. In Quebec, labour mobility is hampered by linguistic factors. According to the present regional development patterns (which we do not expect to change significantly over the next decade except of course if, for example, offshore oil is found in the Maritimes), a 6% national unemployment rate would imply a rate of about 10% in the Maritimes and 8.5% in Quebec as opposed to 5.5% in Ontario.

These higher unemployment rates, while indicators of a serious social problem, do not necessarily point to ever-increasing hardship for Canadians. On the contrary, the severity of problems caused by unemployment has somewhat decreased, at least from a financial point of view. The increase in multi-earner family units is but a case in point. Since 1960, the proportion of unemployed persons who are heads of families has declined by 25%. There has been a similar decline in family units in which nobody is employed. (See Tables 32 and 33.)

The proportion of unemployed who are not members of family units include young persons who live away from home, but can count on support from the family. Unemployed members of family units, on the other hand, enjoy considerable latitude in extending the job search period, thereby tending to raise frictional unemployment.

In 1971 (the latest figures available at the time of writing), in half the cases in which unemployment occurred, the family income was higher than that of families with no unemployment (indicating a seemingly regressive impact of unemployment insurance).

It can be argued that long-term, "hard-core" unemployment has the more serious economic and social implications. Table 34 shows that for heads of households 25-54 unemployment fifteen weeks or more is less than 3%. Nevertheless, unemployment rates for 25-54-year-olds has been rising recently, and this trend cannot and should not be taken lightly. (See Chart 8.)

We would expect the unemployment rate of heads of households 25-54 to increase in a period of protracted stagflation or in the constrained growth scenario. Though this rate would remain below the national average, the social and financial hardships resulting from unemployment in this group will lead to increased social tensions and more difficult labour relations.

Without discounting the impacts of unemployment–especially on this age group and on youth–it should be recognized that over the longer term, in some cases, unemployment insurance may increasingly be considered as part of the regular stream of income and become a way of life, not because jobs are not available but because people choose not to work (for example wives and husbands each working six months and receiving unemployment benefits for the remainder of the year). This will not be widespread, but it will reflect the trend in attitudes. In many cases, employers will co-operate, "rotating" their staff to allow more people to be eligible for unemployment benefits. This is likely to occur more in slow growth regions.

In *The Year 2000*, Herman Kahn and Anthony J. Wiener suggested the following pattern for employment in a "normal" post-industrial affluent society:

50%	Work normal year
20%	Moonlight
10%	"Half-time hobbyists"
5%	Frictional unemployment
5%	Semi-frictional unemployment
5%	Revolutionary or passive "dropout"
5%	"Voluntarily" unemployed
100%	

We are not projecting that this is a description of the Canadian labour force in the next generation, but the trend seems to be towards some arrangement of this type with record levels of unemployment nearly a way of life.

Part of this unemployment results from sucess–economic growth and affluence–not from failure. But a culture of plenty can also become one of complacency. The danger of excesses is very large.

Does this reflect worker dissatisfaction? Many would have us believe it. Yet, a recent survey* of work values found 89 per cent of Canadians interviewed were at least "somewhat satisfied" with their jobs, while at least 40 per cent were "very satisfied." Fewer than 3 per cent were extremely dissatisfied with their work. Sixty-one per cent would take the same job without hesitation; 33 per cent would have some second thoughts; and only 6 per cent would definitely not take the same job. When asked how their job measured up to their original expectations 86 per cent answered that it was at least "somewhat like" the job they wanted, while 47 per cent said it was very much like it.

This did not satisfy the interviewers, who have been reading for years about "blue collar blues," job frustration, job dissatisfaction, and worker alienation. Canadians were asked if, given carte blanche, their job choice would be the same. Of course, if given carte blanche, most people would choose a more powerful or more glamorous job. This does not indicate dissatisfaction with their current situation; it reflects ambition and wishful thinking. Nevertheless, the survey concludes that "if given carte blanche, only 50 per cent of Canadians would remain in their current jobs"; this should have read, "surprisingly, as many as 50 per cent."

Further examination of poll data also indicates less erosion of the traditional Canadian work-oriented values than is often claimed. Work was named by more Canadians than any other factor as being the primary

*Burstein, M., *et al. Canadian Work Values: Findings of a Work Ethic Survey and a Job Satisfaction Survey,* Information Canada, Ottawa, 1975.

means of achieving the most important goals in their lives. (Family was second.)

Will work continue to have the same prominence in the next decade? There has already been a decrease from 42 hours worked per week in 1965 to 37 hours per week in 1976, and we expect an average 32-35 hour week in the 1980s because of increased holidays, longer vacations, sabbaticals, and other forms of relaxing or recycling. Work may become relatively less important, and family, friends, and leisure would gain in importance. However, it is just as plausible that the change in the role of work may cause work as an issue to achieve new prominence. The ideologies that surround work and give it justification and value may become strengthened in support of what remains of work; but they may also increasingly come into doubt, and become the objects of frustration and rebellion. Both these trends could occur simultaneously in different parts of the country, in different parts of society, and may cause increasing labour conflicts.

Labour Relations and Costs

One of the main factors determining Canada's economic future will be the future of labour relations as they relate to stability and costs. The establishment of labour unions and the growth of the collective bargaining process in democratic countries has been a key trend throughout the century. In Canada, this development has contributed to the substantial increase in labour's share of GNP and on the whole its impact on income distribution was a welcome achievement. However, in recent years the focus on anti-business and anti-technology issues, and government intervention have increased worker consciousness and fueled trade union activity to the point that Canada's strike record is second only to Italy's, and its unit labour costs have grown much more rapidly than those of its major trading partner, the U.S.

An important trend in the Canadian labour movement is the very rapid unionization of public sector employees in the past decade. The rate of unionization in the public sector has risen from 21.3% in 1962 to 63.2% in 1977 (the overall national rate is 33%). These unions have tended to be more militant and political, with the resulting impact on strike activity. The disruption of essential services – postal service, air traffic, etc. – has also tarnished Canada's image abroad. This of course results in part from the decision in 1967 to allow public service employees to strike.

Another characteristic of the Canadian labour union movement in the last decade – and this also applies to Australia, another Commonwealth country in many ways very similar to Canada – is the importation of British shop stewards. We were unable to obtain numbers to support this, but officials of the Canadian Labour Congress as well as the major provincial federations confirmed this trend. Quite bluntly, the last thing Canada needs to import from Britain is union leaders. If we were to characterize the attitudes of Canadian unions we would describe them as roughly halfway between the American and the British unions. They were much closer to the American unions a decade ago, but especially in the last five years have moved to the halfway mark. The difference? The American unions adopt an adversary attitude towards management, but are not hostile to capitalism; the British unions are hostile to private and state capitalism. If Canada becomes increasingly anti-business, it is unreasonable to expect the workers to be more capitalist than the capitalists.

These trends combine with a new lukewarm commitment to economic growth and related traditional values in many influential Canadians, who increasingly have been oriented towards "new values." Their argument is that economic policy should be the instrument of social policy; that the thrust of both should be towards income redistribution; that employment and quality of employment are more important than efficiency or economizing in resource allocation; and that more "industrial democracy" is necessary for workers to be associated more closely in decisions which directly or indirectly affect their work environment. They also stress the importance of improving the environmental and "experiential" quality of work.

It would be rather naive, of course, to try to predict, with any degree of certainty, the evolution of labour relations over the next decade. The labour situation in Canada is a function of inflation and unemployment, labour force and unionization growth rates, and the structure of the labour movement. But most immediately, in the short term, it is a function of economic variables.

The economic dislocations of the 1970s have generated attitude changes, have provoked a certain backlash in public opinion, and have put a damper on many union demands. But the longer-term outlook is uncertain, at best. If Canada's economic situation should worsen, the result could very well be a severe polarization of attitudes and heightened social tensions. Even the wear and tear of protracted "stagflation" could have this effect. An important feature of such a society could very well be the spread of syndicalism–a "gang" society wherein groups responsive to only their self-interest compete for economic and political advantage. Increasingly militant unions, especially those operating in the public sector, take a "public be damned" attitude in pursuit of their own narrow interests (e.g., the QPP striking for two-man patrol cars). Conflicts could also develop between different groups of trade unionists for increased shares of GNP, inducing more and more sections of the population to adopt militant trade unionist attitudes in self-defence. Any attempt to limit trade union activity and/or the right to strike could lead to further disruptions.

Conversely, a period of "hard times" might just "force" a greater sense of responsibility and closer co-operation between labour, business, and governments. Some of the residuum of real "hard times" may very well encourage more caution, simply because of the recent years of labour unrest and their costly implications in terms of unit labour costs, of man-hours lost due to strikes, of incompetitiveness and investment. Furthermore, public opinion is increasingly expecting more discipline by organized labour. The majority of Canadians blame big labour, big business, and big government—in that order—for the current inflation. Fifty-three per cent also agreed that the government should take a larger role in running institutions. The political role of unions irks an increasing number of Canadians. In 1977, 66 per cent of Canadians disapproved of union involvement in politics versus 58 per cent in 1967. (But then this compares to 70 per cent in 1959.) Four out of five Canadians feel that the powers of unions should be somewhat more strictly watched or at least that the right to strike in the public sector should be submitted to voluntary arbitration for at least a year. With the high number of strikes in recent years many workers are beginning to question the usefulness of strikes in terms of lost pay versus wage increases. In a number of cases, they have been returning to work before the strike is settled.

A period of steady economic growth with only mild setbacks, as described in our standard scenario, could make it easier for management to grant union demands. Both the standard and accelerated growth scenarios rely on stronger work-oriented and achievement-oriented values than those of the recent past. They also imply that public reaction to trade unionists is more balanced, with less emphasis on guilt of the upper middle class, and more emphasis on discipline and responsibility. In the accelerated growth scenario, there may be some "knocking-off," but on the whole, the economy is dynamic enough to withstand it. Worker and union dissidence are substantially overcome because of intelligent and well-run programs by business and government—and they can afford them.

In the longer term, values and attitudes are a dominant influence on the labour movement. We expect the traditional labour-new class alliance to be increasingly dominated by the new class. This could of course spell the break up of the "alliance," with labour assuming a more traditional, though not less political, role.

110

Rather than an overall national trend in the next ten years, Canada will see a continuing of disparate regional and sectoral trends in labour legislation, wage settlements, strike activity, participation, and political influence. Comparative bargaining is likely to be even stronger, but the trade union movement continues to be characterized by the same organizational diffusion that characterizes Canada as a whole. The same regional issues that affect the country as a whole affect the union movement. The same political and economic conflicts, the same jealousy of functions apply. The result is an overgoverned organization with a rather weak central federation – the Canadian Labour Congress (CLC) – and increasingly stronger provincial and local federations.

The most notable examples are Quebec and British Columbia. The Quebec Federation of Labour (QFL) runs its own show, and very clearly bases its decision on provincial economics and politics, not on CLC directives. The CEQ and CSN have their own "intellectual infrastructure" and take their own decisions. The independence of the Quebec union movement has been reinforced by the recent election of a PQ government. As long as the PQ is around, the unions will carry much more political clout in Quebec, and thus tend to differentiate themselves even more from the CLC. The Quebec labour movement will continue to co-operate with the CLC on specific issues, particularly if the debate involves unions versus the federal government. It would not be at all surprising to see Quebec labour play this card in an attempt to shift the blame for Quebec's economic problems to Ottawa. In a scenario combining increasing political clout of local unions and new-class value trends, it is possible that labour cost increases and anti-business attitudes could exacerbate current economic problems in Quebec. In the short term, the labour situation in Quebec may be more peaceful than in recent years, if only because labour will want to give the government a chance for ideological reasons. But, if economic conditions worsen, if the government is too "moderate" on social reforms and independence, the situation could be worse than it has been.

Whatever the political outcome of current tensions, a different alignment between the Quebec labour movement and the rest of Canada could very well occur. The much publicized "opting out" application recently submitted by Quebec pilots wishing to form their own union could likely be imitated by a number of other groups. This is not new; for the past ten years, some Quebec railway trade unions have been seeking to break away from national unions. It is increasingly evident, as far as the labour movement is concerned, that the focus of power and dynamism will continue to lie with the provincial federations and their constituents. But the pursuit of separate bargaining units based on language could be devastating to the trade union movement.

This trend does not apply only to language issues or to Quebec. Labour leaders in British Columbia tend to believe that everyone east of the Rockies is hopelessly out of date, and the CLC has little or no influence, as a body, in B.C. British Columbia is likely to continue taking its cues more from the West Coast United States than from TQM, in its push for greater "industrial democracy." As in the U.S. Pacific Northwest, the B.C. labour movement will likely be more radical and "advanced."*

Other provinces could also adopt a more independent and assertive line. Ontario is an obvious candidate. Of course we place more importance on the personalities of union leaders, on motivations, opportunities, and constraints than on agendas.

Our standard scenario leads to reduced constraints and increased opportunities in the 1980s. The recognition of these reduced constraints by union leaders and by a better educated work force could combine to broaden the activities of trade unions.

Governments are coming to play a much larger role in supplying protection to workers, in legislating labour and employment standards and working conditions. An analysis of the Minister of Labour's "fourteen points" shows governments attempting to further improve working conditions through legislation.

Very few of the suggestions provide jobs or direct benefits for workers (except for legislation to prevent unjust dismissal, ensure payment of wages, and other basic minimum standards for the protection of unorganized workers or for the suggested improvement of government policies on pension rights and benefits so as to reduce the friction caused by this issue at the bargaining table.) Some points attempt to improve the process of collective bargaining, but most suggestions are clearly jobs for the bureaucracy and new class, i.e., greater educational facilities and opportunities to assist labour leaders (and potential leaders) to increase their skills and knowledge in all areas of labour relations; and the establishment of a collective bargaining information centre.

The accent on information and education would appear to be an attempt by government to reduce adversary procedures in collective bargaining. Past experience would indicate, however, that no matter how antiseptic the statistics provided to labour representatives, they will bargain according to their own economic and political needs. In order to preserve their power, the trade unionists may be even tougher in their wage demands.

*"Anglo-Saxon" North Americans have historically been difficult to organize. The bulk of trade union strength in Canada and the U.S. has been from later immigrant groups, except in the West, where unsuccessful prospectors rebelled at being reduced to "wage slaves." Trade union militance (and violence) has flourished in the West for more than a century.

The unions will clearly want to increase their influence on government if government continues to broaden the scale and scope of its interventions in the labour field. Does this lead us to tripartism? Not likely. It is very difficult to imagine our labour leaders achieving any kind of consensus among themselves for any length of time. The labour movement in Canada is fragmented and decentralized. The CLC has more than one hundred affiliated unions and the affiliates have more than seven thousand local unions. There is no trend towards centralization. The CLC plays an advisory role and enjoys little leverage to bring the provincial federations into line. On the contrary, financial leverage is from the bottom up. The focus of power will continue to lie with the provincial and local federations, and efficiently operating corporatism or tripartism on the federal level will continue to be the dream of planners.

Labour representatives generally have been unable to divorce their union functions as bargaining agents from committee work, and if the collective bargaining system is to be preserved, we see no signs of this changing. Furthermore, Canadians may not want tripartism. It will be seen as by-passing Parliament, for one thing; federal and provincial governments would also have to handle conflicts amongst one another more elegantly than they have in the past.

There will be some experimentation with co-determination. There is labour opposition to this concept; if labour sympathizes too closely with the problems and issues of management, the collective bargaining system can be eroded. Employers have mixed feelings about it, too. Canada is not Sweden or Germany: it is not a homogeneous country, its work force is not as disciplined as that of those countries, and their labour unions are very different. (Can we imagine the Canadian Labour Congress investing in real estate in New York as the German Trade Union is doing in Montreal?) But that is not the only issue. The issue is whether or not participation will make a significant difference. Past experience is not conclusive. While highly disciplined Sweden has suffered little labour unrest, absenteeism has increased significantly in recent years despite very progressive legislation. What the impacts of increased worker participation will be for Canada we cannot predict with any certainty. We are almost certain, however, that Canada will follow the European trend.

The Need to Compete More Effectively on World Markets

Canada is more trade dependent than most other countries. The Economic Council of Canada report, *Looking Outward*, points out that our trade is not only huge, but its role is growing in the Canadian economy:

Between 1963 and 1973, for example, exports of goods rose from 17.2 per cent to 24.1 per cent of Gross Domestic Product (GDP), while imports increased from 16.0 per cent to 22.0 per cent of GDP. This expansion of trade represented, on the export side, an enlargement from the equivalent of one-third to more than one-half of the output of the goods-producing industries...at a time when the share of the goods-producing industries in GDP was declining moderately, from 45 per cent in 1963 to 41 per cent in 1973.*

Thus the impact of trade on Canada, both imports and exports, is much greater than is sometimes recognized. Canada cannot opt out. Nor can Canada operate in an overtly mercantilist manner, without risking selective reprisals, which will bring pain to some regions and sectors.

Canada has seen changes coming with increased competition from less developed countries. The competitive LDC suppliers keep changing. Japan and Hong Kong were strong yesterday; a larger number of countries like Taiwan and Korea and some of the Latin American countries are strong today. There is a process of "rolling adjustment" taking place which will inevitably intensify, as large LDC borrowers push to increase their exports to finance their heavy debt burden.

On top of this process is yet another at work in the development of a competitive trading capacity in eastern Europe and the Soviet Union. These countries, and especially the U.S.S.R., must generate foreign exchange and pay for imports of technology and food. They must go as fast as possible for expanded markets. This will intensify the pains of the "rolling adjustment" generated by industrialization in the LDCs, and indeed the product composition of exports of both sets of countries are likely to overlap considerably. Moreover, the U.S.S.R. will likely become more aggressive in resource supplies, and especially in processing and fabrication based on its raw materials. Even without capitalism, the Russians are learning to be "Yankee traders," and the "workers state" permits no union problems.

The world restructuring of trans-national enterprises, and LDC industrialization, the advent of eastern Europe in competitive markets, and the rapid transfer of high technology—these are the factors which both provide opportunities and make Canada vulnerable, over and above Canada's natural vulnerability to the U.S. and current trade and financial interdependence.**

*Economic Council of Canada, *Looking Outward*, Information Canada, Ottawa, 1975.

** It is important to bear in mind that certain countries have performed well in the face of market limitations and raw material shortages without special trading relationships. The most important example is Japan, which has been an enormously successful producer and trader without joining any customs unions, Free Trade Agreements

One Canadian problem is that success at raw material exporting is expensive. Exports of raw materials tend to drive the value of the dollar up—in fact, the Canadian may still be overvalued at this time (December 1977).* This raises the standard of hiring, making the country less competitive. Avoiding such a situation requires a slower increase in the standard of living and a larger increase in investment.

If investment in Canada is weak, internal structural adjustments will be correspondingly difficult. Our standard scenario assumes that sector deals on resources (mainly energy) with the United States, mainly benefitting the western provinces, could be achieved, but their potential would require a greater willingness to provide *assurance of supply*. Thus, in this scenario, it is hard to visualize the absence of very close United States ties in at least some parts of the economic relationship, especially resources. (Government-guaranteed long-term supply contracts might be a method of achieving this.)

The accelerated growth scenario, on the other hand, is based upon "forced" growth in the areas of comparative advantage, more open trade policies, and probably closer ties to the U.S. Thus, while Canada develops a strong base of economic activity in the processing and fabrication of primary products mainly in the western provinces, it will find itself under intensified external competitive pressure from the manufacturers of the U.S., Japan, LDCs, and perhaps Eastern Europe, with particular significance for industry in Quebec and Ontario. (Textiles would be a special case, since their trade is already highly regulated in most countries.)

This scenario, presuming intensified energy development and intensified development of resource-based industries, would necessarily involve more open markets with the U.S. The "openness" might come about through (i) multi-lateral, most favoured nation liberalization; (ii) bilateral free trade with the U.S.; or (iii) sector agreements or liberalization with the U.S. (or with other nations as well, but with the U.S. the principal beneficiary).

This scenario also would involve rapid growth of Pacific trade, as Japan sought more supplies from the western provinces. If the market between the U.S. and Canada were relatively open, Japan might be induced to invest more in assembly as well as production in Canada, for the U.S.

(FTA), or discriminatory bilateral commercial arrangements. Sweden is another example, more similar to Canada, although Sweden found it desirable to work out a special FTA agreement with EFTA countries initially, and subsequently with the Common Market, in order to preserve its competitive trading position in Europe.

*The fall in the Canadian dollar is all too often attributed to the election of the PQ government in Quebec. True, this did contribute to uncertainties vis-à-vis the dollar, but it was obvious before the election that the Canadian dollar would have to be devalued—soaring costs, labour problems, balance of payments difficulties, etc...

market, as well as for itself. The potential for Pacific trade is much greater than just Japanese demand would indicate. We project that Japan will continue to be the engine of growth for East and Southeast Asia, and for the Australia-New Zealand complex. Japan's basic growth will continue at a rate somewhat higher than the rest of the industrialized world; it will increasingly draw on East and Southeast Asia for labour, producing in these countries for Japan, and for export to third countries, especially North America. It will also seek supplies from the Pacific Region, including Oceania and parts of Latin America (the West Coast and Brazil).

The strength of the Pacific Region is much greater, in terms of both actual and potential GNP growth, than any other region of the world. The western orientation of Canada's future growth in this scenario could therefore be intensified by accelerated involvement of Canada in trade and resource development for the North American/Pacific Basin system of markets. The very special relationship between Japan and Brazil has encouraged Japan to pay more attention to Brazil than to either Australia or Canada. Brazil has welcomed Japanese investment and offered the Japanese opportunities that have made it less attractive for them to invest in Canada and Australia. This provides a context for Canada/Pacific Basin relations in our standard scenario.

The accelerated scenario is first and foremost world-market oriented. It is an accelerated export scenario, with increasing value-added content and increased volume for Canadian exports. Because it relies on markets abroad, and must meet intensified competition in world markets as trade grows from many sources in the next decade or two, the trade policies of Canada must in this case become more liberal. Essentially, this scenario probably requires moving towards freer trade. It requires active Canadian leadership in global trade negotiations. It requires greater co-operation with the U.S. in the evolution of North American trade and investment, and a somewhat less independent stance in the resource relation of the western provinces with the U.S.

In the constrained growth scenario, the growing role of government is likely to be accompanied by growing Canadian nationalism, with more restraint on U.S. and other foreign capital. Periodic use of export controls, and unilateral price-fixing of exports of primary products would be possible instruments in the effort to boost export earnings to replace capital inflow. Because of this, and a gradual but inevitable deterioration in the competitive position of Canadian manufactures, growing protectionism would be likely, as would increasing trade frictions with the U.S.

The link with the U.S. economy might be lessened, but alternatives in world markets would not be easy to develop in the face of the need to restructure the home economy to maintain export competitiveness. This scenario implies growing reliance on the Pacific, because of resource trade, but even there growing tension would be likely from competitive pressures induced by manufactures from the Pacific seeking outlets in Canada. The U.S. would certainly fight against "special" trade agreements between Canada and other countries in such a tension-ridden context.

In this scenario, a declining exchange rate relative to the U.S. dollar and other key countries seems inevitable—with consequent inflationary effects and further deterrence to foreign investment.

Some "shock scenarios might be possible. For example, Mexico's substantial oil reserves might come on stream, and be made available at world prices in North America only on condition that there be *quid pro quos*: more liberated immigration of Mexican labour, and free access for Mexican manufactures. With oil deals, Mexico probably becomes more competitive than we are on the U.S. market. In any event, the Mexican role in manufactures in North America bears close watching.

Economic Culture

Underlying economics is changing values and priorities. As Canadians become more affluent, the value attached to economic progress seems almost certain to diminish. In recent years, in Canada as in the rest of the industrialized world, concern with the size and distribution of the social and environmental costs of growth has led many scholars, governmental officials, politicians, journalists, and even some businessmen to question economic growth. This phenomenon results largely from a basic clash between the prosperous and the rest of the country.

We refer to the growing competition between the "ins," the "rising ins," and the "outs": as the "outs" try to improve their lot, the "rising ins" see their relative position threatened and, likewise, in their attempt to increase their status, threaten the "ins." Thus, the issue is one of jealousy of privileges. There is an increasing tendency to pull up the ladder behind you. Of course in terms of amenities, as income per capita increases, the quality of life and the standard of living of the upper middle classes go down relative to their past. But the tendency is to overemphasize the losses, and to try to overcompensate at the expense of the rest of the society.

The conflict takes a more dramatic form in that sub-class of the upper middle class that we have referred to as the new class.

We believe that in the long run most of these new emphases and trends will be given an overwhelming priority by Canadians. Indeed this is one of the main reasons for the slowing of economic growth in the long run.

Regional Development

The future of the regions and provinces depends mostly upon the value, political, and economic variables developed in the topical sections. In terms of economic growth, the three growth areas are Alberta, Ontario, and B.C. In a standard scenario these regions average 4.5-5% growth to 1980 with 3-3.5% growth rates beyond that slowing to 3% towards the end of the decade. The other regions do not do so well, but benefits do "trickle down."

Atlantic

Most people are very pessimistic about the prospects for the Atlantic provinces and nobody seems to have any sort of favourable projection for these provinces. Most people feel that it would literally take an act of God to make them significant on the world scene, something in the order of Providence providing huge amounts of gas and oil under them or their territorial waters. There are indications that such is the case, but one cannot count upon it. The conventional description for these provinces as "basket cases" is not entirely inaccurate, and no amount of "groundnut schemes," such as the Bricklin Auto factory or the Shaheen oil refinery, will bail them out of their economic difficulties.*

That is one way to look at the Atlantic provinces. Fortunately there is another, considerably more attractive, view. Although the Atlantic provinces are hardly the leading edge and most dynamic part of our economy and society, and are falling behind the more vibrant areas of the nation, in most places they are not in absolute decline. In fact, because of "trickle down" of growth elsewhere in Canada and the redistributive policies of the central government, they are economically better off than they ever have been. Opportunities for individual advancement and upward mobility are certainly limited, so people interested in such opportunities move elsewhere, and leave a remnant who are, on the whole, reasonably satisfied with life in the Atlantic provinces. Most people who live in the Atlantic provinces like them very much–obviously if they didn't, they would have left. Life is easygoing and pleasant, unhurried, decent, and reasonably dignified. Those Canadians dissatisfied with the hustle and bustle of the great cities, with environmental pollution and all the discontents of modern urbanization, would be well advised to consider living in the Atlantic provinces. Many such people already have done so.

Unless the act of God occurs, we project that little of interest to anybody outside will happen in the Atlantic provinces during the next genera-

*The new two hundred mile fishing limit should provide some promise, but where is the potential for a Canadian industry to take advantage of this opportunity?

118

tion. For this reason, the Atlantic provinces do better in both the accelerated growth and the constrained growth scenarios than they do in the standard world. Under accelerated growth conditions, the trickle down to them is greater; under constrained growth, Atlantica is more in harmony with national values.

Quebec

Assuming that Quebec remains within Canada, its short-term prospects are not the best. Unless and until the secession option is defeated at the polls, Quebec can expect little new investment whether internal, from the rest of Canada, or foreign. Indeed attrition and some disinvestment is more likely, so long as the threat of separation is credible. Economic conditions are such that the existing fiscal structure will be strained, and there will be little money available internally for Quebec state capitalist ventures. In 1976-77, the Quebec government's deficit was already higher than its capital expenditures, which means that borrowings went to finance current consumption. The government has shown restraint in recent budgets and has very little manoeuvring room unless economic growth picks up significantly.

Growth rates in the past few years have fed on major construction and public work projects—James Bay, Olympics, Montreal metro extension. Such investment will not be available, at least in the same order of magnitude, over the next few years.

The linguistic policies of the new government could have the effect of eroding the Anglophone minority and discouraging new immigration, and would not be without effect on the Francophone population as well.

Moreover, if economic prospects are brighter in other Canadian regions, Anglophones, Francophones and immigrants may be attracted elsewhere. Thus growth rates will be slower in Quebec than in Ontario (the traditional yardstick) with discrepancies in provincial per capita income increasing.

That is the short-term prognosis. In the long term, things are more rosy. Were it not for what we believe history will show to be the diversion of the present independence-sovereignty movement, Quebec would now be in the midst of an economic take-off. The province now has indigenous skills and technical workers with high morale, and a high level of national spirit to progress rapidly in the world. One might hope that this talent will be increasingly utilized to build Quebec's internal economy, polity, and culture.

Of course, Quebec must expend much energy to modernize and restructure its economy. Quebec has long defended its low-wage, slow-growth industries, but as competition from LDCs intensifies, the pressures to invest in high-technology, rapid-growth, "modern" industries will be overwhelming. Nearly 60% of jobs protected by Canadian tariffs of 20% or more are located in Quebec. Quebec has one third of its population concentrated in Montreal, with serious gaps in regional income persisting throughout the province. Attempts are being made to disperse regional development by granting tax incentives to businesses locating outside Montreal. But Quebec has flourished most when Montreal was strong, and a dynamic financial and commercial centre is necessary for increased provincial growth. Development is likely to continue to take place around the major metropolitan centres, and trickle down to the regions. In some sense, the relation of Quebec's "deprived" regions to the rest of the province resembles the relationship of the Atlantic provinces to the rest of Canada. When the major metropolitan areas–Montreal, Quebec–do well, so does the rest of the province. Under constrained growth, disparities intensify.

Ontario

Ontario is destined to continue to be Canada's dominant province/region. It has so much going for it:

1. *Location:* Ontario is the centre, the keystone, of Canada. In addition, its location near the major industrial area of the United States gives it access to U.S. markets, rapid transportation to U.S. commercial centres, and ready accessibility to U.S. tourists;
2. *Climate:* Except for coastal B.C., southern Ontario has the most favourable climate in Canada;
3. *Population:* 33% of population of the nation;
4. *Manufacturing:* Ontario contains the bulk of national manufacturing;
5. *Resources:* While most tend to think of Ontario in terms of its southern urban manufacturing complex, we should not forget the vast northern regions of the province which are rich in raw materials. Ontario produces more mineral resources than the entire West. Also, despite some decline, Ontario continues to have a large agricultural sector;
6. *The Headquarters function:* Ontario is the capital of Canadian industry, commerce, transportation, and, increasingly, of finance. The political capital is also in Ontario.
7. *Morale:* In a very real sense Ontario feels that it created Canada. Ontario is accustomed to dominating Canada.

With the continuing rise of the West and the expected rise of Quebec later on in this century, the relative strength of Ontario will slip, but not entirely.

Even with the construction of the Northern Gas pipeline, which is expected to provide a boon to the West's economy, Ontario does very well as a supplier of capital goods and equipment, and of financial services and capital. In fact, the pipeline is also a boon to Ontario's economy.

The West

Actually, while they share a common sense of distance from and hostility to the East and to TOM in particular, there are three Wests:

1. The Prairie farming West;
2. The resources West;
3. The coastal West.

The overall prospects for the Prairie farming West are modestly favourable. Prospects for the resources West are very favourable and very interesting. And the prospects for the coastal West are mixed.

What will happen in the Prairies can be summed up in the future of farming and rural Canada. The prosperity of Prairie farming depends almost entirely on the world market for grain, which is a function of world affluence and of the relative production of other countries, and is therefore imponderable. On the whole, we see no reason to doubt that our Prairie farmers will continue to be among the most productive and efficient in the world and that they will earn a major share of whatever that market is. The farmers will more likely be prosperous than not. And indeed, given the highly competitive world market they have to be very prosperous in order to support the capital and technological investment required for competitiveness. In any case, there would certainly be fewer of them.

The cities of the Prairies will prosper as will the farms. The rural parts of the Prairies will almost certainly have a shrinking population, somewhat masked in the population figures by the existence of increasing numbers of "farms" which are really exurban residences spreading out from cities. A close examination of regional growth patterns in the Prairies will reveal that those places doing the best in terms of population growth will be near the larger cities.

The resources West we commonly associate with Alberta because there it is dominant and there it controls provincial government; but it is also those places, institutions and individuals in Saskatchewan, Manitoba, and B.C. that see their principal interest in wresting resources from nature. Their prospects will be those of their industry – the situation is very similar to that of agriculture–and to the degree that west Canadian resources are competitive on the world market and government permits them to be pulled out of the ground, these sectors will prosper.

On the whole, except in the most unfavourable economic and social scenario for Canada as a whole, we think these will prosper very much indeed, although certainly not as much as some of the more enthusiastic believers in limits-to-growth would project. Canadian resources are valuable but not irreplaceable; and their world marketability will depend on very simple calculations of their price compared with those from other sources and substitutions. These are discussed in considerable length in the energy and resources chapter.

Political factors will have much more of an effect upon resources than on farming. National environmental restrictions could seriously curtail resource production and certainly increase its price. Local political considerations come into play also. For example, the temporary reign of the NDP in B.C. had the effect of hindering investment. If this sort of thing were to dominate the West, resource development could only be carried through by provincially owned corporations which, by the very nature of things, will attract executives and professionals from the more conscious members of the "new class." These people will rely on systems and other types of formal learning which, as any resource-company executive can tell you, are useful tools, but must be used in a context of judgement and experience; these latter talents tend towards the private companies.* The construction of the natural gas pipeline will provide a tremendous boost to the western economy, but in terms of future big projects, much hinges on how successful this project is in terms of labour relations, political intervention, and regulation. The same considerations apply to the development of the oil sands.

Coastal B.C. is our California. The Pacific coast of North America has always been occupied by a significant proportion of people highly sensitive to fashions. Our five-year world projection is for a "neo-conservative trend." We are already seeing B.C. settling down, as evidenced by the recent Socred victory. The next five years will be a settling in, and there are some good prospects for development, economic growth, political growth, and prosperity. The excellent climatic conditions and the location of this area make it extremely suitable for growth if the people there want the growth. Given the dynamism of the Pacific Rim and the growth in Canadian trade with Japan, B.C. is likely, at least in the stan-

---

*Under current arrangements, provincial crown corporations pay no income tax to the federal government. The tax savings provide considerably higher returns on any project to a provincial government than to a private owner. Consequently, in open competition for any project, a province can outbid any private investor, using Ottawa money to succeed.

dard scenario and certainly in the accelerated growth scenario, to have as high or higher than national growth rates.

The North

To paraphrase a cliché about Brazil, "The North has a great future, and always will." Our North is not only the last frontier, but a permanent frontier. The principal function of the North in the world system will be as a place small groups of people venture to get resources; they will live there temporarily, strictly for the purpose of obtaining those resources. When the resource deposits are depleted or their exploitation becomes uneconomical, that particular installation will disappear. Most occupation in the North will be in camps, not settlements.

The tiny numbers of native peoples of the North will attract many times more attention than their numbers would seem to warrant on account of their historical role in this country and their uniqueness. However, while they will continue to be exotic, if only because they choose to live in the forbidden North, they gradually become less different from the remainder of Canadians. Sympathetic writers will continue to complain about the adverse effects of our civilization on the native culture, but they are too late–three hundred years too late. The native cultures have long since been destroyed. What remains to be seen is how they will interact with dominant Canadian culture. We believe that the period of greatest trauma is ending. Despite considerable dislocations, the various native peoples are gradually becoming assimilated to the national culture. For example, the production of Eskimo and Indian sculpture and other artifacts is becoming very nearly like another commercial business. Eskimo silk scarves are as expensive as St. Laurent scarves and are being sold in many fashionable boutiques. Native leadership with modern education and orientation is emerging. "Ethnicity" is a symptom of modernization. The native peoples will make continuing claims on us, and will probably gain much from us, as long as we are sympathetic.

On the whole, the process of improved health for the native peoples and the temporary immigration of people to work on the resource industries will lead to a continued increase in the tiny population of territories. But, we find it hard to imagine a circumstance under which any of the territories could be made into provinces during the time frame of this study.

Resources

Energy*

Canada's future energy requirements and supplies are amongst the most controversial issues in our country. Here the clash between the limits-to-growth proponents and the more growth-oriented groups becomes most obvious. Unfortunately, the discussion has been almost exclusively inward looking, with only passing attention being given to the key issue–the impact of energy prices and supply on long-term world and Canadian prosperity.

A number of powerful arguments favour rapid development of Canada's energy potential. First is the need for national assurance of adequate reserves for long-term growth, whether business as usual, constrained, or accelerated. Second is the potential for export income wherever the economic considerations outweigh the need for additional domestic reserves. But third, and probably just as important, is the need for Canada, in co-operation with other member nations of the International Energy Agency (IEA), to help stabilize the international oil market and thereby enhance the prospects for growing world prosperity. This last consideration is especially vital for the Third World nations, most of whom are desperate for economic growth and depend upon the continued growth of the developed countries for their prosperity. Moreover, if the energy issue is not resolved in some way or another, there is little hope of solving the world stagflation problem.

Indeed, one of the principal threats to the scenario of world prosperity is the concern about future energy prices. The conventional disaster scenario visualizes continued world economic growth fuelled by OPEC imports until sometime between 1985 and 1990. By then, OPEC's production capacity reaches its maximum potential, and oil prices zoom to heights

*This and the next section on minerals were written by William Brown.

124

which would induce a worldwide depression. The resulting turbulence in international finance, fuel prices, and inflation would impact upon international trade and could lead to undesirable political consequences including insurrections and, possibly, wars.

Of course, many other scenarios can be written. Those which visualize rapidly changing oil prices, *down or up*, almost certainly will be associated with very unpleasant events. Even worse, probably, would be scenarios in which the international fuel prices fluctuate severely during the rest of the century, first zooming and then falling precipitously only to zoom again and then perhaps to collapse once more. Under such circumstances, private industries or governments would have some difficulty coping with the economic and political shocks.

One of the major requirements for long-term economic growth without political upheaval is that of stable, or at most slowly changing, prices in the more important items of world trade. Today, that means the price of oil, as set by OPEC. Whatever the merits of the argument for or against this cartel's rapid increase of oil prices in 1973-4, and the use of oil as a political weapon by the Arabs, the economic future of the world depends strongly upon the future stability of OPEC's prices. Thus, it would appear to be quite dangerous for the oil importing nations to embark on economic courses which together would lead to a demand for imported fuel that would soon strain OPEC's inherent capability to meet that demand.

Indeed, a prudent course of action, if it can be achieved, would be one based upon an IEA program to insure that OPEC's production capacity would remain substantially below world import requirements. Such a program would require a vigorous effort at both conservation and new energy supplies from each IEA member. Unfortunately, the progress, to date, has been less than completely satisfactory in most of the IEA countries, including Canada. The next ten to twenty years will be a period of transition. During this time a co-ordinated policy among IEA nations, logically, would take all the actions required to restrain the potential threat from OPEC. In this context, Canada's role should emphasize, first, the earliest possible achievement of energy independence and second, an increasing export role, until the perceived threat is over.

Future Energy Demand and Prices Under Three Scenarios

As for most countries, the Canadian demand for energy is expected to grow less than GNP. This is a new phenomenon, resulting from the recent higher prices for fuel and the uncertain future for both prices and supplies since the oil crisis of 1973. A conservative figure for the standard scenario would suggest a ratio somewhere between 0.8 and 0.9. Thus, a 4.5 per cent economic growth would be accompanied by a 3.6-4.0 per cent growth in energy demand. This would be a modest revision in historical growth patterns and could be readily justified by recent price increases and fears of future ones, which appear almost certain to continue until Canadian energy prices reach international levels.

The energy:GNP growth ratio could be much smaller than 0.8 or 0.9, perhaps even about 0.5 or 0.6, if energy conservation becomes a serious national commitment. The lower ratio is assumed in the constrained growth scenario, because this represents a partial retreat from Canada's historical experience with international economic interdependence, towards an emphasis on "small is beautiful" ideologies, on self-protectionism through reducing energy dependence, environmental risk, and economic growth rates. In the accelerated growth scenario, the ratio is lower because GNP growth is higher and because Canada, like other industrialized nations, takes steps to reduce dependence on OPEC while continuing traditional international economic independence. The demand for energy and the growth in GNP in these three scenarios is projected in Table 35. In each scenario the absolute demand for energy increases somewhat less than the EMR projection of at least 67 per cent growth by 1990–about 1 million barrels of oil per day (MBPD) between 1985 and 1990. A net dependence on oil imports could exist in the standard scenario, but would be smaller and more than compensated for by anticipated exports of gas, petrochemicals, and refined petroleum products.

The standard scenario forecasts domestic fuel prices increasing to world prices by 1982, as growing needs for OPEC imports cause considerable concern about the future. Partly as a result of the need to resist reliance on OPEC, GNP growth slows to 3 per cent between 1985 and 1990. Continuing federal-provincial disputes and difficulties in achieving proper financial arrangements with energy companies retard the development of coal, oil sands, and exploration of the frontier regions. Nuclear-power development also becomes more complicated and more costly because of environmental resistance and safety concerns. Nevertheless, during the eighties, Arctic pipelines bring substantial quantities of natural gas from the Mackenzie Delta-Beaufort Sea region. Part of this gas is exported to the U.S., and some is used as an alternative to oil to reduce petroleum imports.

In the accelerated growth scenario fuel prices are adjusted relatively rapidly (by 1980) to international levels and Canada remains a net energy exporter throughout the century. Its energy policy also emphasizes an average 10 per cent annual increase in the development of its oil sands which are producing two million barrels per day by the year 2000. Petroleum products, oil, gas especially, and electric power are all being exported to the U.S. under long-term contracts. This policy is justified by abundant production capacity, effective conservation, and a growing conviction that fossil fuels are likely to become rapidly less important as energy sources during the twenty-first century.

In the constrained growth scenario, development problems arise in every energy area. Because of slow economic growth and the curtailment of all fuel exports, a policy of energy self-reliance is maintained. Construction of Northern gas pipelines is delayed. However, conservation programs and reduced GNP growth prevent any serious energy shortages. The prices for oil and gas which had been held constant from 1978 until 1985 are gradually increased thereafter because of the high cost of transporting Arctic gas, and because of difficulty in increasing indigenous oil or coal production. A major reason for the increase is the need for additional taxes, as the revenues shrink substantially with the continuation of controlled fuel prices.

Future Energy Supplies

Let us begin the discussion of the potential for energy production with a perspective which examines Canada's energy "problems" from an external vantage point. Outside observers (American, European, Japanese) often find Canadian attitudes hard to understand. They see a country with a tremendous amount of land, huge resources in fossil fuels, and a relatively small population which suggests an immense potential for resource development—especially since foreign fuel prices have increased. Yet the exact opposite has happened. As prices were increasing during the middle and late seventies, exports began to drop rapidly, partly due to a fear of inadequate long-term production and partly because some relatively bad luck in exploration during 1974-76 amplified these fears. These attitudes, coupled with a growing concern about environmental and quality-of-life considerations, as well as a rise in anti-American feelings, tended to create a form of energy myopia which, some foreign and Canadian observers claimed, prevented the Canadian public from achieving a clear perspective on the potential abundance of various forms of energy.

Petroleum

Stating that non-renewable resources such as petroleum will become scarcer over time is a statement often delivered more for its psychological impact than for its enlightened content; but it also often suggests that the speaker is literally convinced that the next generation will no longer have oil to burn. Today, the conventional wisdom is that a profligate world is squandering its last reserves of petroleum and that the time remaining is only a few decades. That projection might be correct, but has often been made before; and in the past it has almost always been wildly incorrect, despite a solemn and official sanction of its presentation. An overview of such official foresight in the U.S. is portrayed in Table 36 which offers an amusing perspective on the accuracy of petroleum projections during the last hundred years.

All energy analysts know of the perpetual race between the discovery or development of various commercial forms of energy–today mostly fossil fuels–and energy consumption. As the more obvious or more readily available sources become depleted, others from presently obscure or more costly sources must replace them. This implies that the price of energy naturally tends to increase. However, the history of energy prices for the last two hundred years–until the early 1970s–leads to the exact opposite conclusion, that energy almost steadily becomes cheaper relative to other commodities and income. The forces of technology and competition have been stronger than those of depletion, at least until just a few years ago. And now, the world is being asked to accept the new conventional wisdom that energy will be expensive, perhaps increasingly expensive, from now on.

Although this new wisdom may not last out the century, it appears to be a reasonable point of view for the next decade or two, as the result of the influence of several forces. First, the twenty to thirty year hypnotic effect of abundant and cheap Middle-East oil has hindered the development of new energy technologies. Second, there was a roughly parallel period, especially in the U.S. and Canada, of artificially cheap natural gas which in recent years could hardly have provided much incentive to that industry, except for exploring the relatively few large deposits which could be found without undue expense. Third, the appearance of nuclear power promised to deliver electric power, the premium form of energy, at prices competitive with, or even cheaper than, power derived from Middle East oil prior to the OPEC "surprise." Fourth, this last decade or so witnessed a phenomenal growth of a new environmental, ecological, and quality-of-life sensitivity which, when coupled with cumbersome government regulatory systems, resulted in substantially increased prices for all forms of energy (indeed, for all industrial output)–an increase which was justified for conservation purposes, but which was further exacerbated by the rapidly growing need for taxes as government expanded its activities towards greater welfare and service function, and unions demanded and obtained an increasing share of the national income.

Finally, all the above must be coupled with recent inflation expectations and associated requirements for high interest rates and greater returns on capital investment, thereby tending to increase prices further. It has become very difficult to be meaningful in comparing current oil or gas prices with those of prior decades; the pricing structure is now vastly different. In 1977 the taxes alone on oil or gas production may be greater than the total price in 1957. Moreover, careful comparisons are so complicated that they are difficult to understand without a great deal of study, unless one is a petroleum economist or accountant.

The new wisdom about growing energy costs is at least partly suspect. Canada, the U.S., and other developed countries have been strongly affected by the above-mentioned changes, as well as by the recent OPEC experiences. Any substantial reduction of fuel prices will be difficult and perhaps undesirable—except possibly for OPEC prices. It might even be desirable to keep these high to assure some semblance of long-term international economic stability.

Enough incentives are available for producers to remain active. Because of recent tax and/or price concessions by the Canadian government, 1977 was a boom year in petroleum and natural gas exploration and development. Another reason for optimism is that petroleum exploration is a well-developed high-technology industry, and with sufficient incentives relatively rapid progress can be expected. Recent technological advances enable search for new fields at greater offshore depths, in the very difficult Arctic regions, and in deeper zones onshore. Moreover, a greater fraction of the oil or gas in any field can be extracted than hitherto—perhaps 50 per cent more—with the utilization of enhanced recovery techniques. Indeed, if, as many experts expect, huge new resources (perhaps two trillion barrels of petroleum and an equivalent amount of natural gas) exist somewhere in the world, the technology of finding and producing them (politics permitting) may well keep ahead of world consumption for another fifty years. If this is true, contrary to general expectations, the real prices for these fuels may now be at or very near their peak for some time to come.

Unconventional Sources of Petroleum

If the above estimate is found to be too optimistic and the conventional petroleum reserves gradually diminish worldwide over the balance of this century, Canada will still have time to phase in the syncrude from the Athabasca and other oil sands. This source might *eventually* yield several times as much oil as EMR's projected "ultimate resources" of conventional oil—about 40 billion barrels.* These oil sands reportedly have about 600 billion barrels of oil equivalent in place, and a large fraction of it—perhaps half—could be extracted. Even now many in-situ approaches are being actively researched or developed to economically exploit the deeper deposits and several are in the pilot project stage.**

---

* EMR, op. cit., 1975 demand .62 billion bbls.
**See the *Financial Post*, 2/19/77, p. 36 for a recent interesting and unusual engineering approach suggested by a reputable firm.

Some argued that on the basis of Syncrude's experience, the oil sands are not competitive. This is an odd case where incentives are perhaps too high. Since oil companies can deduct up to 130 per cent of their capital costs, there are few incentives to economize. Furthermore, representatives of the oil industry inform us that the cost of doubling capacity in the existing Syncrude plant is low.

Other countries have similar deposits of oil sands, "heavy oils," or tar sands. Canada has about as much "heavy oils" as tar sands and its "heavy oil" technology is more advanced. Venezuela's heavy oil deposits are reported to be much larger–an estimated three trillion barrels in place, roughly five times that of Canada. The Venezuelans, moreover, are negotiating to obtain Canadian technology to develop their resource. The United States has smaller deposits–perhaps thirty billion barrels. However, the U.S. has immense amounts of oil shale from which it has been estimated that about 1.5 trillion barrels of oil can be recovered from high grade shale alone.

Finally, to complete the picture, we must mention the enormous potential for making liquid petroleum products from coal (a process presently commercially operated in South Africa) and for which a number of second and third generation technologies are under development in the U.S. There is also the potential for substitute fuels such as methanol from coal or wood, or ethanol from sugar cane (now a growing project in Brazil), and many others, including various possibilities of converting trash to fuels.

The major point here is that if conventional petroleum exploration and production remain the most profitable venture, switching to alternatives will not be necessary. Nevertheless, most of the large oil companies have been moving to hedge their positions by developing the appropriate technologies for alternatives to conventional fuels; when the time and price are appropriate a large scale transition will begin. Even now a start has occurred with Canada's oil sands. Other countries are following or will soon follow the Canadians into various synthetics.

In this perspective Canada has bright prospects not only for becoming self-sufficient in conventional oil, but for developing its Syncrude industry and subsequently exporting its technology and/or some oil to countries which otherwise might become unduly dependent on OPEC or its successor.

Natural Gas

Canada appears to be very well endowed with natural gas resources, and up until recently had been exporting about a trillion cubic feet (TCF) annually to the U.S. These exports have since been reduced and it is government policy to completely phase them out. Whether or not Canada should again export natural gas will be determined by future proven reserves, prospects for additional supplies, and the relevant economics and politics.

Anticipating that future gas prices will be increased more or less gradually to compete with oil, on a BTU equivalent basis, the EMR projections through 1990 are that gas production can meet both local demand and a hypothetical export demand of about 1 TCF annually. Indeed, by 1990, production capacity should substantially exceed the sum of these demands. These projections assume that higher domestic gas prices will continue to encourage exploration, and that the Arctic gas pipelines will help meet a domestic demand increasing at about 4 per cent annually to 1990–about the same rate as the projected increase in overall demand.

Because an economy that becomes increasingly dependent upon natural gas needs to maintain either large reserves or an equivalent assured supply, is it reasonable for Canada to increase its annual consumption so rapidly, from 1.4 to 2.8 TCF by 1990? To respond to this question we note first that EMR's estimated "ultimate" reserves at the 90 per cent confidence level are 237 TCF or about enough for 85 years at the projected 1990 demand level, without consideration of new supplies from any areas beyond current drilling capabilities. The qualification above is a very important one; if we still had the drilling capability of 30 years ago there would be no Arctic gas today. Exploration has been, and still appears to be, a rapidly improving technology–perhaps more rapid now than ever before. Thus, estimated reserves must be very conservative. It has been recently estimated that the recoverable reserves of gas from the Beaufort Sea alone might be as much as 200 TCF (in addition to 30-40 billion barrels of oil). The Science Council of Canada estimates that $2.00/MCF gas at wellhead might bring 500 TCF from the frontier regions.

If these reserves reach the high range of their estimated potential, and if the gas pipelines are built, Canada might find itself with a substantial incentive to increase its gas exports once again. Excessive reserves have relatively little economic value when discounted for the future. Who would choose to tie up funds in fuels that cannot be sold for 50 years or more?

Unconventional Natural Gas Resources

Stoking up this argument even further, many unconventional sources of natural gas may soon become commercial at unregulated prices; some of these sources have enormous future potentials; and most of them probably exist in Canada as well as the U.S. and elsewhere:

1. Natural gas from geopressured waters;
2. Trapped gas in coal fields;
3. Gas from Eastern shales;
4. Gas from tight sands;
5. Synthetic gas from coal, especially in-situ gasification.

The deep hot geopressured salt waters that lie beneath the Gulf Coast of the U.S. have recently been estimated by the U.S. Geological Survey to contain more than 20,000 TCF of dissolved methane (the principal component of natural gas) in the on-shore portion of the Texas and Louisiana coastline and within present drilling ranges. In 1976, the U.S. Energy Research and Development Agency estimated that from 500-2,000 TCF might be recoverable with current technology, and has initiated a program to develop this source. This gas is to be produced from the natural flow of the pressurized fluid, which is expected to contain about 1 per cent methane. Moreover, the hot water appears also to have a substantial potential for geothermal power and possibly other economic uses. Geopressured zones of these kinds probably underlie most of the large sedimentary basins of the tertiary period (the last seventy million years) and are expected to be found in California, Alaska, probably in the Beaufort Sea and the Mackenzie Delta region, and perhaps even off the East Coast. Although natural gas from geopressured zones may be more expensive than that from conventional sources, the extraction capability will undoubtedly improve over time, as it is not yet even an infant technology. Moreover, it usually appears where conventional gas has long been produced. Consequently, the required distribution systems would already be in place—an important consideration.

Canadian resources of this type have not yet been examined for their future potential, but it might very well prove to be enormous. ERDA's accelerating program should show results over the next several years. If they are positive there will be important implications for Canada.*

Trapped methane in coal mines, long a source of tragic accidents, has recently come under renewed examination (especially in the U.S., which has enormous coal reserves) because of increasing gas prices, and because of the added values in reduced danger and greater productivity when coal mines are degassed prior to their development. Coal fields in the U.S. have recently been estimated to contain about 1,000 TCF of trapped methane, which in many cases might be profitably produced at current unregulated

*From Unconventional Geologic Sources, National Academy of Sciences, Washington, D.C., 1976; William M. Brown, "100,000 Quads of Natural Gas?" H1-2451/3-P (Research Memorandum #31) summarized in Fortune (October 1976).

prices even if the coal is not.* There is every reason to expect that a similar opportunity exists within Canadian coal deposits. In some cases, producing the gas may or may not be profitable unless a new mine is to be opened shortly, a matter which must be determined by the industry. An estimate of the potential reserves from this source could only enhance Canada's future energy security.

Methane is also associated with the organic matter present in most shales. It tends to be trapped within a relatively impermeable matrix, but when fractures are present in the shale they provide a reservoir or a conduit with a large surface area into which nearby methane can gradually enter by diffusion. Gas can be found in commercial quantities in appropriate geological structures. Until recently, however, most such production constituted only an occasional "consolation prize" after a wildcatter had failed in his quest for a conventional oil or gas reservoir. By now, however, enough experience has been accumulated to make these shales interesting in their own right. This is a consequence of higher gas prices and substantial advances in various techniques for fracturing underground formation in order to stimulate the flow of gas. Current estimates indicate that about 300 TCF of methane might be recoverable in five states of the Appalachian region of the U.S. with existing technology. Even this is less than 0.001% of the gas in place. Needless to say, some thought is now being given to alternative approaches which, over time, might yield increasingly large fractions of this potential resource. In this regard, whatever success emerges from the ongoing research (ERDA, in 1976, started a five-year fifty million dollar research and development program) will be useful for Canada, which has similar resources, as have many nations.

The fourth gas resource is that of the tight sands in certain regions of the Rocky Mountains. This resource is comprised of substantial gas-bearing sandstone formations of low permeability. Various technologies have been employed to free this gas. Estimates suggest that over 1,000 TCF (a billion billion cubic feet) are in the U.S. formations, much of which evidently can be produced once the price is sufficient (over $2 per thousand cubic feet). The most promising non-nuclear technological approach today appears to be the use of massive hydraulic fracturing for stimulating the flow of the gas.

The degree to which Canadian geological formations of a similar type exist is not yet known (or publicized much, if they are). It would be surprising, however, if they were not comparable in size to those in the U.S. In any event, the technologies associated with the American efforts

* *World Oil*, February 1, 1977, p. 13.

may have useful applications wherever the permeability of natural gas reservoirs is very low. Stimulating the flow of gas will be important to the commercialization of most of the unconventional sources—and some of the conventional ones as well.

Finally, our list of future sources of gas includes the synthetic gas, syngas, which can be produced from coal. Gas from coal is an old art* which may be revitalized by new technology in the years ahead. But the most exciting part of this alternative may be that of in-situ gasification. This technology, which the Soviet Union claims is commercial today and which is being studied in many countries, has a special appeal because it can extract gas from coal which otherwise might not be utilized. Many coal deposits are either too deep, or too fractured, or too thin or unsatisfactory as coal mines for other reasons—technical, environmental, or social. Together they constitute an immense energy source from which many thousand TCF of syngas is potentially available during the coming decades. Although Canadian coal deposits are not fully assessed, they are very substantial and might be huge. It would appear that the future evaluation of Canada's coal resources should include the potential for in-situ gasification in addition to the more conventional uses.

This brief review of some of the less well-known prospects for future sources of gaseous fuel provides a context for discussion of Canadian policy. Canada may be endowed with fossil fuel resources that are simply enormous and that will come into view within decades if not years. From this perspective it would seem unwise to become overly concerned with the adequacy of current known conventional reserves. On the other hand, a reasonable amount of concern, especially with the economics of producing alternative sources, is almost always justified as the economics tend to be a little difficult, at least initially.

Nuclear Power

Although the future growth rate of electric power is scenario dependent it appears quite likely that the CANDU reactor will furnish a reasonable part of that growth. Whether the few current reactors will by century's end increase to thirty, fifty, or one hundred is likely to depend more upon preferred domestic policies than upon economic growth. The CANDU reactor by recent evidence appears able to generate electric power at about 1¢/Kwh. This is less than the cost of fuel alone in oil- and gas-fired plants (about 2¢/Kwh using international prices). Few authorities expect this relationship to change during this century. Even for coal-fired plants the delivered price of coal alone would cost more than 1¢/Kwh at most power

*Once upon a time, not so long ago, many Canadian cities had a "gas works" which used this process. They were shut down because natural gas was cheaper.

stations. Only at a site close to a source mine can the coal cost less than 1¢/Kwh, but few mines are located near power consuming centres. Where hydro-electric power is insufficient for meeting future demand, CANDU reactors would be the most economic addition to capacity.

The other potential role for CANDU is for manufacturing export. It is one of the most promising existing reactor designs, and has proved its value in commercial experience. But even with adequate public acceptance, CANDU development is likely to be constrained by the rates with which technical talent for design, construction, operating and maintenance, and the manufacturing capability for plant components can be increased. These needs would require a continuing commercial investment as well as a growing national research and development program to continually improve the reactor, as well as to develop appropriate mechanisms for dealing with radioactive waste, safety, protection against theft or sabotage throughout the fuel cycle, and possibly the potential for recycling and utilizing plutonium.

As in most high-technology development, policy fluctuations can be very costly. They lead to losses of trained personnel who cannot readily be replaced, and tend to increase the number of operational blunders. Thus, Canada must try to decide early and wisely on the appropriate future role for the CANDU system. Whatever the chosen rate of development and for whatever purposes, a long-term program with a smooth growth would be most likely to give optimum economic returns.

The social debate about the environmental, safety, or moral questions associated with nuclear reactors will have to be thrashed out through the political process. It is to be hoped that in this debate the CANDU technology will not be carelessly confused with other nuclear technologies whose designs may be considerably less desirable from the point of view of safety, sabotage, and fuel thefts. The government's role in presenting a balanced picture of its policy, after weighing the arguments and sentiment, will necessarily be a delicate one.

Hydro-electric Power

In nearly all scenarios of Canada's energy future, hydro-electric power represents a fast-growing component. EMR projects a growth of about 5 per cent annually until 1990, roughly doubling the 1975 capacity.

This growth in hydro power appears to be a natural economic development, and from a commercial point of view has the advantage that any anticipated power surplus can be readily exported. Indeed, this appears to be a desirable option to maintain, even though, among some groups, there are sentiments against the export of Canadian resources.

We are extraordinarily well endowed with hydro-electric potential

135

whose clean, high-grade energy over the long term gives the country an enviable position. Of course, there are those whose sensitivities are ruffled by the required disturbances to the natural topography and the changes in local ecological systems that large hydro-electric engineering projects will create. However, Canada may have no better alternative available as the natural course of technological progress moves towards a relatively increasing demand for electric power. The post-1975 contributions from thermal and nuclear power are expected by EMR to exceed that from hydro, although it would be difficult for most environmentalists to argue that these sources of electricity are less objectionable. Nuclear power, in particular, is expected to increase about ten-fold by 1990, although even then it will contribute much less power than either thermal or hydro sources. Whether nuclear power is a greater or lesser threat to the environment is a highly polarized debate, which has yet to be resolved in most nations of the developed world.

At the current time Canada is committed to a substantial growth in hydro and nuclear power. If the total growth in electric power is less than that forecast by EMR, then the preferred economic choices would appear to be a cutback in oil and gas fired power plants; temporary export arrangements for an excess production, and a reduction in planned coal-burning capacity. Thus, it appears that hydro and nuclear power would be the most preferred candidates for future growth in power production in any of the scenarios we have been considering.

Coal

Canada is fortunate to be endowed with substantial coal resources. Known resources have been estimated to exceed 100 billion tonnes, without considering deposits north of the 60th parallel. Considerable additional quantities will probably still be discovered. The energy content of the 100 billion tonnes of coal is about that of 300 to 400 billion barrels of oil and, therefore, is about ten times that of the ultimate oil reserve estimates by EMR. The location of the known resources (concentrated in Saskatchewan, Alberta, and B.C.) implies that their eventual use on a very large scale would depend upon future technology for either converting the coal into liquids and gases or for developing low-cost coal transportation systems or cheap transport of coal-derived electric power. Of these, the conversion to fluid forms appears to be technologically closer, although the potential for obtaining oil and gas from alternative sources, as discussed above, appears to preclude coal conversion processes on a large scale during this century. If and when very large-scale utilization or conversion of coal is desired, the technology probably will have been developed by other countries and could then be adapted to Canadian needs.

Meanwhile, some of the standard uses of coal for electric power, process steams, and metallurgical purposes should grow relatively more rapidly than competing processes requiring higher-priced oil or gas. About 9 per cent of domestic energy demand in 1975 was met by coal; this fraction is not expected to change much in the near term unless a major change in policy occurs.

The development of coal mines and coal conversion will face its share of objections from environmental and local-interest groups. The recent coal policy of the Alberta government appears to have been quite responsive to these groups, in imposing substantial increases in royalty rates. The coal producers have argued that land disturbances during coal mining would only be temporary, and that the land would be restored to a condition at least equal to its present quality. Opposing groups claim that that would be impossible. Evidently experts are available to both sides who can give conflicting testimony.

Although additional coal supplies from Alberta may be in for a period of difficulty, British Columbia appears ready to expand production. Whether the use of western coal in Ontario is economic will depend upon production costs (including royalties, taxes, and environmental protection) and transportation. The cost for rail and lake shipment to Ontario power plants would be a major factor in determining the competitiveness of coal, especially in comparison to hydro or nuclear power. Steam coal for use in Ontario may still be available from Saskatchewan if the lignite they produce is satisfactory technically and economically; if not the needed coal can be imported from elsewhere.

Inexhaustible Energy Alternatives

The two major "inexhaustible" alternatives are solar and fusion energy, often referred to as solfus. To these a third, geothermal energy, is sometimes added and perhaps "geosolfus" would be an appropriate designation. Each of these three has its own special problems as well as future potential and, as a result, may or may not become important in Canada during the next fifty years. Ultimately, a developing world must come to depend upon these renewable or essentially inexhaustible resources.

It is not our purpose here to discuss in detail their economic or technical potential. It is sufficient to say that each of them is expected to become technically well developed during the next fifty years and will be phased into the energy system in which they are commercially competitive. Over the course of the next century these alternatives might become crucial, not because of a basic shortage of fossil fuels, but rather because of the potential danger of excessive carbon dioxide in the atmosphere. If the world use of fossil fuels continues to grow at five per cent per annum, the carbon dioxide in the atmosphere might be increased four-fold by the middle of the next century.

It is barely conceivable that this much change of atmospheric composition could lead to major, irreversible climatic changes; a heating up of the earth's atmosphere by the "greenhouse effect" is now the primary concern. This would lead to a melting of the polar ice caps, a rise in the level of the oceans and a severe change in rainfall distribution and other meteorological patterns. When the potential long-term changes can be reliably evaluated, a major shift by the developed countries away from fossil fuels to the geosolfus alternatives might be required. In this regard it will be important for Canada to be ready to contribute to the solution of a potentially very serious international problem. Even now, forward-looking scientists, especially meteorologists, in many countries are devoting increasing efforts to the understanding of this problem. Even with good international co-operation it could prove to be a very difficult adjustment for the world to make if it had to be accomplished within a few decades. The relatively sudden change in the importance of energy since 1973, the need for relative independence of insecure foreign sources, the need to shift to new domestic sources of supply during this century, and the eventual switch form fossil to geosolfus sources is the long-term trend, probably in nearly all nations, developed or developing.

Energy Research and Development

Canada has been criticized for insufficient funding of energy research and development in past years except for its nuclear program based on the CANDU reactor. Without trying to analyse past policies, a good case can be made for a growing long-range research and development effort in many energy areas–some of which were indicated above. Indeed, a strong case has been made by the Science Council of Canada.* The Science Council's evaluation of Canada's research and development potential for future energy sources states that:

> Canada has no experience in the exploitation of its geothermal resources, it does not have coal gasification experience, it has not generated hydrogen on a large scale, it has not heated homes and offices predominantly with solar energy, and it does not have the companies or utilities to exploit biomass energy. Above all, Canada does not have the mechanisms required to set research programs in motion in a coordinated manner, or the funding necessary to grasp opportunities.

*Science Council of Canada, *Canada's Energy Opportunities*, Report No. 23, March 1975.

Minerals

A Long-Term Perspective on the World's Mineral Resources

In recent years, the neo-Malthusians have also raised the spectre of the potential exhaustion of mineral resources. This would be bad news for humanity, but presumably good news for the Canadian economy–our mineral resources would become increasingly precious. The policy implications of this analysis are that we should curtail exploitation and consumption of our resources and hoard them for the future when they will become more vital and valuable. This analysis is not credible.

Industrial society is not dependent upon the extraction of any single critical mineral. Obviously, every society becomes dependent upon its traditional use of raw materials, and would find it difficult to make a relatively rapid change if a sudden unanticipated shortage appeared. Still, if any of today's commercial minerals had never existed, modern industry would have developed around the rest. The only material which might cause one to wonder even momentarily about this statement is iron, because the widespread availability of iron ore has led to our steel-based civilization.

A fundamental scientific law states that no elementary substances except radioactive ones can be *used up*. They can only be moved around or changed in form. Metals can be taken from ores and used for buildings or vehicles, but this does not make them vanish from the earth. Fertilizers scattered on the soil ultimately may end up in the ocean or in lakes; but, if necessary, they can be recovered or simply made anew from air, soil, and rocks as long as we have energy available.* Water and carbon dioxide can be reconverted into hydrocarbons if need be; indeed, nature does it daily on a grand scale through photosynthesis.

We will claim that very few important materials in the world will become unduly scarce–although the distribution of their prime sources often is so uneven that unless sufficient care is taken, cartels might be formed to boost prices until adequate adjustments are made. For example, tungsten, chromium, cobalt, mercury, tin, bauxite, platinum, and gold are currently being produced in substantial amounts by relatively few countries, making it possible in theory for an effective cartel to form. In practice, however, such cartels are much more difficult to form–and to maintain once they are formed–than economic analysis alone would suggest. Even OPEC, the world's current model of a successful cartel, is vulnerable, beause of disparate and changing requirements of its members.

*A new and much cheaper process for recovering phosphorus from waste water, for example, is reported in the October 1975 issue of *Industrial Research* (p. 50).

Indeed, some weaknesses of this organization became apparent when internal disagreements resulted in the adoption of a two-tiered price system applicable to exports in 1977.

When minerals are difficult to find in concentrated forms or very costly to extract, they tend to command commensurate high prices and their use is substantially restricted. Gold and silver are high-priced metals in part because they are naturally scarce. Therefore we use them less than we otherwise would. For example, electrical wire is made out of copper although silver would be better. When the price of copper gets too high, as it occasionally has, aluminum can take its place in most of its present-day uses. The same economic considerations apply to most metals, indeed, most materials! Some potential substitutes for a few metals in common use are listed in Table 37 to illustrate this point.

In practice, the painful task is not usually finding a substitute, but making the adjustment rapidly. Thus, an unanticipated shortage caused by cartel action could bring about a few, perhaps several, years of economic aggravation. To reduce risk of economic stresses due to sudden price rises, excessive dependence upon unreliable foreign sources should be avoided. In a general sense, these potential socio-economic and political problems relate to human choices, not to any fundamental or potential exhaustion of supplies.

In a world in which all materials were sold at their cost of production, the possibility of any shortages because of exhaustion could be anticipated for decades and gradual adjustments made to avoid undue economic stresses. In recent times, sudden or very rapid changes in expectations created economic anguish. As prices skyrocketed in 1974 we were informed "everything was scarce." One year later "nothing was scarce" appeared to be the accurate description for nearly every commodity. How easy it was for panicky philosophical generalizations to be accepted during the short term (1973-74) commodity-prices boom following the "energy crisis." The "everything scarce" phenomenon quickly became a "permanent" theme about a growing resource dilemma, only to come crashing down after a mere year of reality experience. Nevertheless, the concept of vanishing mineral resources over the course of a century or so needs to be examined carefully and thoughtfully if the argument is to be made that an expanding demand does not exhaust the supplies of a finite earth.

Let us examine the principal metals that are used in the world. (See Table 38).

First, note that over 95 per cent of the demand for metals is for five clearly inexhaustible ones. Of this group, the least abundant is titanium, which constitutes about 0.5 per cent of the earth's crust and which eventually, as technology improves, may become one of the world's most important metals because of its light weight, excellent corrosion resistance, and high strength.

In discussing potentially scarce metals only the other 5 per cent of the demand can be a matter of concern. Moreover, if the specific considerations relevant to each of the next seven metals in the table are studied sufficiently, a persuasive case can be made that any future problem about exhaustion of resources can be reduced to the remaining ones, which together constitute less than 0.1 per cent of total demand. There should be some relief in finding that 99.9 per cent of the probable future demand for metals is easily manageable. The balance of this section will present some arguments to support this point of view.

Known Reserves

As discussed in the long-term trends section of this study, commercial production only requires known reserves a generation ahead, so it would be a waste of money to look for more reserves. It should not be surprising to learn that if the lead industry had proved reserves sufficient for about thirty years at anticipated demand that they would be only mildly interested in searching for new reserves.* If any new resources found today could not be sold for thirty years, it would hardly be a fantastic investment opportunity. Indeed, success in locating new reserves would put severe pressure on current prices. Consequently, new lead mines are more likely to be found because of fortuitous discovery than from concerted exploration for the mineral.

In many commodities world reserves have grown so rapidly, as Table 39 shows, that any further exploration would be more likely to occur for reasons of national security or fear of incipient foreign cartels, than from a concern about fundamental shortages. If we know of recoverable identified zinc resources sufficient for about fifty years at current demand rates, who would be interested in exploring for more *now*? On the other hand, when reserves diminish to only a ten-year supply, the marketplace will reflect that condition with increased prices until new mines have expanded reserves to higher levels.

Because of these economic considerations, known reserves which exceed expected demand for more than a few decades should be the exception, not the rule. It does happen occasionally, but not because shortages have prompted a search for additional supplies. Thus, if we have stumbled upon coal reserves sufficient for more than two hundred years and iron ore for more than one thousand years they have been found for reasons other than concern about near-term exhaustion. As a result,

*U.S. Mineral Resource, 1973, reports world lead reserves at 140 million tons in 1971, annual production 3.5 million tons.

those who make conservative predictions about future availability of materials based upon known reserves naturally tend to underestimate future production capability. The literature is full of such predictions. As one example, the prestigious U.S. Paley Report of 1952 forecast that U.S. copper production would not exceed 800,000 tons by the mid-1970s. In 1973, it was, in fact, 1,700,000 tons. Maximum lead production was projected to be 300,000 tons, yet in fact it exceeded 600,000 tons. This tendency for authoritative groups to underestimate future production is so strong that similar mistakes are made over and over again. (In the case of petroleum, they have been repeated for a century, as discussed in the Energy Section.)

The reality of economic adjustments will correct most errors of projecting reserves, but sometimes the correction can take several years and is costly. Since each mineral has a fixed production capacity, the rate at which it can now be produced commercially is limited. Producers are wary of over-investing in capacity that might lead to losses whenever demand falls off. Consequently, the demand for a mineral or several minerals occasionally exceeds the total capacity of the industries. At such times the prices tend to rise along with the expectations of persistent shortages. This occurred during the 1973-74 inflationary period when prices of many minerals reached all time highs and provoked a U.N. General Assembly Session on Raw Materials (May 1974) to debate the associated issues. However, capacity shortages tend to be overcome by new investment, by use of substitute materials, or by an economic recession. All of these occurred during 1973-1976.

Recycling

The belief in the "fundamental reality" of the energy crisis of the early 1970s followed by the raw materials crisis of 1973-74, together with both the recent general interest in environmental protection and the recession of 1974-75, effectively created a much greater interest in recycling of minerals than ever before. The potential for recycling of most metals certainly appears to be very great. Ultimately, perhaps after one hundred years or more, an advanced recycling system can be imagined whose effectiveness is so great that nearly all extracted minerals would be in inventories or in actual use. Only a very small fraction not worth recycling would be allowed to run into the sea or would be buried, and would need to be replaced.*

Consider the supply of copper, which some have claimed may last only fifty years at the required rate of consumption in an expanding econ-

---

*Increasingly, the sea is also becoming a new source of mineral supplies.

omy. Let us accept for the sake of argument the estimated potential of world resources on land (given in *U.S. Mineral Resources*) of 1.1 billion tons of copper, which eventually will be available somewhere above ground in various metallic or chemical forms. At current prices this is over $1-trillion worth of metal. If it can be preserved through effective recycling and any residual losses made up by mining expensive copper from the igneous rocks, the stock could last indefinitely. This choice would be for people to make. Almost certainly the technology required for efficient recycling could be made available during the next one hundred years. If people choose some other alternative then, presumably, it will be a better one. For example, they may decide not to recycle dilute copper wastes because the ocean does it by producing nodules on the sea bed, and may prefer gathering these nodules to recycling.* Or perhaps they will find that copper is no longer an important metal, that other alternatives are functionally superior for most purposes. The central argument is that a permanent trillion-dollar stock of the metal can be kept available by recycling efficiently. Any minor losses can be replaced from ores or sources now considered sub-economic. What our descendants will actually choose to do is not a matter for our concern; we will have left them a substantial legacy in copper alone.

The above argument appears to be valid for nearly every "scarce" metal, except radioactive substances which can be destroyed through fission. Through the efficient mining of our resources and with conservation of minerals through recycling, nearly all of the metals which have been extracted and which will be extracted in the future can be readily available to the people of the world for whatever purpose they choose to use them—over and over again.

Mineral Prices

The argument has been made that a basic structural change has taken place in the economies of the industrial countries and in their relations with the less developed countries. Actually, classical economics may provide a sufficient and straightforward explanation of the price movements in all commodities with the possible exception of oil. A recent study by W.D. Nordhaus has shown a trend in commodity prices since 1900. He notes the ratio of the price of some of the most important minerals to the price of labour. The examples of copper, iron, zinc, aluminum, and crude petroleum are given in Table 40.

This continuous decline in the cost of minerals relative to labour over the last seventy years came to a dramatic halt during 1973 and 1974, when

*These nodules have been estimated to contain up to 5 times as much copper as the land resources given in Table 42.

the commodity boom saw most raw-material prices double or triple. But a recession in the major consuming countries during 1974 and 1975 put an end to this. From mid-1974 to mid-1976, most mineral prices fell, some by more than 50 per cent.

The fact is that the *constant-dollar* prices of many important raw materials declined between the early 1950s and 1971 (See Table 41). In the medium term, average prices will probably be somewhat above the depressed pre-1973 levels. Over the long term the fluctuations of the commodity cycle will undoubtedly continue around a slowly changing trend line.

Future World Demand and Supplies

Technology is the key factor in estimating just what resources will be available during the next century and after. Data about "known reserves" or "ultimately recoverable resources," deals with the technology of the immediate or near future, and assumes that the main changes in mining will involve equipment and techniques similar to those in use today, although exploiting lower grades of ore. In the nineteenth century for instance, only copper ores containing 4 to 6 per cent of copper were regarded as useful. At present, ores are worked with a content of as little as 0.4 per cent. It is virtually certain that in twenty to thirty years, ores with as little as 0.25 per cent could be profitably exploited. Flotation methods of enriching polymetallic ores have been developed, and hydrometallurgical and other processing techniques make the extraction of zinc, lead, silver, copper, nickel, cobalt, and many other metals from low-grade ores possible. Until recently, for example, the mineral nepheline syenite (about 20 per cent aluminum) was considered to have little or no value. Now a technique has been developed for extracting its aluminum content, and it has been reclassified as a valuable raw material. Technological advances of this type will no doubt occur frequently in the future.

Certain other corridors of technical development are beginning to look feasible. The first involves the possibility of extracting minerals at deeper levels of the earth than are worked today. At depths of more than 5 kilometres, some rock formations are thought to contain huge deposits of iron, manganese, chromium, cobalt, nickel, uranium, copper, gold, etc. In order to extract these metals, very sophisticated scientific and engineering research and design is necessary to develop instruments and equipment that can be used under greater heat and extreme pressure. Although intense research and development efforts are underway, it may be beyond the year 2000 before such equipment has evolved; but this is a conservative view.

Furthermore, technology for mining the ocean floor is developing rapidly. Interest in this concept began in the 1960s, and the basic technology for mining depths to 15,000 feet appears to be available today. In addition to a number of large U.S. corporations, the Japanese Sumitomo group of companies and the German AMR group are among those who are initiating deep-ocean exploration programs. The manganese, nickel, cobalt, copper, and other minerals that are found on the floor of the Pacific Ocean in the iron-manganese nodules (Table 41) could increase their supply enormously. The experience gained in this field in the next ten years or more should result in a rapid acceleration of activity before the end of this century. This kind of mining should be especially attractive for nations such as Germany and Japan that are currently "have-nots" from the point of view of natural resources, but are highly developed and organized in industrial research and production techniques.

It is still too early to give accurate estimates of the amount of the nodules. Some experts have claimed that the Central Pacific alone contains 1,600 billion tons. Table 42 shows estimates of the potential mineral content of these nodules (based on a 1,000 billion ton total) and compares them with other resources.

Other long-term possibilities include extracting ores from sea water or even from processing rocks if energy becomes relatively inexpensive sometime in the distant future. Calculations indicate that every cubic kilometre of sea water contains approximately 37.5 million tons of solids in solution or suspension. Most of this is sodium and chlorine, but there is also a huge amount of magnesium and varying quantities of iron, gold, copper, nickel, and certain other minerals. For comparison, a cubic kilometre of granite or shale on average contains 230 million tons of aluminum, 130 million tons of iron, 260,000 tons of tin, 7,000 tons of uranium, and 13,000 tons of gold.

Past scientific work already enables us to obtain some minerals from the sea and from the sea floor. Others will follow as incentives develop. The Japanese are now preparing to extract uranium and other metals from sea water. In time, the rocks and the ocean will constitute an essentially infinite resource base, although it probably will not be needed except to a minor degree.

An admittedly optimistic scenario is implied in the above: a growing rate of resource exploitation via conventional methods for the next few decades or so, accompanied, towards the end of this century, by a commercial mining of the ocean nodules; in the next century and after, deeper drilling into the earth for important concentrates; and after several centuries, technologies for the extraction of minerals from sea water and from ordinary, but higher-grade rock, where needed. Such a flow of events is, of course, open to much doubt. Nonetheless, the long-term outlook appears far more promising than the limbo of resource exhaustion to which it has sometimes been condemned in recent popular debates and publications.

Canada's Principal Industrial Metal Exports

A discussion of Canada's mineral policy naturally separates into the fuels and non-fuel minerals. The fuels are discussed in the energy section. Here we are concerned about the non-fuels, principally the industrial metals. Canadian production of major non-fuel minerals is given in Table 43 in order of export value.

From the table it appears reasonable to discuss the first four minerals: copper, nickel, iron ore, and zinc. These four constitute about 66 per cent of the total non-fuel mineral production (in value), and would be basic to any minerals policy.* What is the outlook for these minerals?

Copper

In our earlier discussion it was estimated that long-term copper production from conventional land resources might be limited to about a billion tons. To this we might add about 3 billion tons from deep sea nodules. We will ignore for now the potential of other sources, even though about five thousand times as much copper exists in the upper mile of the earth's crust (Table 6). Four billion tons would provide about 500 lbs. per person, if the world's population stabilized at 16 billion people–a high estimate by the recent projections of many demographers. To give some indication of potential need, the total copper production in the U.S. has been roughly the same–500 lbs. per person. By this measure the world's future supply of copper, if reasonably conserved through recycling, can hardly be considered to be meager.

A more important point, however, is that copper has some ready substitutes for its primary uses. About half the copper produced for the developed world today is for electrical purposes. But aluminum is becoming a very strong competitor. The same amount of electricity can be transmitted by half as much aluminum as copper (i.e., half the weight; the cross sectional area is about 25 per cent greater). One of the drawbacks to the use of aluminum for electrical wire has been the difficulty of making good connections by soldering. However, a satisfactory solution to this problem was announced very recently.**

*It is worth noting that Canada's position with regard to asbestos is unusual. Although it produces about 40 per cent of the world's asbestos, it enjoys an estimated 70 per cent of the world trade in this commodity. Quebec has the major portion of this export market. Thus, Canada–or Quebec–appears to have the potential to dominate the world market in asbestos for many years to come, although it is doubtful whether this would remain viable for long if higher than competitive prices were charged. Many substitutes are available, e.g., Dupont's "Nomex" fabric.

**"Solve Aluminum Soldering Problem," *Industrial Research*, February 1977, p. 44.

146

Another widely publicized technological development is the substitution of fine optical glass fibres for large copper cables in telephone lines. Some have claimed that the replacement of existing copper cables with glass will soon be possible for less than the value of the copper scrap. In any event glass appears quite certain to replace copper in new telephone cables within the next decade.

Perhaps the next most valuable use of copper in industrial countries has been due to its thermal and corrosion-resistant properties. This combination makes it a desirable material for heat exchangers. However, here again aluminum is becoming increasingly competitive in applications where volume is not critical: As in the electrical application, an equal weight of aluminum can transfer heat faster than copper, although more physical space is required. Increasingly over time aluminum is expected to take a greater share of the market for heat exchanger material.

Other competitors for copper in building materials are stainless steel, plastics, and aluminum. Various alloy steels increasingly replace brass in shell cases. Many previous decorative uses of copper are now merely copper plating or substitute materials. Also, the use of copper in coins, while significant, is mostly traditional and essentially arbitrary. Thus, it appears quite clear that copper is often a desirable, but seldom a necessary, material. For most of its bulk uses it can be replaced relatively readily and, indeed, often has been. Should the price increase very much relative to aluminum, we could expect major shifts to occur within a few years.

It is a matter of fact that a glut of copper has existed since the commodity hysteria of 1974, and it seems unlikely to disappear soon – discounting severe strikes, revolutions in major producing countries, or the formation of an effective international cartel. These latter possibilities are generally of a transitory nature, if they occur at all. We note that copper consumption in the U.S., the major consumer, has increased by 15 per cent in two decades, while consumption of aluminum has tripled. The future requirements for copper may be even less than they are today. The demand for copper could even decline – at least in the developed world.

Fortunately for Canada, the U.S. is a net importer of copper. However, the U.S. produces enough for about 90 per cent of its needs. Without a growing demand for the metal, the U.S. market might not be open for much longer – or at least is unlikely to be a growing one. In the early 1970s about 21 per cent of Canadian copper production was exported to the U.S. (constituting 37 per cent of U.S. copper imports).* It appears likely that the principal growth of Canadian copper exports, if they occur at all, will come from consumers outside North America.

*Energy, Mines and Resources, *Towards a Mineral Policy for Canada.*

Nickel

The chapter on nickel in the authoritative U.S. Geological Survey publication *United States Mineral Resources* opens with the following "Abstract of Conclusions":

> At the present time the free world requirement of nearly 1 billion pounds of nickel per year is supplied from deposits of nickel sulfides, mostly in Canada, and of nickel laterites, mainly in New Caledonia. World resources from these types of deposits are estimated to total 70 million tons (140 billion pounds) of nickel in 7 billion tons of material averaging about 1 per cent nickel. An additional 7 billion tons averaging 0.2 per cent nickel, or 14 million tons of nickel, is estimated for sulfide deposits in the United States. The 0.2-0.4 per cent of nickel universally disseminated in peridotites and serpentinites throughout the world amounts to a figure several orders of magnitude greater than 70 million tons, as does the quantity of nickel contained in deep-sea manganese nodules; but new technological developments will be required to recover nickel successfully from these two types of occurrence. The discovery in 1949 at Thompson, Manitoba, of a major new type of nickel sulfide deposit suggests the possibility that similar deposits may exist elsewhere in the world.

The current major advantage that Canada has over other nations appears to come from the rich Thompson mines which have 3 per cent ore—a concentration at least double that of any other known large nickel-sulfide resources. This mine, together with the others shown in Table 44, indicates that Canada has a very large fraction of the world's known nickel-sulfide deposits whose nickel content averages 1 per cent or more. However, the other major group of nickel-bearing minerals, the nickel laterites, exist in large quantities in many countries, as shown in Table 45. When all of these various known resources are evaluated we find that there are two hundred years of nickel production (at the present demand of about a half million tons annually) available from the higher-grade resources alone. At a growth rate of 3 per cent these resources would contain a sixty-year supply.

To the above reserves must be added the huge potential of producing an estimated nine billion tons of nickel from ocean nodules. This enormous resource is about one hundred times greater than those of the high grade ores shown in Tables 44 and 45. Finally, the potential for finding new conventional resources appears to be large, as most of the world has not been well explored.

Thus, the story of nickel resources is one of relatively great abundance. Canada can probably remain the dominant supplier for many years if it wishes to do so. Probably the greatest potential threat, although one which is at least a decade or two hence, is that of competition from the mining of the ocean nodules. These nodules are expected to yield nickel, copper, cobalt, and manganese in substantial commercial quantities, in addition to several other minerals in lesser amounts. Concern has been expressed that a successful development of this form of ocean mining might flood the market with relatively cheap nickel and copper. Of these two metals, the threat to conventional mining of nickel is by far the greater of the two. Because of the imminence of this possibility, it appears that the long-term position of Canada as the world's leading nickel supplier might be somewhat unstable. For the balance of this century, however, this overhanging "threat" might discourage new competition from conventional sources.

Iron Ore

Iron is the second most abundant metal in the earth's crust; it constitutes about 6 per cent by weight (aluminum is first with about 8 per cent); consequently, the amount of potential iron ore resources is simply enormous. Thus, the preferred iron mines are those which contain the greatest concentrations of ore, which have ores of preferred chemical composition, which contain other valuable minerals, and for which transport costs are relatively low because of their proximity to navigable waters or to existing steel mills. Thus, economics dominate. Iron ore trade is very competitive because of this abundance and ubiquity. The mines in the most preferred locations tend to be the first to be produced.

Technological changes also can have a major impact, as has been shown in the Lake Superior region, where relatively recent processes for upgrading (beneficiating) and pelletizing ore that was once considered low grade (20-25 per cent iron) has added immensely to the potential reserves of that area (which has the excellent advantage of water-based transportation).

Iron ore will undoubtedly continue to be a steady export commodity for Canada, although it is unlikely to enjoy high growth unless we develop a large integrated steel industry—an unlikely direction for Canadian development.

Zinc

Zinc is the fourth most important metal in world trade, in terms of tonnage produced. Deposits of zinc are relatively ubiquitous and are generally found with lead. World zinc requirements grew roughly at a 4 per cent rate from 1950 to 1970, at which time they were about five million tons annually.

The reported identified world reserves in 1970 were about fifty times the annual demand while the total resources, including those currently subeconomic and/or requiring new technologies, are about one thousand times the annual demand. For example, about 750 million tons are estimated to be in the deep sea nodules discussed earlier.

The three largest industrial uses of zinc in North America are die casting alloys (41.4%); galvanizing sheet & strip (18.4%); and brass products (13.1%), for a total of 72.9% of total production. While there may be no economic alternatives for zinc in many products, substitutes are readily available for the three principal uses above. Magnesium, aluminum, and plastics are now competing in die casting; aluminum is often substituted for galvanized sheet steel; brass usage is often a matter of convenience, tradition, or decoration for which substitutes are generally not difficult. Thus, about 66 per cent or more of the present demand for zinc might be considered to be readily vulnerable to competition. However, zinc is not an expensive metal. Its price, roughly 33 per cent of that of copper, and quite volatile, allows it to compete quite readily.

Canada has a substantial stake in zinc as an export commodity; resources are adequate to maintain its position for many years to come. If the cost of producing zinc for export becomes excessive in Canada—indeed, in any country—undoubtedly many other producers would be eager to increase their share of the market. Between 1950 and 1970 Canada's production of zinc increased from 9 per cent to 23 per cent of the world production—an outstanding performance. It probably will have difficulty maintaining the present share during the balance of this century.

Conclusions

From the evidence presented in this chapter, protracted shortages of the minerals providing the important industrial metals appear extremely doubtful. This is especially true for Canada's major mineral exports.

Indeed, the opposite situation may be more likely—that a potential surplus of minerals could occur, partly as a result of other countries desiring a reduced dependence on imports, and partly as the result of competition from improving technologies (e.g., the harvesting of the deep sea nodules). Therefore, Canada may have to remain alert to these potential developments if it is to hold its present share of the current export market—if, in fact, that is feasible.

Of course, it is always possible that future technological developments may create shortages of relatively scarce metals for which substitutes may not be readily available and which are only found in a relatively few locations. Perhaps niobium or mercury or yttrium might eventually be found to have new uses which would create shortages and therefore high prices. However, there is no apparent threat of this kind today. In any event, these are the normal hazards of minerals production, and are of little importance in our context.

In this survey, we ignored the role of many commodities, in part because there did not appear to be a special reason for examining them individually, and in part because any one of them would not significantly affect Canada's future if its demand should rapidly increase or decrease. The likelihood of several such changes happening simultaneously appears to be, at most, a temporary self-defeating phenomenon such as that which occurred in 1974, or which sometimes occurs during wartime.

It appears that the concept of preserving Canada's mineral resources for the use of future generations who might otherwise be deprived of their "natural legacy," is without physical or economic foundation. Such a policy might bring moral satisfaction to its advocates, but the cost would be large to Canadians of this generation whose income would suffer from lost export earnings–and perhaps to the next generation also, if the lost share of the export market were not readily recoverable. This eventuality appears to be a possibility in the constrained growth scenario, although even there it seems doubtful that it would occur to a significant degree–at least not for any scientifically or economically rational reasons.

Agriculture

Agriculture is best understood in terms of a "resource." The demand for agricultural produce is a product of the level of world affluence; and the production is a function of the price. It is not possible to look at Canadian agriculture in isolation, because we are part of the world market, not only as producers, but also (as we often forget), as consumers. The economics of agriculture have created a situation which can be classified under three headings:

1. Canadian production for domestic market (e.g., dairy products, eggs, poultry);
2. Canadian production for domestic and world market (e.g., grain, beef);
3. Canadian consumption of world goods (e.g., tropical fruits, coffee, tobacco, cotton).

Like almost all countries, the rule of "comparative advantage" leads us to import many more agricultural products than those few we concentrate on exporting. It is not in the cards that Canada will produce significant quantities of cotton, tobacco, or grapes.

151

Domestic production for the domestic market is and will continue to be primarily of those goods which are highly perishable and are most economically produced near their consumption. These include milk products, eggs, and various types of truck goods. Because the market is there, these tend to be produced close to the great urban centres.* As the demand for this type of produce increases, we have more than enough land to supply it, if only by increasing production of existing farms which are underutilized or not used at all. Only about 5 per cent of Canada is improved farmland. Although our population is so small that this gives us more than twice as much cropland per capita as the U.S., the average productive capacity per acre of Canadian cropland is about half that of U.S. cropland.

When we think of Canada in the world market, our first thought is of the vast granary of the Prairies. Hudson's world projection implies a continued strong demand for this produce, but not brought about by world starvation or lack of food supply. The demand will not come from malnutrition, but from affluence; the principal determinant of demand for food is not numbers but wealth. While it is true that there is a limit to how much anyone, however wealthy, can eat, prosperity is accompanied by higher consumption in the form of food products which require larger and larger inputs. The most obvious example is the well-documented tendency of prosperous folk to shift from eating bread to eating meat, the meat requiring a much larger grain input than bread. Thus, the trade aspects of Canadian agriculture will probably be much along the same trend line in the next twenty years—more grain and certain types of livestock.

Whether or not it is Canada's grain and beef that a prosperous world eats depends mostly upon the relative cost we charge for produce, which is primarily a function of the productivity of our farmers. There is no reason to doubt that Canadian farmers will continue to be among the most efficient in the world. It would not be practical to project Canadian agriculture production in the next decade, but it is not difficult to show that an increase in productive capacity is certainly possible from the point of view of strictly physical constraints. There is no sign of reaching the peak of the yield trend.

Spring wheat, barley, and oats are adapted to Canadian growing condi-

*One often hears a concern raised about urbanization devouring our most valuable agricultural land. But, the land is valuable because of proximity to the urban markets. If urbanization "devours" the existing cropland then land farther out will be the nearest to the urban market and therefore more intensively used for agriculture and the most valuable. To the extent, also, that farm retrenchment in areas fringing cities has outstripped actual changes from farm to urban land uses, a considerable acreage of underutilized land exists, ripening for development.

tions, so climate is not a limiting factor. The probability that production can be increased to meet heightened demand is high if land use is increased slightly and some land is taken out of summer fallow. Yield improvements through the use of fertilizer, improved management practices, the reduction of losses due to weeds, pests, diseases, harvesting, and storage, and the development of higher yielding activities are relatively easy to achieve. New technologies, such as "zero tillage", should not be overlooked either.

There are many different possibilities for increasing production of oilseed crops, although Ontario soybean and Manitoba sunflower acreages appear sufficient, even at constant yield, to meet significant increases in demand in the next decade. Numerous selections of early-maturing soybeans have been made, and with appropriate management and more inputs, soybeans could probably also compete for land in the southern Prairies, in the unlikely event that Ontario "runs out" of land. Sunflowers could become a rotation crop in southern Saskatchewan and Alberta in high-density planting or in combination with summer fallow.

Beef output and beef prices have tended to follow a cyclical pattern (the "cow cycle") as output prices interact. If farmers feel the price is right, total output can be increased by raising carcass weight or by expanding beef herds in the West by improving forage production. Land presently unsuited for grain production could be reconverted to forage land, particularly in northern areas. This could bring several million acres into use. Official estimates show that improved forage varieties, intensified fertilizer use, and improved harvesting systems—all current technology—could raise production of forage crops by at least 50 per cent and perhaps 100 per cent in the Maritimes. We forecast that the major increases in beef production will occur in western Canada, but modest expansion will also occur in northern Ontario, Quebec, and the Maritimes.

New technologies, improved reproduction, reduced calf mortality, cross-breeding for better overall reproductive performance, lowered post-calfhood mortality, and various measures for improved nutrient utilization are also likely to come on stream in the next decade. Labour and mechanization can be employed more extensively to improve production. This is a question of economics, not of physical constraints.

In fact, we need not concern ourselves unduly about some of the common agricultural nightmares. Soil exhaustion is more a problem of pre-industrial agriculture. Today, the nutrients originally in the soil are of increasingly less importance compared with the artificial inputs provided through scientific farming. Obtaining petroleum-based fuels and fertilizers is a more realistic concern. However, as pointed out in the fuel

153

section, we expect continued reliable supplies. The price may be higher, but this will not affect Canada's competitive position because we will no doubt pay as much or as little as anybody else. It is possible that at some time in the twenty-first century, water pollution from the run-off of fertilizers will become a serious problem in some areas; if and when it does, agriculture will move towards more self-contained closed-cycle forms which the much richer world should be able to afford. In any event, we need not worry about this issue during the time frame of this study.

Recent fears about running out of agricultural land or Canada becoming a net food importer would seem to be without substance. The amount of land in production and the output per acre is a function of technology and investment, not natural limitations.

It should not be forgotten that agricultural production is concentrated in certain areas for economic reasons, not because those places are the only ones with agricultural capabilities. A Dutch study has calculated that most of the Laurentian Shield reaching up almost to Hudson Bay could be developed for agriculture and produce as much as 700 million tons of grain a year. The drawback is that the investment to make these areas suitable for agriculture would be extremely expensive, and better yields can be achieved at lower cost elsewhere in Canada and in the world. To repeat, this is an issue of economics, not of limits to productive capability.

It might be interesting here also to recall the "brown line" policy of the British Government in the late 1940s. According to this policy, no more farmland was to be released to urbanization, because of concerns that farmland built over was lost to food production. But it was soon discovered that since the British were avid gardeners, the intensive cultivation of land in housing areas equaled the land's production when it was farmland. Once again, the issue was not one of limits to productive capability.

As pointed out earlier, it would not be practical to try to project what will be Canadian production and exports of major agricultural commodities in the next decade. As in the past, these will depend upon world market conditions, which will largely be the effect of the interplay of local climatic, political, and social conditions.

Of the three, political conditions are probably the most important. If, for example, the Soviet Union should abandon its incredibly inefficient system of state farms, its markets could be lost to us and the Russians and Ukrainians could become formidable competitors on the international market. Similarly, should the Indian government abandon its essentially anti-agricultural policies (for instance, the artificially high price of fertilizers), that country would become not only self-sufficient but an exporter. It is our view that the Soviet Union is too deeply committed to the collective system and that the Indians could run into numerous difficulties, so our principal competitors will continue to be the United States, Australia, and perhaps Argentina.

One sure thing in agriculture is that relatively fewer people will be directly involved in it, and those few devoting less of their labour time to it. We qualify the phrase with "direct," because the number of persons actually on the farm vastly underestimates the number of Canadians who are involved in agricultural production. To say that ony six per cent of our population is in agriculture is rather like counting the strength of our armed forces only on the basis of the number of riflemen. For every Canadian on the farm, there are at least two who engage in agriculture by producing farm equipment, fertilizer, agricultural research, distributing farm produce from farms, and providing all the services involved in this huge industry. It is probable that the relative number of people engaged in agriculture will decline; but we will not be able to measure how much: Because so many of the supporting industries devote only part of their time to servicing agriculture, it is not practical to measure what percentage and how it is shifting.

However, the absolute number of farmers will probably remain substantially unchanged. The long-term decline seems to have bottomed out in the early 1970s. Unless there is some major surprise, we can expect a permanent agricultural labour force of a half million. This raw number is just a little misleading. Many of these people will hold other jobs in addition to their farming function.

Perhaps most important is the waning of farming as a way of life, and its replacement by farming as an occupation in the urban style. This is one aspect of the effective urbanization of the entire society. Indeed, we should expect a continuation of the division of Canadian farmers into several different types, distinguished by their outlook towards agriculture. These can roughly be characterized as follows:

1. *Agribusiness:* These are the big operators who are managing what amount to rural agricultural factories. Their operations are characterized by heavy capital input, a high degree of technological and managerial skill, and large size. The leading Canadian farmers of the late twentieth century are moving far from the traditional image of "horny-handed sons of the soil" towards becoming highly sophisticated and cosmopolitan international businessmen. Already, 30 per cent of our farmers produce 70 per cent of the output.

2. *Part-time Farmers:* Especially in the older rural areas of Eastern and Central Canada, fewer and fewer farmers are deriving the bulk of

155

their income from agriculture. Their principal sources of income are factory and service labour, and small proprietorships. They continue farming as a useful supplement to their income, largely because of a historical attachment to their land, which frequently came to them from inheritance. We should not underestimate the social, indeed moral, value of this type of operation in maintaining local stability; but it is increasingly less of a "serious" contributor to national agricultural output.

3. *Pseudo-farms:* These are "farms" which are not really farms, but very low-density exurban large-lot developments within a few hours driving of our cities, which serve as weekend or even year-round homes for the upper classes. From the air we can see how these "farms" thicken as we approach almost every city. Farming may be performed as a hobby by the owner ("gentleman farming") but more likely the proprietor will make some arrangement with a local farmer to plant and crop a few fields for a modest return to help him pay the taxes. This represents a trivial contribution to our agricultural output, though one not to be sneered at. But these sorts of "farms" greatly misrepresent the real amount of serious farming in Canada.

With the waning of the traditional family farm, the considerable political clout of agriculture should diminish. It will be increasingly difficult to justify the deployment of State power to guarantee the incomes of what amount to prosperous businessmen. Over the next generation the consumer interest in the cities will build up relative to the producer interest on the farm, and it must be expected that this will weaken the power of various marketing boards and other apparatus to set artificially high prices. Of course, the consumer interest will be concentrated in the eastern provinces and B.C., while the farmers will continue to be very powerful in the Prairies, particularly Saskatchewan and Manitoba; therefore this prospect has in it the potential for exacerbating regional differences, especially since we must project a continuation of the gradual shift of agriculture from east to west.

The Environment

"Environment" has two meanings. The first sense, used by many environmentalists, means the entire physical world; so, in that sense, this entire study is about the Canadian environment. In popular usage, however, "environment" refers to pollution of the natural environment–the air, water, and landscape–and this section of the report uses this definition.

This is a particularly difficult section to write because the general tone and trend of official and popular literature would lead us to believe that our environment is seriously impaired, is getting worse, and in many cases disaster is impending. We do not believe this to be generally true. To begin with, let's put some things in perspective: first, pollution is a condition. Nature pollutes. Particulate matter, ozone, and carbon monoxide are produced by nature as well as man. Seepage from natural deposits sometimes creates water pollution. Natural oil spills are more frequent than any other type of oil spill. It is not that nature is pure and man is soiling that purity, but that man adds to and in some cases reduces the pollution of nature.

Second, most aspects of environmental concerns, or at least those most often discussed by members of environmental groups, are not as severe as they were half a century ago. The air in the major cities is unquestionably cleaner than it was in the early part of the twentieth century for the very simple reason that we have largely substituted oil for coal as fuel. Coal gives out very nasty particulate matter, leading to the famous fogs over industrial centres which clearly had serious health effects. Oil is by no means as bad.

Our potable water is much cleaner than it was half a century ago. It was not so long ago that cities had higher death than birth rates, and had to be constantly recruiting from the countryside to maintain and increase their population, because of the foul water which spread endemic diseases through the population. The simple expedient of separating potable water from sewage has reduced this to a minimum.

The emissions from motor vehicles are trivial compared with the excrements of the draft animals which preceded them. Junked cars are ugly, but not as noxious as the dead horses which once littered our streets.

Third, moving from the popular to the total environment, we should never forget that the total system of industrial society provides for a healthier and a more pleasant environment. While it is true that some industrial processes produce undesirable pollutants which have adverse health conditions, these are the effluents of a system which has provided an overall level of health that was inconceivable in historical terms. Thus, life expectancy continues to creep upward and overall health is far better—by objective standards, of course; by our relative standards we are more sensitive to the slightest deviations from perfect health.

Furthermore, the increased mobility made available to us by the industrial system permits us to experience a wider variety of physical environments, most of which in our country are hardly touched. Fortunately, of all the nations in the world, ours is the one which needs least worry about these issues on the basis of our great land mass and scattered population.

In the above context, we argue that current debate on "environmental" problems has focussed on the more trivial issues, and has all but ignored the more serious concerns for the environment. The affluence which has produced our superior overall environment makes us extremely sensitive to its negative aspects. We are troubled by the adverse health effects of pollution and, more important, by the aesthetic effects. For example, it has not been possible to demonstrate that any individual person has ever died from auto-induced smog. But in a place like Vancouver, that ought to be an earthly paradise, seeing a dirty line in the sky like a ring around a bathtub is a continuing aesthetic annoyance, and we wish to take steps to alleviate it. We want to preserve areas where the air is so pure and the skies so clear that you can see for miles and miles ahead. We would like to have more secluded beaches, less crowded ski slopes. We want as many parks as possible. We want our cities to be "garden cities." We are right in wanting these, but it is important to recognize that our qualms are based more on aesthetic than on health reasons.

Unfortunately, the quality of environmental data, i.e., the availability and accuracy of measuring devices, makes it very difficult for us to tell whether or not attempts over the last decade at alleviating environmental pollution have had any serious effect. We believe, on the basis of data from the U.S. and Europe, that they have, though doubtless much more can and will be done. Basically, the efforts of dealing with pollution are straightforward and simple. First, the problem must be recognized. This has been the major achievement of the environmentalist movement. Second, we reduce the pollution, either by cleaning up after the pollution or, more commonly, by preventing the original emissions or restraining them to a local area in which they can be cleaned up. This is mostly a question of money and technology, once the will is present.

In some cases, it may be necessary to stop the activity producing the pollution as a by-product, but we believe that such cases will be very few. For this reason, we are rather skeptical of the motives of many of these so-called environmentalists. The solution they too often recommend is to block the activity rather than prevent the pollution. This leads us to believe that they are less interested in the environment than in stopping the activity. For example, if automobile emissions are creating an urban air-pollution problem, the solution would seem to be to reduce the emissions from the cars. But some of the most vocal environmentalists would have us stop driving altogether. We suspect they object more to the car than to the emissions.

Our projections are that investment of capital and human resources in dealing with the environment is now a permanent part of the economy. From now on, engineers will have to add emissions to their historical design parameters of performance, safety, reliability, and costs. This will be done without question. Our economic projections assume that 2 to 3 per cent of GNP (compared to less than 1 per cent today) will permanently be invested in dealing with pollution. Again, this is not new. Our cities have long been investing in pollution control, (i.e., sewage and water treatment), but in the future, standards will be higher and more rigorously enforced. The very existence of an economic surplus will allow us to increase our standards and afford to develop new technology or processes to deal with our problems.

This is not to say that no new pollution issues and problems will appear. Remember that when the automobile was introduced, one of its most heralded boons to mankind was that it would eliminate the pollution from draft animals that blighted our cities' streets. Other fixes will themselves create new problems.

Perhaps even more important are the "unknown" environmental problems that are likely to emerge. Some of these—heating or cooling of the earth, possible destruction of the ozone layer, etc.—are very complex. Furthermore, we know very little about the possible outcome to these problems. It is virtually impossible to internalize the costs of these externalities, nor to be sure that proposed solutions are correct. Nevertheless, we argue that these esoteric questions will best be resolved if we are technologically advanced and rich, and thus have the resources necessary to deal with such complexities.

Returning to the less esoteric and more aesthetic concerns for the environment, our economy is too heavily reliant on resources which must compete in the international market, to suffer too much excessive cost in environmental considerations. Already, some of the steam is going out of the environmental movement. Even with total awareness and the best will, reforms take time. The polity must first respond to those aspects of a problem which are either the most serious or the most easily solved. We cannot give priority to all aspects with the same intensity. Probably more important is the current economic climate. Environmentalism costs money and jobs, and often improves one aspect of the standard of living to the detriment of others. To some degree, we make, but we do not actually choose, our society and our future. We want to widen the spectrum of choice as much as possible, however, and it would appear that in this area, the generation of economic surplus, if carefully achieved, (not at all costs), will make more choices available in the future. We predict that when the economy picks up again there will be a resurgence of interest in the environment, and by the 1990s even more ambitious environmental controls and investment will be routine—but on the whole they should be more efficient.

This is a key variable in our scenarios. Under accelerated growth, environmentalism will slow in the short-run, but as the economy picks up it will probably become more intensive. Under constrained growth, environmentalism becomes even more central to the national consciousness, and even more conventional economic prosperity will be paid for it.

Of course, serious concern is now being expressed over pollution of our lakes and rivers, and the resulting destruction of our recreation areas. We expect Canadians to react even more strongly to any such pollution in the future–and understandably so. An affluent society should not have to put up with too much of this. We confidently predict that by the mid-1990s air and water pollution will be a fraction of what it is today, yet some people will not be entirely satisfied with air and water quality.

Urban Development*

We expect the following fundamental long-term urban trends to continue throughout the remainder of this century:
1. Growth in population and size of metropolitan cities;
2. Suburbanization, or the spread of cities, with increasing numbers of residents living in lower density housing with larger lots;
3. City size growing faster than population, resulting in a decline in overall density;
4. Continued reliance on highway transportation–automobile, bus, and truck.

Though the authors share this view of Canada's urban future, they acknowledge a considerable and influential body of opinion which challenges many of the assumptions on which these forecasts are based. The dissenters view the growth in our cities as not an unmixed blessing, and as giving rise to many new problems in society, the effect of which will be to limit the extent, direction and shape of the growth of our cities. They see these trends as giving rise to environmental deterioration or to problems arising from the role of the automobile as a commuting vehicle, the enormous infrastructure costs of suburban sprawl, the loss of arable land adjacent to our cities to roads, buildings and small holdings, and the excessive consumption of a costly imported energy source, oil.

We believe many of these concerns to be ill founded, and in fact more defensive action by the upper middle classes (who see their own gains threatened by the desire of the masses pushing up behind them to acquire the kind of life they now lead), than to a reasoned appraisal of the net benefits of urban growth to society as a whole. But these views are widely held by opinion makers in this country, and cannot be dismissed lightly. Thus we will attempt to present both sides of the argument in this

*Our projections are based on calculations done for us by John Kettle.

chapter, but our own conclusions indicate that urban development over the next two decades will follow a path more or less similar to that of the past thirty years, that this is economically fesible and promises an improved standard of living and quality of life for the average Canadian.

First, the quality of life question. Are our cities becoming less attractive places in which to live? If older city-dwellers cast their minds back twenty or thirty years, to compare their present way of life with their life then, and allocated changes for the better between their own rise in material well-being through rising incomes, and improvements in the city itself, we suspect that most would agree with us that in most respects life in Canadian cities is a good deal better than it was before and immediately after the Second World War: Fewer slums, better roads making access easier in our cities and out to the countryside, improved public transit in most cities, more cultural amenities. Against this must be set greater bustle and congestion; the omnipresent automobile; and the destruction of old neighbourhoods. But on the whole, city-dwellers are living a better urban life than they or their predecessors did a generation ago.

For the average Canadian family, the continuation of long-term trends promises a heightened standard of living/quality of life. Participation in metropolitan life offers the individual Canadian a wider variety of opportunities for jobs, services, entertainment, and friendship. The larger the metropolitan area the more choices he has. Larger metro cities permit the formation of a "critical mass" of people to support all manner of minority tastes. From within the metro population one can find a suitable group of like-minded friends or people with similar tastes.

While the large city falls short of rural areas in providing open space and privacy, near universal auto-mobility permits the individual to reach the open country. And even within the metro area one simulates open space and achieves a measure of privacy by opting for lower density development in suburbs (which we define physically, not politically; suburbs can be within the central city limits).

Suburbanization is caused by very simple phenomena: The vast majority of our people want to have their own single-family houses on their own lot, and government mortgage policy has encouraged them. We come from European rural cultures which highly valued land-owning. Indeed, the only full citizens were those who were landowners, freeholders. Most of our ancestors came here to get land. But they also wanted money and the other benefits of urban life, so many of them came to the city, yet they did not entirely lose the idea of having their own piece of property which they now achieve in a small way in a suburban home. With widespread mass affluence and flexible transportation, millions now have the means to achieve this desire.

162

There has been much discussion in recent years about "changing life-styles" or people wishing to reject the traditional, family oriented, home-centred suburban life. It is true that social trends towards more divorce and rejection of traditional forms of materialism among the educated classes are leading in this direction, but only on the margin. If two or five per cent of Canadians wish to give up the traditional lifestyle, it makes very little difference in the sum of things (unless, of course, that small minority is able to impose its standards on the rest of the society). To be sure, young people will continue to flock to certain "ghettos" of our big cities, there to play and socialize. But for most of them–and now we have over a decade of experience with observing the lifestyle of "liberated" young people–city life begins to pale, they become tired of public enter-tainments of various sorts, and they even come to be bored with them-selves. Whether through inherited genetic factors, cultural conditioning, or merely a desire to have something new to talk about, they have chil-dren and get a house, usually in the suburbs. This will hardly change, if at all, during the next fifteen years.

We suspect that the desire for land has always been the case, even among our city dwellers, but they were unable to achieve it because of the primitive transportation facilities of the day. This mobility has only been made available to the mass of people in recent years through the wides-pread availability of cheap mass-produced automobiles. On the whole, the conventional wisdom in urban affairs is anti-automobile. It is seen as a destroyer of urban life, the creator of congestion, pollution, and other anti-urban by-products. The fact is that the automobile is a very efficient way to travel, and with the automobile people can cover what were previ-ously unthinkable distances in the ordinary course of their day's business.

A misleading term in the concept of transportation in cities is that of "distance." This means very little. What counts is time. Most people think nothing of spending twenty minutes going to work. When the mode of travel was walking, they were restricted to the tight little cities of the old world. With streetcars and commuter trains the range was extended. With automobiles averaging thirty miles an hour, ten miles to work is nothing. Furthermore, many people think nothing of travelling an hour for a special occasion–going to a restaurant or visiting friends–or to prac-tise sports; in off-rush hours, forty miles an hour average is usual, so they may go forty miles. Going up a stage, people think nothing of travelling two hours for a week-end with the family or a day of shopping and the theatre in "the city." So a hundred mile trip becomes ordinary for week-ends, for holidays. Draw a two-hour circle around our twenty largest cities and you have encompassed a majority of the population of Canada. Draw the same line around the smaller towns or extend the range to take into account prairie farmers who are accustomed to travelling long distances that would appal Easterners, and for all practical purposes we have encompassed the whole population of Canada.

This view of the beneficent impact of the automobile on our society is not of course wholly shared by its opponents. The automobile becomes more a master or even a tyrant when it is the principal form of mass transit in cities. They argue that insatiable demand for street space forces municipalities and provinces to lay out increasing amounts of scarce capital, raised by higher taxes or borrowing, on roads, arterials, throughways, and autoroutes. To provide space for these, neighbourhoods are penetrated, houses destroyed, barriers erected, and slums encouraged in areas close by. Parking lots replace parks in city centres; the city suffers from the results—visual, aural and air pollution. In other words, they see our cities getting worse not better.

That is not their only argument against excessive dependence on the car. In large numbers, in limited areas, it becomes increasingly inefficient. If one accepts that time replaces distance in measuring the length of trips, that portion of a driver's time spent idling, and fuming, in traffic jams, has to be taken account of. They also state that new roads provide only short-term and increasingly costly expedients, and bring with them all the accompanying liabilities noted above. Most of these problems of congestion arise from the simultaneous attempts of suburbanites to reach their city-centre work destination, alone in their large North American automobiles; they argue that a system of good commuter transit, with trains, streetcars, and buses on their own rights-of-way would be faster and cheaper with few of the environmental defects.

We must, therefore, anticipate continued hostility (by the "official" classes) to the process of urbanization, suburbanization, and automobility. Let us consider this. One of the cant terms in broad-brush social commentary is "urbanization." As we move towards the end of the century, it will be more and more apparent that this term is becoming a historical anachronism of little or no analytical utility. Once upon a time, not so long ago, most Canadians, like most others in the world, were rural and lived by agriculture and husbandry. A few lived in cities and villages. The material and social life of the urban dweller was in sharp contrast to his country cousin. More important, his outlook was different: City folk were better educated, more cosmopolitan, sharper, further from nature, and more liberated from traditional ways of doing things and looking at the world. The distinction between urban and rural was vital to understanding the society and how it worked. Today, this distinction is of little value. The concept of "urbanization" is of decaying importance because, in a considerable sense, almost all Canadians are now "urban." Communications, media, public education, and high-speed, long-distance individual transportation have bridged the gap between the city and country. Except for a few isolated groups, all Canadians are "urbanized," think in urban terms, and live in an urban manner.

The key issues of urban development today are of the density and concentration of urbanization. Unfortunately, most of the conventional discussion of these issues treats urbanization as "a problem." For most people in the world urbanization has been a great opportunity. By coming to cities they improved their individual lives. But this was not necessarily so good for the people already established in those cities; thus urbanization became "a problem."

Once urbanization is established as "a problem," one can exaggerate that problem by extending the definition of what "is urban." A recently published book about our most densely populated area (along the St. Lawrence) shows vast areas painted in dark shades as "urban", provoking visions of this whole area paved over in the image of central Toronto or Montreal with 20,000 people per square mile. But a look at the legend shows that "urban" is defined as 119 persons per square mile or more than five acres for every person and sixteen acres for every family. This line of thought is by no means limited to Canada; indeed, it comes out of the U.S. and England with the concept of "megalopolis," which implies that we are being jammed into more crowded cities. Quite the contrary is true. Even granting that 90 per cent of our land area is for all practical purposes uninhabitable, it is difficult to image that Canada is running out of land.

Another misleading phrase is "urban sprawl." This conjures the same images of vast cities spreading over the landscape, devouring the land. Actually, what is happening is that our cities are spreading out into almost limitless space. Except in southern Ontario, where the expanding cities tend to blur into one another (but at very low densities), and a few Atlantic cities where the space is limited by unfavourable topography, all of our cities can spread at existing rates into the existing countryside areas for generations to come with no loss to the nation.

This statement will sound so bizarre that it must be elaborated upon. As pointed out in the agriculture section, the idea that cities are eroding our farmland is highly questionable. The amount of urbanization in the last generation is less than the error in estimating the amount of agriculture land.*

*By the end of the century Canada will not have more than 10 million households. Assume a million are on farms or in the wilderness. Give each of 9 million urban households an acre. For every residential acre provide two acres for commerce, industry, utilities, highways, parks and institutions—this is generous. Yet, this "plan"

But let spokesmen for the conventional wisdom reply to these assertions. To them, urban sprawl is very much more than paving over large suburbs. It is "ugly ribbon development" stretching out (if uncontrolled) in all directions from our cities, haphazard and spotty development based on accidents of speculative land ownership which is enormously costly in terms of providing roads, services and schools, apart from any aesthetic considerations. The automobile makes the suburbs possible, and the suburbanites' use of it becomes the principal problem of the city from which they are fleeing: the shape and nature of suburban growth make the suburbs difficult to service by public transit.

As for the impact of loss of arable farmland to urban development, they argue that in certain areas and products particularly, development has threatened our future ability to meet our own needs. The loss of land is not simply land used for building and roads; it is also the land beyond the suburbs accumulated by speculators and left idle, or farms bought by escapees from urban and suburban living, and similarly sterilized. They cite examples around Vancouver, the fertile St. Lawrence Valley land south and east of Montreal, the Niagara fruit belt near Toronto and Hamilton. Canadian space may be "limitless"; good farmland is not. (This argument is taken up in the agriculture section of this report.)

Use of the term "urban sprawl" has come to indicate a hostility to suburbanization or the spreading of our cities at lower densities. Density is an abstract notion. People in their individual lives do not think in terms of density. With a lot of people and a lot of activities using a given amount of land, there will be a lot of people around, particularly in periods such as rush hours, when a lot of people want to use the same space at the same time. The cure to congestion is the spreading out of people at lower densities or so-called "urban sprawl" created by suburbanization.

Another widely heard phrase is "urban problems," which suggests that our cities are in bad shape and getting worse. This is a concept adapted from the U.S., and however applicable it may be there, with a very few exceptions it has no relevance to Canada at all. Our cities are a marvellous success. Compared with the Western world–with Europe and Japan, as well as the United States–our cities are clean, honestly and competently governed, relatively free of crime, and offer a wide range of services and a high quality of life to our people. If anything, their worst

for urban Canada requires only 27 million acres or 43,000 square miles, less than the area of Nova Scotia and New Brunswick (48,000) or 2 per cent of Canada *without* the Territories and Labrador. Assuming 3 persons per household, the overall population density of urban Canada would be 630 per square mile. For comparison consider these 1971 Census Metropolitan Areas densities: Calgary–2600; Toronto–1900; Quebec City–1400; Halifax–850.

fault is that they are too good and therefore too dull. This is the kind of "problem" that most Canadians are happy to endure.

Some Canadians fear this process will lead to the "megalopolis," presumably characterizing U.S. urban development. This too is a myth. American cities are more spread out than ours, but still occupy less than 2 per cent of American land area. A glance out the window of an aircraft flying "the Boswash corridor" reveals that it is mostly green. Los Angeles is another presumably horrid exemplar, but is a special case because it is ringed by mountains, requires piped water, and its overall density is higher than most U.S. and Canadian metro cities. In any event, to the extent that L.A. is crowded, it is because people find it desirable to live there. Except in the desert, "megalopolis" and "urban sprawl" mean less, not more crowding.

Those who question this analysis say that density in itself is a non-issue, that some of the least attractive features of American urban life are caused by the impact of low-density suburbs–and automobiles commuting from it–on the fabric of the inner cities. European cities provide a far better model of how high density urban areas, linked to suburbs by first class public transit and freeways, can function vastly better than low-density American cities.

If our analysis is accurate, why have these misleading images been perpetrated? Several factors are involved and they are common to some of the themes that we develop elsewhere in this study regarding views of the future of other aspects of society.

First of all, as we would expect, there are questions of power. If the existing system is working badly, reforms must be made; the preferred modifications usually seem to have the effect of increasing power of urban planners and other bureaucrats at the expense of the business interest and the average citizen. Related are questions of privilege: Clearly, the existing system as it has developed over the last generation is a great benefit to the bulk of Canadian urban dwellers, but it is not so favourable for the established elites. Commentators do not list one of the real costs of unconstrained urbanism–the threat to the quality of life of the existing privileged suburbs. As long as the bulk of the population lived either on the farm or in a small town or crowded within the central city, the suburbs were an ideal place to live. However, as the working people move from the country to urban areas, and from the city to the suburbs, traffic congestion increases and the price of housing is pushed up, causing some of the advantages of suburban life to diminish. This is a general cost to the established classes of mass affluence and of levelling.

Halting or slowing down the suburban trend has been widely advocated. We do not think this is a viable option. To do so requires the deployment of considerable state action. This has been attempted in Europe since the Second World War. The European governments have set themselves against suburbanization and have power and authority unthinkable here. Still, even there, suburbanization continues; the population of most large European cities (excluding their metropolitan areas, i.e. their suburbs) has been declining for decades.

Metro Structure

Within our metropolitan cities, the allocation of land use will remain essentially unchanged. Broadly speaking, the following pattern has dominated the past century:

1. The prosperous classes settled on the high ground. This is the characteristic pattern in an "Anglo-Saxon" country*–those with more wealth take the higher ground with interesting rolling terrain or, in lieu of high ground, settle near a waterway (as in Winnipeg).

2. The city centre spreading from the original transportation focus (the port or railhead) in the direction of the fashionable residential areas. Instinctively, the developers, store owners etc. move the new construction towards their own homes.

3. The flats and row housing for the lower-middle and working classes. Here are the rail lines and the factories. This pattern of the less prosperous on the flats and the more prosperous on the heights makes good economic sense because the flat terrain is better suited for mass housing developments, while the rolling terrain adapts itself to the custom-built homes and winding street patterns preferred by the more prosperous class.

Three New Trends

In addition to the four principal trends listed at the beginning of this chapter, we must expect the acceleration of three trends now becoming apparent:

The Suburbanization of Industry and Commerce

As we move towards the end of the century, the image of a metropolitan city consisting of jobs in the centre surrounded by a suburban residential ring will be less and less valid. Increasingly industry, commerce, and

*Quebec will remain somewhat more "Latin" in having relatively more rental housing with the prosperous more likely to live nearer the centre; but increasing affluence should move the province more towards "Anglo" settlement patterns, as is happening in France today.

offices will also be located in suburbs, usually near motorway interchanges, e.g. Ville St-Laurent, Don Mills. The reasons for this movement are obvious: stores wish to move near their customers and employers near their labour force. Not to be ignored is that many managers have chosen suburban living and find it easier to drive to a nearby location.

In addition to locational advantages, the suburbanization of commerce and business offers distinct economic benefits: suburban land is cheaper. Free parking is a desirable asset to a contemporary commercial establishment; customers are less willing to carry purchases home on mass transit or, with more women working, are loath to subject themselves to the uncertainties and expense of home delivery. Contemporary industry relies on low-built horizontal factories mostly supplied by truck, with internal movement by forklift truck. Here, too, free parking for employees is extremely desirable. All of these criteria lead managers and entrepreneurs to seek out space not available in the city centre.

By forecasting the suburbanization of industry and commerce, we are *not* projecting a decline of the traditional centres. There is no inherent reason for the established centres to decay.

There are economies of scale and specialization for business in concentrating in the centre of cities; New York, for all its problems, still exists and functions because businessmen want to be "where the action is."

But the bulk of the growth will be in suburban locations. Obviously, such a shift has important implications. Unless the suburban locations are comprehended within the centre city, tax revenues are lost. Movement of the leading edge to the suburbs also affects the morale and cohesiveness of the commercial interests. The old downtown leaders have a sense of the city slipping away from them and the increased distance between establishments reduces the personal interplay among the leadership cadres in clubs and other contacts.

Conversely, there is considerable benefit to the public purse. It is certainly less expensive to move the shoppers and workers closer to their residence than it is to invest in increasing the transportation facilities—whether highways or mass transportation—which are particularly expensive and politically difficult when it is necessary to "retrofit" by cutting through existing development.

Of our cities, Toronto, Montreal, and Vancouver are large enough to support the next stage in urban development, the building of large satellite urban nodules. Huge regional shopping centres, new factories, and perhaps most striking of all, suburban office parks will be commonplace in those three cities by the 1990s, and will be appearing in smaller cities as well.

Exurbanization

However, the suburbanization of industry and commerce will not reduce commuting by as much as is implied above. Since the centre does not decline, and most people wish suburban living, the residents of the inner suburbs will continue to commute to the centre. Those who work in the suburban factories and offices will commute from farther out. This outer suburbanization we will label "exurbanization." Characteristically it will be of a density so low that it cannot be identified as "urban" in any traditional sense of the word. It will take three forms:

1. Low-density, planned developments with generous provisions for open space as required by local zoning authorities;
2. Additions to existing villages. All towns and hamlets within an hour's driving time of every metropolitan centre must expect bit by bit piecemeal growth as the metro cities spread towards them;
3. "Pseudo-farms." These are "farms" which are really country residences for the relatively prosperous.

One reason for the very low density of exurban development is the desire of our people for more land. Exurbanization is, according to this point of view, merely the logical extension of suburbanization. However, the developing peripheral communities will take steps to keep densities down, in order to push prices up, in order to slow development. This is the "pulling the ladder up behind you" phenomenon.

Many urban commentators believe that the continuation of these long-term trends portends the death of cities. This position gains some support from the recent history of the older U.S. cities, but here we think the American experience is not appropriate for us. Because our per capita wealth is lower than that of the U.S., the average Canadian cannot afford quite as much land and space as his American equivalent. Our less favourable climate compounds the economic issue: commuting by car is more expensive in terms of wear and tear; Canadian spaces require more heating; and our bitter winters put a premium on enclosed malls and other protected spaces requiring higher density to be economic. Fortunately, we lack U.S. racial problems; our cities are relatively competently and honestly governed compared with the U.S. Our metro governments help counter the tendency to relocate towards lower tax jurisdictions. Perhaps most important in preventing our cities from going the way of Buffalo, Cleveland, and Detroit is the stronger social power of the Canadian upper middle classes. They have determined not to go the way of American cities.

Perhaps as affluence and exurbanization continue, we can expect that

170

more and more Canadians will live like the rich today, with a swank city apartment or townhouse and a country house at home or abroad. Eventually, this may make the suburban compromise unnecessary – the suburbs might then become the slums – but that is at the soonest a twenty-first century nightmare.

Localism

What we call "localism" is a heightened awareness of the conflict of interest between an individual locality and whole region or nation. What is valuable for the region is valuable for every locality in that region, but the local interest is in having the regional facility located elsewhere. For example, it is in everyone's interest to have cheap and abundant electric power; it is also in everyone's interest not having electric power plants located in their vicinity. Of course, the people elsewhere feel the same way about not having it there. The same is true of highways, airports, drug treatment centres, prisons, and even low-income housing.

Conflict between the local and the regional interest has always existed, but some recent tendencies have exacerbated it and are rapidly bringing it to crisis proportions. A very strong factor involved here is the increasing disillusionment with progress. Moreover, the developer or other person who wants to institute change of some kind has always been at a great disadvantage in dealing with the local people who do not want the change. Local people in almost every community are "conservative" in regard to that community.

The reasons for being conservative are very simple: every family in that community had a choice of living there or in any one of hundreds or perhaps even thousands of other neighbourhoods. They chose a particular neighbourhood because they preferred it for one reason or another to all other areas in the region. Once there, they don't want it to change much.

Of course, every change has some effect on the environment. It is not even necessary for local interest to bar all development; they need only to put in such high standards of environmental control that it becomes uneconomic for the developer to go ahead with his project.

Needless to say, if this sort of thing were to go on in an uncontrolled fashion almost universally there would be little building of anything anywhere; the desire of most Canadians to own their own homes would be terribly frustrated and, no doubt, government action would be required, perhaps even to the degree of forcing a regional or provincial overruling of local interests and laws controlling development.

Historically, the prestige and authority of the organizations that controlled most new developments were rarely challenged. But recently, hardly an institution has escaped attacks against its competence and honesty. Resistance to local changes is part of a national suspicion of established institutions. And all too frequently this suspicion has been proved valid by incompetent, arrogant, and high-handed behaviour by officials.

Believe it or not, local government in Canada is gradually becoming less corrupt. In local government, only the present residents elect local officials, while the interests of would-be residents are represented only by the developers. The developers have few votes; however, they can "vote" with money. It is no secret that this sort of "voting" is commonplace in many local governments. As governments are subjected to increasing scrutiny, and honesty in government is promoted, this "incentive" to develop is reduced.

Increases in federal and provincial subventions to local governments will further decouple local government from local taxes and thus from local economic activity. If municipalities are indifferent to real property taxes, what motives have they to incur all the varied costs of having factories and shopping centres on their territory? Primarily residential communities–particularly upper middle-class communities–care little about jobs.

We forecast that, in the short run, the jobs of local decision-makers are going to be even more difficult. They will continually be torn between the immediate desires of their constituencies and the larger needs of the region and nation. Still, we need not be excessively gloomy about these issues. After all, the balancing of individual, group, and overall interest is the principal business of government. The polity has successfully dealt with worse conflicts of interest in the past. It will be interesting to see how these new conflicts are ultimately handled. What will happen to our cities will result from an interplay of the forces involved. By the end of the century those parts of our cities that exist today will have had some redevelopment, but will be essentially unchanged and remain healthy while surrounded by newer, lower-density development. Any reader of this study can drop into almost any city in Canada in fifteen years and find his way around with little trouble. There will be a few new buildings, some new highways, and perhaps a rapid transit facility or two. Cities will be bigger in population, occupy more space, and be of somewhat lower density,* but not as low as in the States. Planners and politicians will continue to complain about "urban problems."

Now let us turn to the prospects for some specific metropolitan cities.

Toronto

In 1991, Toronto will more than ever be the great Canadian city. Indeed, it will be a great North American city. There will be no question that Toronto has outstripped Montreal in numbers, wealth, and influence. No particular innovations are required to achieve this goal; the natural work-ings of the existing system are more than sufficient to push Toronto (by which of course we mean metropolitan Toronto) in this direction. It is safe to forecast that the current efforts to restrain Toronto's growth will be less than successful. At most they will cause dislocations and annoy-ances by pushing up land prices. (See Table 8.)

Within metropolitan Toronto the historical patterns of urbanization will all continue. Toronto City long since achieved population saturation, and is in population decline. The Yorks have also reached saturation and are beginning to decline; the outlying boroughs in Metro Toronto will certainly peak before 1991, and the major growth will be in the surround-ing regional municipalities of, for example, Durham, Peel, and Halton. Towards the end of the century the most rapid growth will be even farther out. But it must be noted that a "step" phenomenon will be experienced; the farther from the centre, the lower will be the developed density.

Other Southern Ontario Cities

Toronto will be the hub of a huge urban region. Around the western end of Lake Ontario the concept of "megalopolis" has some limited validity. In 1991, the triangle between Lake Simcoe, London, and Niagara will contain approximately six million people in ten thousand square miles, for an overall density of one person per acre** spreading to Oshawa to the northeast, to Hamilton, around the corner of Lake Ontario to Niagara, and west to Kitchener, Waterloo and even London. This should not be interpreted to be solid urban development. Most of the development will be in cities and small towns with the largest block in Metro Toronto itself, and most of the land will remain open or "developed" at very very low exurban densities.

*Official published data of Census Metropolitan Areas may give a specious impression that suburbanization is slowing. This is a result of the way the CMAS are defined in terms of a certain minimum density which does not pick up "exurbanization."

** Many serious people have expressed concern for the peach-growing areas at the west-ern end of Lake Ontario which seem to be threatened by urbanization. This repre-sents an interesting clash of values. Let us ask these questions: First, is this area the best place for Canadians to obtain peaches? Obviously not; many other places in the world are far better suited for peach production. Importing peaches would cost us some foreign exchange, but a trivial amount in the total picture of international trade.

Second, is it better to grow peaches or people in these areas? Those who do not want people there, do not want the suburbanization, obviously prefer peaches. While we cannot read other people's motives, the terms of the discussion of the peach area in the context of the arguments that have long been made against suburbanization suggests to us that the peach issue is not so important as the anti-people, anti-suburban issue.

The fortunes of the other cities in lower Ontario will depend upon the relative interrelationship of two trends: the relatively declining importance of secondary manufacturing which has long been their base, combined with the rate at which they move into services and post-industrialization. On the whole, we believe that southern Ontario, that is from Niagara to Windsor, will be one of the boom areas of Canada, with a steady shift towards low-density exurbanization, with people living on lower and lower densities scattered throughout the region. Nevertheless, this will go on almost unnoticed by the society, because we are accustomed to thinking of south Ontario as the richest area, and because public attention will almost necessarily be concentrated on the negative aspects of Ontario's development.

The process of "creative destruction" will be most visible in the decay of certain cities who have old-line manufacturing industries; and their problems will dominate public discussion. We do not expect these problems to be severe nor intractable; but places like Hamilton (see Table 9), Kitchener (see Table 10), St. Catharines (see Table 11), London, and Windsor will feel that they are suffering from change, will howl for help, and their "plight" will dominate public discussion of this area. We feel the spreading out of the population will be an increase in the standard of living for those who so spread out; but we are sure that the spreading will be caricatured as "a problem," a cost, not a benefit, of change.

Montreal

Were we writing this study a decade ago, what was written for Toronto would apply to Montreal as well, but even more so. A decade ago Montreal had the potential to be not only a great Canadian city, but a great world city—the crossroads of North America where Anglophone and Francophone Canada met, and where both met the U.S., Europe, and the Third World. Montreal was and has been dynamic, a city of great promise. However, it has been seriously hobbled by political developments. The uncertainty regarding the future status of Quebec must have negative effects on Montreal's vitality and growth for at least five years (see Table 12). If Quebec remains within Canada, the uncertainty about the potential for sovereignty will not go away quickly. If Quebec leaves Canada, uncertainty about the future of the Quebec Republic will also be a negative factor for its main concentration of population, Montreal.

In either event, Montreal must face up to certain difficult facts: First, an outflow of Anglophone population, talent, and money. It is not necessary to project an Anglophone "flight" to get this condition. In the normal course of human affairs individuals change their location. A certain percentage of Anglophone Montrealers will get jobs elsewhere, will relocate their families for other reasons, or will retire. This will happen regardless of the political status of Quebec. The uncertainty and the real possibility of an unfavourable future for Anglophone Montrealers will discourage the replacement of those who leave; so the Anglophone population will age and wither away gradually, and could even flee under seriously adverse conditions.

To which a dedicated Quebec separatist would say "good riddance." Unfortunately, Quebec is not large enough to support such a great city as Montreal. The analogies of Uruguay and Denmark do not apply. Montreal's growth was derived more from the growth of Canada generally and from its role as a shipping terminal and manufacturer of tariff-protected industries than from the rise in Quebec's population. A country of six million could not support a city of two million which developed out of the growth of a nation of twenty million. Montreal would be seriously injured by separation, especially if under a socialist government which, by its nature, would try to concentrate power and jobs in the capital city. An analogy of what could happen to Montreal would be the fate of Constantinople after Ataturk removed the capital of the Turkish Republic to Ankara.

The flight of the Anglophones is enough of a problem, but the same is true of the businessmen who are necessary to make the city a great commercial centre. Many will be annoyed at the inevitable enforced francization of Montreal or hesitant to invest because of political and economic uncertainty. New jobs will not be created, and new investment will not come in. And we must not forget the possibilities of some attrition of Francophone money which would hurt all Quebec but especially commercial Montreal. Again, very little can be done about this problem in any positive way.

The best goodwill on the part of the Francophones in Montreal and Quebec can but mitigate these problems. The question is uncertainty: People will not invest their money or the future of their families in situations where the future is in doubt. One could even make a case that Montreal would be better off if Quebec separated from Canada. At least the situation would be clear. Some would argue that the best possible scenario for Montreal is if it seceded from Quebec.

Mayor Drapeau pointed out that there is something to be said for Montreal as a free city outside of Canada and sovereign Quebec. Under this scenario, Montreal could play a similar role to Singapore in Southeast Asia as a commercial centre serving the whole area. The analogy is not entirely valid because Singapore is a Chinese city in which the talents of its mercantile inhabitants are far more advanced than those of their Malay neighbours. Montreal would have no such advantage relative to Quebec and Canada. Nevertheless, some feel that Montreal, separate from

Quebec, under a government which could not survive except by servicing international business, would be a relatively favourable outcome.

These negative remarks about Montreal's short-term potential for growth should not be construed to mean that we are expecting an absolute decline or serious difficulties in the city. We are merely pointing to a lack of growth. On the positive side, Francophone businessmen will replace Anglophone ones and (except under a disaster scenario) the government will be obliged to be agreeable to the business interest if only for economic survival. And the city will have a vibrant cosmopolitan life that will be the envy of North America.

We expect, in any event, that the Montreal city government will be obliged in the future to be considerably more prudent in its fiscal matters.

Vancouver

Again, were we conducting this study a decade ago, we would have flagged Vancouver as having the most promising future of any Canadian metropolitan area. Of all Canadian cities, it has assets most suitable for development in the last quarter of the twentieth century. The most obvious, and probably the most important, is its moderate climate. In an era in which everyone seems to shun the cold, the Lower Fraser Valley has the mildest and best climate in Canada. A factor often ignored in discussions of urban potential, but increasingly important in the post-industrial era, is Vancouver's superb setting: Surrounded by mountains, yet on the sea, it offers wide opportunities for varied recreation and leisure activities, from sailing to skiing. Also not to be ignored is that Vancouver is simply beautiful.

Nevertheless, we ought not to forget the city's conventional assets: the major port and principal financial, commercial, and wholesaling centre for a rapidly growing province, and a wide variety of local industries supporting and supported by an enormous real and potential resource base in the hinterlands ranging from traditional furs and lumber to aluminum and rare metals.

All of these traditional economic assets could be expected to multiply as Vancouver becomes a major element, and Canada's link to the emerging Pacific Basin. The nations around the Pacific, led by Japan, are that part of the world economy which has been booming the most rapidly in the last ten years, and must be expected to be the leading edge of the development of the world's economy for the rest of this century. The fundamental strength of these nations and their ties has been demonstrated by their success in absorbing the recent increase in oil prices with relatively little difficulty. By full participation in the Pacific Basin, Vancouver could have become one of the great cities of Canada and in the next century perhaps even in the world. It could have been the Montreal of the west.

The "could have beens" are necessary because it appears that, at least in the short run, Vancouver has decided against this future. The "limits-to-growth" mentality is extremely powerful in Vancouver; the current residents, or at least the dominant elements among the population, believe they have more to lose than to gain from further development. And their position is probably justified in terms of their own interest: further growth will mean more traffic jams; it will push up the cost of the lovely communities on the north side of Burrard Inlet; the boat basins will become more crowded; the airport will become busier and therefore more difficult to use casually; and all the institutions, facilities, and comforts will be more heavily used and consequently less exclusive.

It seems to us that these concerns probably have a greater influence than do concerns to maintain the small farms down towards the American border, or concern about pollution or "Los Angelization" of the Lower Fraser Valley. The Fraser Valley could probably hold ten million people at very low densities indeed. The issue here is will; and Vancouver, at least in the short run, does not have that will and is probably right in its collective judgement.

The further growth of metropolitan Vancouver is impinged upon by several objective elements as well. To begin with, the city is in the wrong place. The location of its centre on Burrard Inlet makes it extremely difficult to provide road access over the water crossings. Expanding the downtown in its logical direction towards the southeast is not now practical because that would lengthen commuting for the bosses in North and West Vancouver.

Nevertheless, despite the will of the upper classes and the ferociously militant trade unions, Vancouver will grow and prosper to a modest degree. The economic pressures are too strong. Government cannot clamp down on all development, it can merely push up the cost and delay it. The crunch in housing prices is bound to have especially severe political effects in B.C. The linkage with other Pacific Rim nations is inevitable, and Vancouver will see more and more Japanese, Chinese, and Korean faces and institutions. It will continue to be a great paradise of Canada, will continue to be a Mecca for many Canadians, particularly from the Prairies; and it will attract all groups from swinging singles to retired workers, who appreciate its climate and location. (See Table 13.)

Victoria

The same factors that apply to metropolitan Vancouver must also be assigned to Victoria and the rest of the Georgia Strait. In the rest of the area,

177

the main problem is transportation. Just as the Lion's Gate Bridge (built by private promoters) permitted the boom in land values in North Vancouver that more than paid for the bridge, similar projects farther up the coast, and perhaps even over to Vancouver Island, could achieve the same result. Bridging the Georgia Strait would be an expense that could more than be made up in the increase in land values and tax assessments on the island. But neither is likely to be done, because the people who are already on these places do not wish to be overwhelmed by newcomers, and government lacks the will. Again, however, this attitude will prevent a boom, but will not block all development. Victoria will continue to be a haven for older, retired Canadians from the Prairies and farther east, as well as for younger bohemians. (See Table 14.)

Ottawa-Hull

Ottawa is Canada's most characteristic company town; the company is the federal government, and Ottawa prospers or fails with that government. At the present time, Ottawa is the richest of our metropolitan cities because of our generous civil-service salaries. We expect this to continue, except in the improbable event of a serious "populist" reaction against the federal government.

Whatever are the federal salary levels, we must expect that Ottawa will continue to grow; but whether it will grow at the pace of the past decade is another question. At the heart of this question is the Quebec issue, linked with growing regionalism in other parts of Canada, and the prospective decline in federal power and authority. If Quebec leaves confederation, then the federal capital could decline or even change location. In the much more likely event that Quebec remains in Canada, this could involve compromises to the provinces. The decentralization and belt-tightening measures taken by the federal government in 1976 and 1977 have slowed the capital's growth, but are not, however, expected to be serious enough to stop growth altogether.

The government will continue to grow at least as fast as the nation. Decentralization schemes are seldom successful, because bureaucrats cannot be easily torn from the capital close to the centre of action, power, and opportunity. Almost every country throughout the world, of whatever political colour, has attempted to decentralize the bureaucracy, but the centripetal forces are too strong. Decentralization has not slowed Washington's growth, although the proportion of federal employees that work in the U.S. capital is less than half that of the corresponding Canadian figure. Ottawa may also benefit from businesses emigrating from Montreal.

Taking all these conflicting forces into account, we submit the forecasts of population growth for the capital area set out in Table 15. Those taking the more pessimistic view of Ottawa's future will find the B and C figures in Table 15 more acceptable.

Calgary

From a futures point of view, Calgary is the most interesting city in the country because it is likely to change the most. It has a marvellous location on attractive rolling hills within an hour of the huge recreational resources of the Rockies. Its existing rapid growth is such that a self-perpetuating boom has been created which attracts ambitious people from around the world who contribute to even greater boom. The city is well governed and, with its network of "trails," has the best road system of any Canadian city.

Of course, its prosperity ultimately rests on oil, and in the rather unlikely event of an international oil price collapse, its growth rates would be stunted, to say the least. However, we believe that the city has already reached the point at which it has enough strength to survive and prosper despite a crippling of the oil business. Its vibrant, go-getter, booster spirit, so despised by the cosmopolitan elites of the east and west coast, is an almost sure formula for growth and prosperity. Calgary has money, talent, and most important of all, confidence. This will push it through even a collapse of world oil prices.

However, having made a confident projection of Calgary's prospects, we ought not to overdo it. Even at the rapid growth rates that we project for the next fifteen years, Calgary will still not be a major city by world standards, and even by Canadian standards will still be far behind Toronto, Montreal and Vancouver. It will not yet have sufficient size and resources to support a full range of those urban services that are considered necessary to be a city of the world class: cultural facilities, restaurants, communications, and an international ambiance. (See Table 16.)

Edmonton

We must rate Edmonton slightly lower than Calgary in terms of its overall prospects for two reasons: first, its climate is particularly adverse, even by Canadian standards. Second, Edmonton's relationship to the oil industry is mainly that of exploration and production. It lacks Calgary's administration, finance, marketing, and head office roles, so it is necessarily more of a blue-collar town subject to fluctuations in the business cycle. This has to be counterbalanced somewhat by the fact that it is the capital of Alberta and therefore will benefit from the inevitable inflation and expansion of government, as well as from its position as the gateway to the North. Edmonton will continue to be the jumping off place for northern develop-

179

ment. Nevertheless, while Edmonton will do very well indeed, will fiercely compete with Calgary (which will help both cities), and will continue to be larger in population, we expect that the end of the century will see Calgary winning the battle for status. (See Table 17.)

Prairie Cities

In our view, Winnipeg has a favourable, but not very exciting future. For Winnipeg, we merely project more of the same: slow, steady, and healthy progress, but a growth rate that will almost certainly be less rapid than that of the nation and the economy as a whole, because it rests ultimately on an only modestly expanding economic base. Of our major cities we project the slowest growth for Winnipeg.

The other metro cities of the prairies–Regina, Saskatoon, and the smaller cities–may do a bit better, indeed Regina's growth is booming at present but we are not forecasting sharp increases in growth rates for any of them over the long term. (See Table 18.)

Quebec City

Whatever the status of Quebec Province in the 1990s, we project a growth in numbers and prosperity for Quebec City, as it becomes more and more of "a company town" for the provincial/national government. Even if the province of Quebec should separate from the rest of Canada, Quebec City will do rather well because the bureaucracy will insist upon first class accommodations. (See Table 19.)

Maritime Cities

About these, little needs to be said. They will reflect the conditions of their hinterlands, relatively stagnant and increasingly living off direct or indirect government subsidies. This does not mean they will not be pleasant places in which to live, quite the contrary. They will be well groomed, and have a leisurely pace that will be very civilized, especially to increasing numbers of retirees from Ontario–a kind of North-American England. Aggressive young people eager to make their way in the world will go elsewhere. Halifax will remain the largest of these cities. (See Table 20.)

In summary, the ranking of the largest Canadian metro cities ought not to be revised substantially, except for the changes resulting from the rapid growth of Calgary and Edmonton.* The projected relative decline of Winnipeg should not blind us to the fact that it will continue to grow, just not as fast as the Alberta cities. (See Table 21).

*Some make the case that both could even surpass Ottawa.

Housing

The 1980s will see the biggest housing boom in Canadian history. As the post-war baby boom comes to the age when it forms families and requires single detached homes, the demand for housing will be enormous. No one should imagine that young Canadians are abandoning the traditional desire for their own house and lot. Even if some proportion of young people retain their youthful affection for high-density housing, the desire for the single family home is so overwhelming that the exceptions will not affect the total demand in any significant way. Some "advanced" contemporary cultural trends work in the same direction—the love of nature and hatred of urbanization is reflected in environmental protection laws, but also in the desire of such people to get away from our crowded cities to the countryside in their own houses on their own piece of land.

The demand for homes must be satisfied or there will be serious political unrest. Currently, our nation is becoming divided into two classes: those who can own houses and those who will never be able to own houses.

The problem today can be attributed partly to government: excessive regulation is pushing up the price of housing construction and, particularly, of land. The theory that the real villains are private land monopolists is largely untenable. All land within sixty miles of any city is developable except where there are waterways or miserable terrain; so there are at least ten thousand square miles or six million acres of developable land within commuting range of any Canadian city. It is impossible that any combine of land owners could own any substantial part of that to monopolize land prices. It *is* possible to monopolize "developable" land if developable land is only that certified as such by government. As in many things, land development in Canada has seen a close working relationship between big business and government. Local government has only authorized development of the land that developers were willing to put on the market. No doubt the developers could have made more money with less regulated land development, but Canadian businessmen have usually preferred a modest and safe return to a large but erratic one. In recent years, the role of government in this equation has increased under the influence of urban planning ideology, limits-to-growth agitation, and the interest of existing suburbanites. Now even the developers are unhappy.

This is not mere speculation. As one would expect, there is a strong correlation between Census Metropolitan Areas housing prices and CMA growth rates; the more rapidly growing CMAs have a stronger demand for housing and have more new, and therefore more expensive, housing. But there were two major exceptions, where housing prices have not grown as quickly as those cities' growth rates would indicate: Calgary, where developers have had an extremely sympathetic government, and Saskatoon, where the government itself has been engaged in land development. Note that we use the past tense. In the case of Calgary we are informed that prices are increasing faster now as development becomes more regulated. This suggests to us that the way to promote housing construction is not so much through positive acts by government as by ending restrictions on low-density, residential development. Those who have ideological objections to land developers making a lot of money should then support the Saskatoon system of having the government get in on the business and making the huge profits which come from such development, but not continue the existing system.

It has been argued that government restrictions could only have marginal effects on prices. Our response to this is that in the housing market both supply and demand are highly inelastic; that is, small changes in quantity force large changes in price. After all, everybody must be housed; and every Canadian expects to be housed according to certain quality standards. If the housing supply is restricted, the claimants for that housing will bid the price up until a few regretfully drop out. Since most Canadians live in used houses, restricting the production of new housing forces up the price of older housing. However, if housing supply is highly inelastic because of government restrictions, even much higher prices do not bring in much greater supply. The solution, in economists' jargon, is to move the supply curve by opening up land to development.

Inevitably, in discussions of housing construction and the related issue of housing prices in Canada there is reference to the U.S. experience. Some people have proposed that we imitate some American housing policies. Two are proposed which may be of benefit in themselves, but will not help the housing market: U.S. taxpayers are permitted to deduct local taxes and mortgage interest payments from their federal income taxes. This is partially a subsidy of homeownership and partially a subsidy for local government and for banks; but reforms of this type in Canada will merely increase the demand for housing; unless the supply is also increased, housing prices will be pushed to even more astronomical costs. In other words, these reforms will only benefit those social elements who already own homes or can expect the high incomes to pay for housing at the higher levels.

One possible form that we could adopt from the U.S. is summed up in the term "serviced lot," which is hardly known south of the border. CMHC and local government regulations require on-lot water and sewerage in huge areas, particularly in central Canada, where it is usually unnecessary. As demonstrated throughout the eastern and mid-western

182

United States, low density housing with wells and contemporary septic tanks is a perfectly safe and adequate means of providing water and sewerage, and there is no special reason why it should not be copied in Canada. Related to this is that low density development does not require investment in streets, sidewalks, or even utilities as does the "planned mass development" so desired by urbanologists.

Another thing government might do to promote housing is to eliminate rent-control laws. These are a response to the restriction of housing supply. With new housing supply restricted, rents are forced up, and the owners of existing rental housing earn a windfall; and it seems quite reasonable to protect the tenant from that windfall. But the problem is that, if the return on capital is less than the investor has reasonable reason to expect, people will not invest in new housing and, more important, the value of existing rental housing, and therefore property-tax ratables, will be retarded to the detriment of local government. Rent control should go, but it should go at the same time that there is expansion of building opportunities in the country.

Another positive step that government can take to promote housing is to build more roads. The best thing that could be done for housing prices in central Toronto is to push roads due north towards Georgian Bay. This would open up land for development, and would divert some of the urbanization now creeping along the shores of Lake Ontario. We only mention this as a possibility—not that we think it will be done; the people who run Toronto have too many country places up towards Lake Simcoe.

The current efforts to block suburbanization and urban sprawl have very important economic and social effects. By restricting the land available for intensive development, a sharply segmented land market appears. Within the approved development area, land and housing prices are artificially high; beyond it, land and housing prices are artificially low. This means that the average urban Canadian must pay more for housing than he would under a less restricted market. Conversely, those persons with sufficient means to purchase "farms" beyond the development area get bargains. Of course these "farms" are not primarily agricultural units, but exurbanization. And this is why they are unlikely to be substantially modified: not by PC businessmen, Liberal bureaucrats, or NDP professors.

Housing: A Dissenting View*

The above analysis obviously does not receive unanimous acclaim in Canada. An increasing number of Canadians are beginning to feel that new housing developments spreading from our cities will, in the coming years, be a luxury Canada will not be able to afford. Enormous infrastructure costs, the loss of agricultural land, energy costs, etc. will make the housing boom described above an unattainable dream.

While it is true that investment in new housing has increased rapidly in recent years, I would argue that a significant part of this investment reflects as much an attempt to hedge against inflation as it does growing demand. In a period of high inflation real estate investment is seen by many–and increasingly by young couples–as a means to protect capital. However should such inflation persist, the cash-flow problem involved is likely to discourage home ownership.

Housing prices have been increasing more rapidly within cities than in the suburbs which reinforces the point that, in Canada, people would prefer to live closer in, avoiding commuting, traffic jams, lost time. Most congestion on Canadian roads is caused by people driving to and from work (from the suburbs to centretown) alone in their cars. Municipal and Provincial governments are fed up with the mounting costs of new road construction, congestion and parking problems in centretown, and are seeking a better way out. They would appear to favour housing developments that are less spread out and which can be served by collective transit facilities. The idea that greenbelts are making housing expansion within cities impossible is absurd. Ottawa is often cited as such an example but there remains within the Ottawa city limits land which developers choose not to develop or put on the market. And at present within the greenbelt, the housing market is soft–a buyer's not a seller's market. Moreover, closely adjacent to the green belt there is enough land available to meet our housing needs, and it is in close enough to be serviced by efficient public transportation. This, together with construction within cities and urban renewal, and housing supply is very likely to be adequate. In this vein, I would agree with the above discussion of rent control.

Analyses of our domestic housing situation all too often ignore the total costs of suburban development It is my view that Canadians will not be able to pay these costs much longer, especially in the light of soaring construction costs in all sectors of our economy. Or at least, Canadian city dwellers, when they become aware of the costs involved, will become more and more reluctant to pay for the roads, bridges, and other amenities required to open up suburbs. In a policical and economic environment in which pressures for cost control and spending restraints are increasing at all levels, a housing boom of the kind described above is highly unlikely.

* This was written by Douglas Fullerton, member of the Board of Trustees.

Social Policy*

The enlargement of governments' social roles has been a dominant trend in all of the major democratic countries since the Second World War. This development has entailed a substantial increase in government's share of total national expenditures. However, for most of the post-war period in most of these countries, most people were enjoying a rapid enough rise in their own purchasing power to mute the pain of a disproportionate rise in taxes. Indeed, when citizens were able to vote directly on government outlays, willingness to spend more money was commonly evident.

The economic dislocations of the 1970s have generated attitude change. However, in most western countries–and very clearly in Canada–the influence has had much more to do with the protraction than with the intensity of "hard times." Relatively few people have suffered a loss in real income. Indeed, in a December 1976 international Gallup poll, 53 per cent of Canadian respondents (compared to 38 per cent in the United States) claimed that they "almost never" worried that the family income would be inadequate to meet expenses. Also, the liberalization of unemployment insurance, and the indexing of many pension and welfare benefits have limited the material hardships of the less fortunate.

Thus, while the climate in which social policy operates today is different from that of a decade ago, it is not at all certain that it should be regarded as fixed for more than the next year or two. If Canada's economic situation should not improve or should worsen, a greater polarization of attitudes on social policy might emerge. Even the wear and tear of protracted "stagflation" could have this effect. Conversely, a return to a period of steady economic growth, with only mild setbacks, might be

* This chapter was written by Jane Newitt and edited by Douglas Fullerton.

expected to swing attitudes of various population groups back closer to those of a few years ago, while others might find their attitudes tempered a bit by the lessons of recent economic adversity.

Some of the caution caused by current troubles would likely have developed in any case, simply because a decade of rapid and costly innovation tends to produce opposite reactions. More people have come to favour at least a temporary moratorium on new programs, a period of consolidation, perhaps of selective retrenchment. It may well be that rapid growth in the scope and scale of social policy has satisfied the appetite for innovation for a generation. Any speculation on the future of social policy in Canada must take these conflicting factors into account.

The Factor of Government Scope and Scale

The growth of social and welfare outlays in Canada has been a product of many forces: political platforms, population growth, inflation, rising unemployment, and lagging growth in certain regions. Chart 9, which is limited to cash transfers to persons, shows how, in the 1970s, exceptionally high rates of inflation and unemployment, coupled with the liberalization of unemployment insurance, higher family allowances and old age pensions, and the phasing-in of the Canada and Quebec Pension Plans, brought about a very sharp increase in spending. The question which concerns us is the slope of the spending curve over the next few years. Clearly the extrapolation of recent trends is not in the cards, for all the reasons we have noted earlier. But how much will it be cut back? Line A assumes a 13 per cent increase in 1977 and 9 per cent thereafter (it was 23 per cent in 1974).

Lines B and C represent, respectively, the basic and "high transfer payment" projections developed in 1972, using the CANDIDE model.*

Chart 10 indicates how the Line A trend appears if the cost rise is expressed in constant 1961 dollars. There was a tripling of transfer payments between 1964 and 1976, a period when real GNP roughly doubled.

The Economic Council may have erred because it assumed the inverse movement of inflation and unemployment, although it did allow for new programs being continually introduced. In looking ahead, given the larger than usual range of uncertainty in our economic prospects, we therefore do not attempt to describe growth in social spending as a function primarily of Canada's economic performance. Instead, we adopt the simplifying assumption of a moderate growth economy over the next ten years. To be more precise, we assume a relatively steady economic

*as reported in the Economic Council of Canada's Ninth Annual Review.

growth, in the 2.5-3.0 per cent range of GNP per capita per year. A possible new surge in inflation is not unlikely; unemployment will be high by historical standards but will be accompanied by adjustment of attitudes regarding how "full employment" should realistically be defined. This is the standard scenario.

Other Factors Affecting Future Spending on Social Programs

Administrative Issues

Cost changes attributable to administrative practice may stem from "running in" problems of new or reformed programs; lax controls associated with general prosperity, budget surpluses, etc.; greater liberalism or conservatism of administrators than policy-makers or of social workers than supervisors, etc.; radicalism at the operations level, a desire to "break the system" and force sweeping reform; federal-provincial power squabbles; divided accountability; or low morale in the bureaucracy.

These factors exert an upward pressure on costs at all times, both directly and through their encouragement of fraud and self-serving error by benefit recipients. In our standard scenario for the next decade, they function at an endemic level that tends to rise with economic growth and the revival of psychologies of affluence. The standard scenario does not entail either improvement or deterioration in the contribution of joint federal-provincial program administration to inefficiency and fraud. However, this factor is of sufficient current interest to invite brief speculative descriptions of the bracketing cases for policy trend. These might be sketched as follows:

Decentralization Extreme

1. Policy to alleviate provincial governments' deficit position;
2. Fade-out of economic controls;
3. Substantial provincial autonomy in shared-cost programs;
4. Toleration of sloppy bookkeeping, waste;
5. Low morale in federal bureaucracy;
6. Few program innovations.

Centralization Extreme

1. "Grand design" for Canada;
2. Phase-out of some shared-cost programs, tight rein on others;
3. Continuing or expanded economic controls;
4. Bluff-calling tactics towards Quebec;
5. Carrot-and-stick tactics;
6. Innovations;

7. Expanding federal bureaucracy.

At least as delineated here, the decentralization emphasis would exacerbate some major causes of inefficiency, but avoid the high rates associated with innovation. The centralization emphasis connotes a "tight ship," but it also includes social-program "sweeteners" that carry the high administrative costs incident to innovation.

A decade ago, speculation on the future importance of decentralization and provincialism to social policy was put, if in extreme form, by Paul Gerin-Lajoie's statement (1967) that.*

Social security and welfare, including health, are too directly linked to the structure and values of society for Quebec not to have exclusive responsibility for them.

At the other extreme would have been listed the factors commonly adduced to support the thesis of long-term trends towards cultural homogenization, economic interdependency, large-scale organization in both public and private sectors, and the emergent role of national government as the embodiment of the "national conscience." In selecting a most persuasive scenario for ten years later, i.e., for the present year, a thoughtful and reasonably well-informed Canadian would probably have leaned at least slightly towards the dominance of "centripetal" over "centrifugal" forces.

Today the resurgence of regional and separatist forces in a number of countries has sapped the aura of inevitability of the centralizing scenario, which becomes imbued with the hazardous and ugly politics of confrontation. These tensions may ease as prosperity and confidence grow. Still it appears probable that dynamism in the social policy area will revert to the provinces. Rather than a national trend in the next ten years, we might see various provincial trends in innovations and outlays, conceivably with Ottawa largely out of the picture. However, the forces for national action, especially in the area of income transfers, remain strong.

Impact of Innovation on Past Trends

The growth curve in recent years has been skewed by the many innovations in new programs and expansion of old ones. Thus Canada Pension Plan/Quebec Pension Plan (CPP/QPP) outlays have doubled and redoubled in brief periods of time. Unemployment payments tripled between 1970 and 1974, even though the number of initial and renewal claims rose

*Quoted by W.A.J. Armitage, in "The Emerging Realignment of Social Policy – A Problem for Federalism," *Canadian Welfare*, September/October 1971, p. 5.

by only 7 per cent and the number of weeks for which benefits were paid by only 44 per cent. In the medical area, net physician earnings responded to the introduction of government insurance with increases of 22 per cent in Ontario, 48 per cent in Manitoba, 51 per cent in Quebec, 34 per cent in New Brunswick, and so forth, between the last full year prior to the innovation and the first full subsequent year. These major changes could not be expected to continue, at least at the same pace.

Demographic Variables

Spending is influenced by changes in the population distribution, affecting old age pensions, family allowances, and welfare.

Attitudes

All the above affect the future curve of health and welfare spending, but limit the utility of past trends for forecasting. Of equal importance is the way Canadians feel about these programs. Do they welcome new programs? Or are they more concerned about the costs, and their impact on their taxes and take-home pay? There is no doubt that recent economic uncertainties have affected the willingness of governments to innovate (as have their budgetary deficit positions); their reactions also appear to reflect their view of constituents' attitudes. But will these cautious attitudes change as the economy improves, and as governments' share in total spending levels out or even declines a bit?

Most recent opinion surveys suggest that the average Canadian is not too concerned about the government's role in his life being excessive. Thus we find (August 1976) that only 26 per cent of CIPO* respondents feel that government interferes too much in their own lives, while 51 per cent say "about right" and 12 per cent "not enough." By contrast, pluralities of 46 per cent and 41 per cent, respectively, would like to see more interference with labour unions and large corporations.**

Earlier in 1976, 53 per cent agreed with Prime Minister Trudeau that the power of unions and corporations should be further curbed; this is roughly the same percentage that expressed a similar view in 1971, when there were no comparable economic ills.*** And recent public opinion polls indicate strong support for wage and price controls.

The general impression conveyed by a review of 1972-77 attitude

*Canadian Institute of Public Opinion (CIPO), August 1976, reported in *Current Opinion*, Roper Public Opinion Research Centre, November 1976, p. 123.

**CIPO, February 1976, in *Current Opinion*, May 1976, p. 46.

***CIPO, 1971, in *Current Opinion*, various issues.

survey data is that the rather dramatic social-program innovations and liberalizations which characterized Canada in the 1960s and early 1970s did not satiate the public's appetite for further programs. The polls suggest continuing support for governmental regulation of "big business" and "big labour," at least while unemployment and inflation rates stay high. They suggest enduring suspicions of the government relationship, as well as a strong belief that government should do more for the poor, but nearly as strong a belief that more should be done for the middle class. While the proportion of the public which thinks that Canada is moving towards socialism has jumped from 14 per cent in 1950 to 28 per cent in 1967 and 33 per cent in 1975, we found no measurable evidence that this trend is viewed with alarm.

This corroborates the impression that in the early seventies, as Canada was growing faster than the U.S., Canadians differed significantly from Americans in attitudes towards government participation. This may explain why the Canadian governments' share of GNP has risen further and faster than the United States governments', despite Canada's much smaller commitment to military and other non-domestic outlays. It warns us against too-ready an extrapolation to Canada of the qualms about "big government" and rapid social-outlay growth that have characterized the U.S. in recent years. However, the current stagflation has had the effect of increasing pressures for cost-cutting and better control of government expenditures at all levels; and we believe that Canadians will move closer, if not all the way, to U.S. attitudinal positions on this issue. Therefore though we do expect a slight increase in government's share of GNP, unless growth accelerates more than we expect. In our standard scenario we assume that in the late 1980s governments will account for not more than 45-48 per cent of GNP. That is already high, but the Canadian public will find it acceptable.

Psychologies of Affluence and Uncertainty

What were the principal components of the psychologies of affluence that promoted social-program growth for a generation after the Second World War? The flame was lit by the Depression background of policy-makers. It was fuelled by the fact that rising incomes made the rising tax burden acceptable. Continuing prosperity gradually generated confidence that serious economic instabilities were a thing of the past. It did not seem irresponsible to enact bold new programs which mortgaged the future; the dividends of growth would pay for it all.

While social policy retained its pre-war commitment to improve economic security and facilitate the upward mobility of the average citizen–"the worker"–the climate of affluence and optimistic expectations promoted a broadening shift of primary emphasis to include the indigent poor and disadvantaged minority groups. Attitudes of a more distant past, the fear that public largesse would pauperize the working class, gave way to a view that extreme poverty was an unconscionable and remediable blot on an affluent and just society. Thus political support for enacting or liberalizing anti-poverty transfers and services increased dramatically. The results were visible. Transfer payments comprised 27 per cent of the income of the lowest fifth of Canadian families in 1951, and 46 per cent twenty years later.* At the same time, regional differences in income tended to converge; and it is estimated that 70 per cent of the convergence for the Atlantic provinces between 1950 and 1973 and all of the small convergence for Quebec was accounted for by transfer payments.**

Expansionary social policy was also popular because much of the resulting redistribution of income had favourable economic effects. More government jobs were generated, especially in professional, managerial, and clerical occupations. Thus, much of the transfer of dollars occurred within the middle class, enlarging the part of that class which had a vested interest in social-program growth. There was also a pattern of redistributing income from the middle-aged to the old or young; the benefits of such programs are often perceived as accruing to oneself in the future, or to one's children or grandchildren.

Finally, until recent years it was difficult to believe that the growth of the welfare state imperilled economic incentives in any important, much less poentially disastrous, way. In 1978, the era of unthinking optimism about the future seems remote. To borrow a phrase from the 1960s, there has been a reordering of government's priorities to place principal emphasis on the restoration of vigorous economic growth, the control of inflation, and the reduction of unemployment. In his budget speech in May 1976, the then Minister of Finance asserted:

> In recognition of the widespread feeling among Canadians that present circumstances demand restraint in government spending, the government has stated that the "trend in total spending by all governments in Canada should not rise more quickly than the trend in gross national product...
>
> This statement is not put forward as a short-term goal: a brief slowdown in the rate of expenditure growth to be followed by a resumption

*Canada Year Book, various issues.

**Economic Council of Canada, Twelfth Annual Review, 1975, p. 30.

of excessive growth. Rather, it is put forward as a basic change in the trend of expenditure increase.

We quote this particular statement in order to illustrate the ambivalence of current upper-class thinking. "Widespread feeling" about "present circumstances" results in a policy which "is not put forward as a short-term goal" but "as a basic change in the trend of expenditure increase." Clearly, a context is required for interpreting such a statement.

The Minister of Finance's ambivalence reflects the two-track thinking that characterizes Canadian politics. The long-term problems, monetary and other, associated with spiralling social-program costs may be essentially distinct from Canada's short-term economic ills; but they are not perceptually–and hence not politically–distinct. At the moment, this means that short-term ills may be used to promote a relatively conservative interpretation of long-term national interests. However, as we have noted, unless economic ills persist, this view may not endure very long.

In a protracted hard-times scenario for Canada, pressures for less government control of the economy and less spending would increase. An alternative hard-times scenario would have economic activity come under increasing government control, both directly and via massive expansion of government-subsidized jobs; and the interaction of social and economic policy would be considerably advanced.

The primacy of economic policy in the past few years has imposed (or superimposed) at least a vague measure of order on social policy, with economic objectives functioning as a bias towards caution, as a pressure to improve housekeeping and reduce waste, and as a tendency to view proposed social legislation in terms of risk rather than merely social justice. In Canada, a more ready acceptance of government's responsibility for managing the economy suggests a continuing Canadian willingness to accept social programs as the complement to economic policy, but also to accept that social policy itself influences economic policy's objectives and consequences.

Speculation on the Character and Timing of Social-Policy Innovations

We believe that federal-provincial relationships ameliorate in our standard world's conditions of relatively steady economic growth, but that these problems perpetuate a climate of uncertainty sufficient to inhibit major social-policy innovations in the next five years.

The desire to innovate is present. We note a June 1976 communiqué in which the federal and provincial ministers of welfare commented, in the style of a "throw-away line," that the tripling of family allowances is "the first substantial step towards ensuring that family incomes match family responsibilities." A recent headline is relevant: "Guaranteed Income in Works, Quebec Says." However, the gist of the article is that an earlier study is being reviewed, and a former Quebec official is quoted as saying that "the plan could not be implemented until 1978 and depended heavily on the state of the economy, agreements with Ottawa, and administrative changes."

If the immediate future is clearly to be a time of constraint, where may we expect the next thrust to come?–assuming the economy picks up enough by, say 1980, to make new adventures in social spending possible. As we have noted, the "guaranteed annual income" is waiting in the wings, with plenty of support for it at both the provincial and federal levels. The case for it will continue to be that it rationalizes existing social programs (unemployment insurance, family allowances, old age security, etc.), inhibiting waste and evasion. It allegedly will reduce income disparities and provide new support for the economy; it is an instrument of social justice. The cynics will also regard it as a new way of increasing welfare spending; no innovative measures have yet succeeded in curtailing anything already on the legislative books.

We place more importance on motivations, opportunities, and constraints than on agendas. In the manner of whether a glass is perceived as half full or half empty, we define the short-term future as a time of reduced constraints, the 1980s as a time of increased opportunities. Recognition of reduced constraints is probably led by special-interest groups, including the labour unions, the clients of social programs, the providers of social services, and the more specialized "do-good" lobbies.

Table 46 summarizes findings of a 1974 survey of Canadian attitudes towards a range of possible social reforms. It may illustrate the trend of popular thinking, subject always to the impact of current (1977) economic conditions on the public at large.

The table indicates that nearly seven in ten participants in the CCSD poll felt that Canadian old-age pensions were not high enough in 1974, and 78 per cent felt that the eligibility age should be reduced to sixty. The highest percentage shown on the attitude table is the 92 per cent who favour government job creation to aid the unemployed (95 per cent if the "both" category is folded in).

Canadian governments for many years have adopted fiscal policies and "make-work" programs designed to reduce unemployment; the extent to which they succeeded or not has been difficult to measure. But certainly in the past few years there has been growing doubt cast on the ability of governments to solve the problem of unemployment by massive spending programs. The side effects–monetary expansion, higher taxes, administrative and federal-provincial problems, and waste–tend to be counterproductive. The current size of the federal deficit–$9 billion in

1977-78—and the deficits of most of the provinces, are another factor inhibiting new spending programs, regardless of the scale of unemployment.

When it comes to new ventures into education, there appears to be little public support, as the table suggests. Our colleges of education are turning out annually many more teachers than the schools can absorb, and our universities appear to have overexpanded and to be overstaffed. Recognition of this has become increasingly widespread and, indeed, educational retrenchment at the provincial and municipal levels is now taking place. The educational boom in Canada, spurred in the 1960s by a desire to "catch up" to the Americans in income, appears over.

There might be pressures to modify the federal Canada Assistance Plan, by adopting national standards for amounts that welfare recipients can earn without penalty; or for the maximum reduction in welfare payments; or by regularizing provincial practice with respect to the "working poor." The CAP is the only major Canadian social program that has a marked apparent potential for explosive "unprogrammed" growth under existing legislation. Among the reasons why this growth has not already occurred is the crucial one: the expectation of elite activists that the CAP would be supplanted by a new and less demeaning system of income transfers to the poor and near-poor, such as the guaranteed annual wage. The alternative, making the CAP do what its reformer-proponents hoped it would do, has attracted relatively little interest and effort. It may soon be back in favour if we are correct in expecting constraints on enactment of bold new welfare programs.

As for unemployment insurance, there is a growing concern about abuse of the system, particularly by the young and housewives. Many observers feel that the existence of generous unemployment benefits has artificially raised the unemployment figures by drawing marginal workers into the labour force; they work simply to qualify for benefits, but for many, benefit levels are considered legitimate. Nevertheless, the unemployment rate stays high and may move higher. Is this situation tolerable indefinitely? Probably not, and we would like to look briefly at a few of the ways our society may try to cope with the problem in future.

One, of course, is the guaranteed annual income, a negative income tax, or whatever title is used to describe a system that provides grants or supplements to those whose annual income falls below a certain level. All income the person receives from employment or from grants from the state (family allowances, pensions, unemployment benefits) will be counted in determining his entitlement.

Another is providing more employment choices outside the regular labour market, e.g. Local Initiatives Programs, Opportunities for Youth,

194

etc. They imply the enlargement of the definition of "work," and could eventually lead to salaries for going to college, or payments to mothers for child care. This approach may be expected to broaden out as new and experimental job-creating programs are introduced to try to reduce historically high unemployment rates. Such efforts also create more jobs for the bureaucratic elite, whose enthusiasm for experimentation is usually directly linked to what it can do for their own incomes and status.

Conclusions

One familiar scenario for the future of social policy in Canada sees orderly progress towards the cradle-to-grave security of a thorough-going welfare state. This might be termed a 1940s and a 1950s British scenario. A second adds to the first a heightened emphasis on the poor, a garnish of post-industrial values, and either the passive acceptance or enthusiastic approval of slow rates of economic growth. This might be termed a 1960s British scenario. A third scenario, which would be termed today "the British scenario," proposes that the government's social commitments and the vested interests their growth has generated have led to a crushing burden of taxes and regulations that seriously damages the Canadian economy and its competitive position in the world, and corrupts the national will to work.

In the near future – say until the early 1980s – it does seem likely that Canada's social policies will come close to the British 1960s model. A stepping-up of attempts by government at job creation, and a reduction of age for pension eligibility seem the likeliest candidates. Income support schemes are likely to be deferred, although some tax concessions to lower income groups might be expected.

In the second, probably less retrictive, half of the decade to come, such possibilities as "salaries" for full-time mothers and/or income supplements for lower-wage worker families seem likely, as does "free" dental care and a range of medical or quasi-medical counselling services, and the expansion of "home-maker" services, services for the elderly and disabled, adult education, and recreation programs. An exceptionally high proportion of Canadians will be of an age when family responsibilities strengthen work incentives (even if the family is small). The sense of what Canada can "afford" will be high. This we call our "standard" scenario.

Two Possible Variations from the Standard Scenario

The character of the next decade will not only be affected by good-times hard-times alternation. Attitudes will matter more. What will people consider important? What will they work for? What will they be willing to sacrifice? In this section, we speculate briefly on other possible developments. In an accelerated growth scenario, Canada becomes more outward-looking; economic growth is emphasized, achieved, and celebrated. The times will be more propitious for sweeping reform of income-support programs. This possibility develops out of the appeal of rationalizing existing programs in order to eliminate duplication, reduce disincentives to work, and facilitate cost control. As the country is prospering, fairly generous benefit levels might be set, and provision might be made for their future adjustment, not only for inflation, but to some extent for economic growth.

These changes would be accompanied by serious efforts to curb the growth and control the costs of social services. Strict accountability for use of federal hospital and medical care funds would be enforced; deductibles or co-insurance provisions might be instated. Federal subsidies for job creation and for social work would be sharply curtailed. There would be few "demonstration projects" and little funding for research in the social sciences. Efforts would be made to reduce government bureaucracy and red tape.

With rapid growth of real GNP a sense of what the country can and cannot afford would not constitute much of a restraining influence on social program growth. Rather, accelerated growth would be associated with the image of a well-functioning, relatively free-enterprise society, in which governments play supporting roles.

In contrast, the low-growth scenario could view government's central mission as creating a good society, with democratic roots. Central government must be powerful in order to effectively counter big business and big labour, but its role in social policy is basically that of finding money for "interesting," experimental, low-budget LIP-type programs. Administrative and professional superstructure mushrooms, but there is no serious effort to keep track of how money is spent. Costs for all programs invariably exceed budgets or projections, but people who worry about this are viewed as irrelevant old fogies who don't understand what New Canada is all about. The "irrelevant old fogies" will claim Canada is going the way of England–to the dogs.

Favouring decentralization, and little concerned with administrative detail or costs, the elite supporters of slow growth are committed to income redistribution. However, there are political obstacles to income-support changes. Annual growth of real GNP in the 2.0-3.0 per cent range is considerably outstripped by the "normal" growth of federal and provincial social budgets. This is not of concern in itself, but it poses a barrier to

196

enactment of new schemes with high incremental costs. "Welfare" has almost entirely lost its stigma, and interest at both the federal and provincial levels shifts to liberalizing the Canada Assistance Plan and to expansion of job-creation programs for the marginally employable. The one-time ideal of a negative income tax comes to be scorned as "computerized charity." In the New Canada, income support would be accomplished by means that promote integration of recipient and community, and satisfy emotional as well as material needs.

One way to view the "constrained growth" scenario in its social policy is that it reaches an evolutionary point by 1985 that standard or accelerated growth reaches by 1990 or 1995, i.e., the scenarios merely progress at differing speeds towards a "post-industrial" society (or a debacle). Another view is that the preference for traditional structures, values, and aspirations of the accelerated growth scenario will find new forms of expression in the next century, such as Arctic, ocean, and space development. The cultural product of the great wealth this scenario generates could be both, *viz.* Elizabethan England or Bourbon France.

Do such developments, given reasonable luck, seem plausible for Canada's next decade? Do they point towards a "happy ending" or towards economic and political collapse? In briefly considering this question, we need to adopt a larger perspective than we have used thus far, and we need to ask more carefully, "What really *is* social policy?"

While this term is used in various ways (and rarely, if ever, defined), all of its usages relate to activities of government which supplement or modify the productive and distributive actions of the private sector in the name of the public interest. These activities are rationalized by norms to which universality is attributed, e.g., such values as order, freedom of conscience, equality of opportunity, equality of condition, more place for the individual, the just society, the right to an adequate subsistence, the promotion of knowledge and the arts, and stewardship of the natural environment. We use a particular kind of governmental intervention to stand for all of the essentially ethical social functions that, in our secular age, have gravitated from church and local community to the state.

The exercise of such functions has always been motivated by a mixture of compassion, ideology, and self-interest. Also, it has always been true that the limits to aiding, protecting, and improving one's fellow men were determined rather haphazardly by resource limitations, cultural traditions, and resistance of intended beneficiaries to being aided, protected, and improved.

A question deserving closer consideration than we can give it is, What happens when these functions are assumed by the state? Problems are translated into statistical terms; solutions are debated from the viewpoint of ideology; decision-makers can no longer deal at an individual level, but with aggregates and groups.

Second, the absence of logical boundaries to ethical or social action gains new meaning, given the taxing powers of the modern state. But in the absence of revolution, the limits to actions that can be taken in the name of the public interest or of social justice are not transformed overnight, although they can be changed in a few generations.

Third, the switch of social roles to the state leads to a redistribution of power and privilege to the functionaries of social policy. Bright and ambitious young people are drawn to jobs that formerly attracted only pedants or "do-gooders." New occupations, even new industries, are created in planning, evaluating, promoting, computing, advising, studying, and implementing. Interest groups proliferate among the suppliers as well as the consumers of government goods. And each makes its demands in the name of ethical verities.

Fourth, it appears that the private economy suffers as more people identify their interests with government expansion, and as more potential managerial talent is attracted to government-related opportunities. This latter appears to entail a vicious circle: more aggressive people in government and among its advisers brings more regulation of business, and more regulation of business means reduced attractiveness of business careers for the bright and aggressive. Business becomes accommodating. The industry or the firm advances its interests by accepting government's legitimacy in its enlarged social roles, and by exploiting it.

How will individuals react? Essentially as they always have: "What's in it for me?" Social policy expenditures create their own constituency, and the vested interests so created combine to virtually rule out significant spending cutbacks. The only avenue of relief is to get more oneself, yet the "more" one gains from government is rarely perceived as exceeding the "more" one pays in taxes. The real test is the take-home pay, the "bottom line." Thus, rising taxes push up wage and salary demands in a manner which suggests that the price of a successful expansive social policy for Canada is continuing high inflation, and, of necessity, policies to contain it. It is not at all clear that Canadians are willing to pay the price, yet it would seem essential to check inflation to sustain Canada's competitive position in world markets. The implications for social policy seem fairly clear; this continuing inflationary pressure will be the factor limiting its further growth. Even if we return to a relatively prosperous economy in future, Canadians may be less inclined to push for the kind of rapidly expanding social programs that have characterized this past decade.

Foreign Policy and Defence*

Reconsiderations of foreign and defence policy occur frequently in most countries, but continuity in fundamentals is the general rule. Physical, economic, and cultural geography sharply diminish the practicality of many policy options that look interesting as theoretical ideas. With a population of only twenty-three million, severe problems of unemployment and inflation, and uncertainty over the political unity of the country, Canadian freedom to select a foreign- and defence-policy course that best suits national aspirations is in a sense marginal. However, this restricted condition of choice matters little, because of scant evidence suggesting a desire for substantial change in foreign policy. Canada's fundamental orientation towards the world is the product of geopolitical circumstance and of the character of her society.

Yet a clear trend in Canadian foreign policy to the 1990s is not easy to discern because either one or two substantially different paths could be dominant: on the one hand, Canada may be returning almost four-square to the internationalist alliance theme that was dominant from the late 1940s to the mid 1960s. On the other hand, the nascent isolationist (vis-à-vis military security ties, not international relations in general), "Canada First" sentiments of the late sixties, could harden into a policy that truly would upset the expectations of Canada's traditional security partners in the Western world, perhaps to the injury of Canada itself.

The Disappearing Middle Power

As late as 1972-73, it was little short of commonplace to observe that Canada emerged from the Second World War with her economy much

*This chapter was written by Colin Gray.

199

strengthened, and that this domestic base—together with recent memories and expectations of major international security involvement—encouraged our governments to play what was termed a "Middle Power" role in Western alliance and UNO affairs. The transfer from Allied partner in the Second World War to NATO member in the Cold War was both painless and apparently inevitable until the mid-to-late 1960s. Then Canadians began to doubt the wisdom of their total security involvement with the United States; they tired of "chipping in" to multinational security enterprises, and wondered whether or not more distinctively Canadian duties were not going by default as a cost of the very heavy NATO-European-North American security connections. Canadians began seriously to question whether American perspectives on international security issues were not increasingly atavistic (e.g., Vietnam), and as the 1930s and 1940s had seen many Canadians concerned about the identity and cultural integrity of their country vis-à-vis Great Britain, so the late 1960s and early 1970s saw a growing debate over the American threat to things Canadian. "Continentalism" became an abusive term to characterize activities that seemed to lock Canada into American-dominated endeavours.

Rarely does history fall neatly into periods and the major international policy structures that bound Canada to common Western security causes continued in force after the 1960s. However, with very few exceptions, commentators upon our country's foreign policy have seen the late 1960s as a transition period, as Canada toyed with the impulse to put more and more policy distance between herself and American-dominated "Cold War" institutions. As of 1970-71, the most pertinent question seemed to be just how far would we go in asserting a more independent stance? And in what direction would we go? A sense of movement, of a willingness to explore the feasibility of substantial policy change, was engendered by the conduct of a basic foreign policy review in 1968-69. The results of the review, *Foreign Policy for Canadians*, published in 1970, did, in however guarded a language, express a desire for change and provide a sense of movement. Canada might be leaving much of the past, but where was the future?

Foreign Policy for Canadians said very little about the rougher aspects of international life. Readers were informed that Canada now had six basic national goals: to foster economic growth; to safeguard sovereignty and independence; to work for peace and security; to promote social justice; to enhance the quality of life; and to ensure a harmonious natural environment. Even bitter opponents of the government would have difficulty challenging the content of that list. But, in terms of actions as opposed to words, how could Canadians change course? More fundamentally, could Canadians change course? In the very early 1970s, it seemed to some that they could. The debate occasioned by the foreign policy review tended to be cast in terms of "what should we do?" rather than "what can we do?"

The defence policy analogue to the foreign policy review appeared in 1971 with the publication of the White Paper, *Defence in the 70s*. The defence "new look" proclaimed that Canada had four defence priorities: "the protection of our sovereignty"; "the defence of North America"; "the fulfillment of such NATO commitments as may be agreed upon"; and "international peacekeeping roles." Some commentators and very many members of the Canadian armed forces saw *Defence in the 70s* as the beginning of an anti-defence policy, emphasizing a set of roles that were scarcely military at all. In the same document, the Minister of National Defence also stated that Canada needed armed forces compatible with duties in Canada (and for that reason, the obsolete *Centurions* with the Mechanized Battle Group in Europe would *not* be replaced by a new main battle tank). Since there were no exacting military roles within Canada (unless one wished to venture into the very dangerous area of "aid to the civil power" on a very large scale), it seemed not impossible, nor even improbable, that Canada's armed forces really had no future worthy of mention, at least with regard to traditional fighting-oriented roles.*

Apparently disregarding the traditional framework of international political life (e.g., that defence policy should support foreign policy, and that "foreign policy" does not exist as something free-floating, independent of defence support), the government chose to parallel its more domestic-looking defence policy with a broad foreign policy concept that came to be known as "The Third Option." In 1972, the Canadian Government issued a policy paper on U.S.-Canadian relations in which three options were specified: (1) to maintain the present relationship; (2) to seek closer integration; or (3) to "pursue a comprehensive, long-term strategy to develop and strengthen the Canadian economy and other aspects of our national life, and in the process, to reduce the present Canadian vulnerability."**

"To reduce the present Canadian vulnerability [to the United States]"

*For a discussion of this issue, see Roddick B. Byers and Colin S. Gray, eds., *Canadian Military Professionalism: The Search for Identity*, Wellesley Paper No. 2 (Toronto: Canadian Institute of International Affairs, 1973).

**There is a fourth option:

Increased nationalism, economic autarchy, with intensified protection of the industrial sector, utilization of export controls, and strong management of foreign interests in Canada.

This, of course, is the historic Conservative policy.

required the co-operation both of security dependents of the United States and, indeed, of the United States itself. It should not be forgotten that most Western Europeans are aware that 23 million Canadians could not protect them from the Soviet Union, while 215 million Americans just might (and certainly could, if motivated adequately). How important this fact is for Canada's freedom varies with how frightened Western Europe is of the U.S.S.R.

In principle, the Third Option is eminently sensible and seems to have been the policy of every government since that of Sir John A. Macdonald. That most of these governments failed miserably to protect the Canadian economy from American influence (though they have prevented complete economic domination) may reflect less Canadian incompetence than the structure of Canada's situation. In short, beyond marginal accomplishment, which may still be valuable, the Third Option has little future just as it has little past – and for many of the same reasons. Nonetheless, to eschew skepticism for the moment, it is possible, though decreasingly so, to argue that the early 1970s, with the foreign and defence policy reviews, and the outlining of the Third Option, marked the end of an era for Canada. As Canada came of age and outgrew British influence, so the American era also was coming to an end. As the then Canadian Secretary of State for External Affairs said in 1975:

> What we have witnessed since the early 1970s has been the ending of one era and the beginning of a new period in Canada-United States relationships. This change involved the ending of the "special relationship" between Canada and the United States.

This is one vision of the Canadian international future. It would be a Canada looking first for the alleviation of distinctively Canadian problems; remaining in NATO but having no forces deployed forward in Europe in peacetime; and diversifying its trade relationships so as to reduce markedly an unhealthy measure of dependence upon the state of the American economy and the will of American governments.

The other vision or trend, by way of substantial contrast, is to the effect that, although the Third Option and the foreign and defence reviews of 1968-71 did reflect deep and enduring sentiments (and solid reasoning) on the part of Canadians, they were merely an interlude. The "Cold War" may be over, but our security (military, political, and economic) connections with the United States, Western Europe, and Japan are as indissoluble as ever they seemed in the 1950s and early 1960s. Trends in world politics, so this argument goes, brought Canadian politicians and officials back to face reality by the mid-1970s. The Third Option is still very much official policy in Ottawa, but we cannot have a foreign economic policy of our choice without a defence acceptable to our major trading partners.

Recognizing that trade diversification away from the United States must mean increasing business with Western Europe and Japan, Canada sought to accomplish a contractual trading link with the European Economic Community. However, the West Germans and others made it very clear that such a success for the Third Option policy would have to be paid for in the coin of a serious Canadian contribution to NATO's frontline defences. As a consequence, late 1975 to mid-1977 has seen almost a total about-face in Canadian defence policy as presented in *Defence in the 70s*, which is supposed still to be an authoritative document. Canada is buying 128 *Leopard 1* medium tanks from West Germany, has purchased 18 *Aurora* long-range patrol aircraft to guard the North Atlantic shipping/reinforcement lanes, is buying TOW (anti-armour) and *Blowpipe* (anti-aircraft missiles), and has begun the selection process to find a new air defence/ground attack aircraft to replace both the 48 obsolescent CF-104Ds in the air group deployed in Europe, and the CF-101 *Voodoos* employed in Canada. Late in 1975 the government committed itself to a five-year program intended to achieve a level of capital expenditure of 20 per cent of the total defence budget. In short, we were signalling our friends, allies, and trading partners that Canada is returning to serious military business.

While it may be unduly deterministic to maintain that defence procurement restricts foreign policy choice, it would be foolish to ignore the fact that Canada is in the process of embarking upon a defence modernization program that only makes sense if we maintain current NATO commitments. A Canada breaking away from "obsolete" Cold-War ties needs fisheries protection vessels, ice surveillance, hydrographic research, search and rescue capability, and very cold climate engineering competence. The kind of armed forces that Canada will be buying over the next five years will not be capable of operating in the North (which is perfectly justifiable on the grounds that armed forces are not needed "North of 60"), nor is it easy to see what need we would have at home for battle tanks and ground-attack aircraft.*

This somewhat cynical view of events–that Canada has rediscovered her NATO military tasks because Helmut Schmidt threatened to prevent a contractual economic link with the EEC–is probably both true and incomplete as an explanation. The world of the mid-to-late 1970s is different from that of the late 1960s and early 1970s. Canadian voluntarism in foreign and defence policy could flourish in an era of apparently burgeon-

*This author has reviewed the entire range of Canadian defence issues in his *Canadian Defence Priorities: A Question of Relevance* (Toronto: Clarke, Irwin, 1972).

ing *detente*, when the United States was hyper- (and mis-directedly) active in defending the marches of "The Free World," and when world trade was growing and domestic inflation and unemployment looked distinctly manageable and tolerable. By 1975 it was apparent that *detente* might mean little more than old practices under a new name, that the *objective* Soviet threat (in terms of relative capabilities) was growing rapidly, that the United States, if anything, needed encouragement to defend its allies and dependents, and that galloping inflation and rising structural unemployment gave a new though not novel meaning to the phrase "economic necessity" vis-à-vis foreign policy. In short, many of the most important, though under-articulated, premises of the late 1960s and early 1970s with respect to the character of Canada's international environment, had been overtaken by events.

The NATO-oriented and/or "continentalist" Canadian could simply comment in 1977 that Canada is back on course as a fully functioning member of the Western community of nations. Such a judgement would be overly simple and may yet prove to be in error. The global economic problems and the deterioration in East-West relations that marked the mid-1970s were not predictable in the period 1968-72. The vision of Canada pursuing a more distinctive course in world affairs was not foolish, nor is it precluded permanently.

Canada: Roles and Identity

Canada does not need to posture in world affairs in order to provide a high and distinctively Canadian profile, so that foreign observers might appreciate that Canada is indeed different from the United States. The outside world knows that Canadians are not Americans be it only as a result of the experience of two world wars and our role in the western alliance. Any identity problem is a Canadian one; it seems that only we have doubts about our national label–others, perceiving Canada, do not. Countries and cultures that share a region tend to have many features in common (e.g., Norway, Denmark, Sweden, and Finland), but the fact of a common language does not serve greatly to diminish perceptions of degrees of cultural distance. The world outside tends only to doubt the Canadian identity to the extent that Canadians themselves appear to doubt their identity. One suspects that Canadian identity problems, so-called, really are problems for low-morale intellectuals rather than Canadians-in-the-street. Foreign and defence policy options (and non-options, but intriguing ideas) designed to project an image, and even perhaps a reality, of Canadian distance from the United States would probably speak to the psychological needs of relatively few people.

Save with respect to some unlikely domestic emergencies, we really have no more than the most minimal need of armed forces. However, for reasons of support of foreign policy, sub-Middle Power Canada has very great need of a respectable (though small) military establishment. Would-be radical innovators in the foreign policy field have to take account of the following facts: Like it or not, by reason of geography, history, and culture, Canada is an affluent, white, Western capitalist power. Our internationalist and humanitarian credentials are good, substantially by virtue of a long record of assuming a relatively high profile in United Nations activities. Nevertheless, Canadians have to appreciate (as, indeed, most do) that their security is dependent almost entirely upon the course charted by our allies. A neutralist foreign-policy posture certainly is feasible–if likely to be expensive in the attenuation of trade and investment opportunities from Western and Japanese sources–but such a posture would remove us from the role of player in the security game most central to the safety and welfare of Canadians. Aside from membership in the Western Alliance, there are no alternative security roles of importance which we could fill (which is one reason why we started the Alliance). Some Canadians may be unhappy with the role of "chipping in" to a vast multi-national enterprise like NATO, wherein Canadian perspectives and opinions sometimes are less than fully reflected in overall alliance positions; but Canada's modest stature in NATO is a direct consequence of size of economy and population, and of location of territory.

Canadian "nationalists" need to be reminded that the alternative to close involvement with NATO-Europe is continental near-isolation with the United States. Economic counterweights to American influence over the Canadian economy require a military down-payment for NATO in Europe. This linkage may seem somewhat absurd in the late 1970s (Hasn't Canada done enough already?), but it does exist as a consequence of settled European expectations concerning proper Canadian behaviour.

The Third Option

Does the Third Option make sense for Canada? One would like to say yes, but is compelled to say no–if, that is, one means by the Third Option a truly major change in the pattern of Canada's international economic linkages–but does anyone really mean that? The Third Option expresses a traditional prudential Canadian concern, and is eminently sensible if a true diversity of potential trading partners is just waiting for Canadians to interest themselves in their markets, but it stands little prospect of affecting the direction of Canada's import-export flows beyond the margin. To repeal, on a non-marginal scale, the facts of economic geography and the established practices of both federal and provincial governments would require a political decision that might well threaten the basis of Canadian prosperity, fragile though that prosperity appears in the mid-to-late 1970s.

In the face of predictable American displeasure, not to mention the question of GATT complications over the putative establishment of preferential trade agreements, it is quite implausible to believe that much more than a trivial rearrangement of Canada's trade pattern away from the United States is possible in the next generation.

One area where Canada might want to emphasize its distinctiveness is that of international politics: North-South relations, the Commonwealth, la Francophonie, etc. As the world continues to become more interdependent, international links, associations, and summits will become very important. In the area of economic relations—for example, relations between the rich and the poor nations—Canada can play a particularly important role in international fora. Canadians are respected worldwide and, while we are one of the richest countries in the world, we are in a position to understand many LDC problems, particularly in the area of resource development, foreign investment, etc. Strains in politics often arise as much because of ambivalence of attitudes as because of complex issues per se. In recent years especially, Canada's role within the Commonwealth has, in a considerable sense, been one of bridging the communications gap between countries. Given her bilingual and multicultural character, Canada should not ignore the possibility of playing a similar role within the Francophone world.

Canada and NATO

Does the NATO connection serve Canadian interests? Even without prior discussion of the detailed meanings that could be applied to the term "connection," one has to register a clearly affirmative answer to the question. NATO defends those western assets that are critically important to the well-being of Canadians. The importance of NATO to Canada may best be appreciated by considering the implications of two propositions. First, if NATO did not exist, or were weakened very severely, the Soviet Union would establish hegemony over western Europe. Second, if western Europe effectively were taken out of the western camp, Canada's independence of decision vis-à-vis the United States would diminish very markedly.

For reasons that far transcend the scope of this study, it is prudent for Canadians to presume that the Soviet Union does harbour ambitions of hegemony respecting the future course of European history, and that NATO is a barrier critical to the frustration of those ambitions. Both presumptions could conceivably be wrong; but there is no way of testing them short of the taking of unacceptable and certainly imprudent risks.

Cost-benefit analysis of the current NATO connection is very difficult to quantify. NATO roles, that is to say potential fighting roles against a first-class enemy, unquestionably have a major impact upon a very small military establishment. If it were not for the NATO roles on the Central Front, the Northern Flank, and in defence of North Atlantic re-supply routes, the entire character of the Canadian Armed Forces would be very different indeed from its present one. The question Canadians need to ask pertains to the opportunity costs of the NATO roles. If we were not purchasing 18 long-range patrol aircraft optimized for anti-submarine duties, were not acquiring 128 *Leopard 1s*, were not about to spend $2-$2.5 billion on an aircraft capable of both North American air defence and NATO-European roles, and were not embarking upon a major blue-water ship-building program, what domestic duties, and at what levels, could a Canadian Armed Forces specializing in surveillance roles perform?

Some circles cannot be squared. Unlike the NORAD involvement, NATO duties are not a cost-free exercise. Some domestic surveillance/national development roles (in the North and over foreign fishing fleets, for examples) could be much better performed were critical resources not being devoted to a putative North European battlefield and to the tracking of Soviet submarines in the North Atlantic. However, it is not plausible to argue that current and projected levels of "protection of sovereignty" activities are manifestly inadequate. In the best of all possible worlds Canada would decide to take seriously its official defence priorities, and would vote defence budgets adequate to support both domestic duties and NATO commitments with the purchase of specialized equipment appropriate to each. However, given a political climate that sets very finite limits upon defence expenditure, the rediscovery of the capital equipment needs of our armed forces for serious NATO military business is a vital sign. One or two additional Canadian over-flights of the Arctic Islands per month makes no difference whatever to Canadian "sovereignty" in the region; the enterprise, in legal terms (and sovereignty is a legal term), needs only minimal physical expression, whereas the re-equipment of the Canadian Armed Forces for NATO roles has an impact upon Canadian trade, upon the quality and quantity of Canadian access to allied information and decision processes, and just possibly upon the stability of the NATO structure. (Europe must notice that a North American member is purchasing equipment for NATO that will be operable at least until the late 1990s.)

The Armed Forces and Quebec

Is there a domestic role for the Canadian Armed Forces in the event that Quebec secedes? Should a large majority of Québecois vote for sovereignty in a referendum, and should the Government of Quebec then request of the Government of Canada that legal steps be taken to effect separation, there could be no role for the armed forces, save as reserve capability to deter–and if need be, suppress–civil disturbance. The armed forces become far more relevant in either of two scenarios: First, violence, latent or actual, could be threatened or occur if the outcome of the referendum is very close, with the losing opinion claiming that the form of words in the question biased the outcome. If this happened, either camp might believe that a display of well-organized, "spontaneous" muscle on the streets of Montreal and Quebec City would work to the advantage of its cause. Each side could well feel that it was in extreme danger of being "robbed" of a victory of historic significance. Another scenario is after a decisive vote against sovereignty in a referendum, the losing faction decides that the revolution has to be created through action. Police forces, even para-military police forces (such as the CRS in France), cannot cope with armed insurrection. It so happens that Canada does not have any para-military police; any conflict that was beyond the competence of the Quebec Provincial Police and imported RCMP would have to be addressed by the Canadian Armed Forces. Can we forget that in 1970, the Government of Canada, by invitation of the Attorney General of Quebec, deployed the Armed Forces in Montreal? Compared with the kind of armed insurrection envisaged here, the FLQ challenge of 1970 was almost trivial, yet the FLQ crisis saw the Armed Forces overstretched severely as support units were employed in potential combat roles.

Quebec may be the country's largest province, but its political life is critically dependent upon control in only two cities, Montreal and Quebec City. In short, he who controls those two cities effectively controls Quebec (which is not to deny that rural unrest could well continue for years). Military action to put down secession clearly would be impracticable, as well as impolitic, were the vast majority of Québecois to favour sovereignty. However, as discussed later, it seems unlikely that such a majority could be mustered.

The Canadian Armed Forces (at a total strength of 78,000) could not coerce back into Confederation a Quebec determined to be sovereign. But Ottawa would be bound to consider its options were the majority in favour of soveriegnty to be in the order of 52-55 per cent–which it could well be–and were Quebec to act unilaterally to achieve political sovereignty. However, Ottawa would not have available for its purposes the 78,000 men in uniform plus reservists: Nearly 1,600 men are aboard on U.N. peacekeeping duties; nearly 5,000 are deployed in Central Europe, and some fraction of the Francophone troops might well decide that their loyalties lay with Quebec City rather than with Ottawa. Moreover, by way of further complications, just as many Francophones (or *demi*-Francophones) in the Armed Forces could feel that Canada rather than Quebec had first call upon their loyalties and professional services, some Anglophones almost certainly would feel that aid to the civil power in Quebec was not proper military employment. In short, the morale of Canadian forces operating in Quebec to maintain/restore an unsullied Confederation could be low indeed.

With regard to the possible military and para-military operations in Quebec by Francophone members of the Canadian Armed Forces, no clear picture emerges. By their calling and training, Canadian soldiers are loyal to Canada. But few, if any, Francophone soldiers could tolerate, let alone participate in, the "pacification" of their provincial homeland. The critical question, as always, is "what is the scenario?" Should Quebec vote overwhelmingly for the continuation of Confederation, leaving only a small number of "semi-terrorists" to contest the popular will, then the Armed Forces (including Francophones) would deliver whatever level of violence the civil power considered necessary. Such duties would run counter to the Canadian military professional ethos, but–virtually to a man–the Armed Forces would recognize that what they were doing was necessary and desirable. That is the simple case, but the future may not be so obliging as to provide such a clear-cut context.

By way of an overall judgement, taking account of the many possible scenarios of Ottawa-Quebec City developments, the Canadian Armed Forces have to be judged to be relevant to the domestic future of Canada. The Armed Forces clearly would not intervene in the event of an over-whelming mandate for sovereignty in Quebec, but in all other situations a more cautious judgement has to be registered. Canada's recent purchase (in stages) of 700 Swiss-designed armoured cars, and the movement of the elite Canadian airborne regiment (1,000 strong) to Ontario (with the Francophone 1st Commando to Ottawa, and the Anglophone elements to Petawawa) have to be appraised in the context of domestic policies, even if that was not the dominant official motive.

Conclusion

The very large American presence in our economic and cultural life is probably unduly substantial, and should be both reduced and subjected to greater Canadian discipline. The problem is that a sensible idea like the

Third Option encourages perception of a non-existent alternative. By means of domestic and foreign policies which enhance the desirability, in foreign eyes, of trade with Canada, Canadian governments should be able to achieve progress at the margin in reducing vulnerability both to American policy and to American economic fluctuations. However, the key phrase is "at the margin." It is a non-repealable economic fact that Canada is locked into a continental economic structure. As stated earlier, the vision of a truly radical switch in Canada's trading orientation is totally lacking in support and substance. Furthermore, it is not at all obvious that Canadians should favour heavy dependence upon economic links with the EEC and Japan, as opposed to the United States.

In practice, the Third Option, as with the foreign and defence policy "new looks," has suffered from changes in the international climate. The United States remains the principal security producer for Canadians as for West Germans and Japanese. Canada's freedom of action, politically and economically, is critically dependent upon the overall state of East-West relations. Moreover, the late 1970s and the 1980s do not threaten a return to "Cold War" conditions in familiar terms. The United States of the late 1970s is not the United States of the 1950s or 1960s. The American Empire, or the American Century, hailed by a few in the mid-1960s, died in the rubble of Hué in the Tet Offensive of 1968. The United States will forever be an economic and political giant vis-à-vis Canada, but it is a giant that is changing.

As Britain has discovered over the past decade, freedom of action in foreign policy is very directly related to economic performance and political stability at home. A foreign policy satisfactory to most Canadians, i.e., one that "chips in" usefully to the maintenance of international order, yet which does so in ways most appropriate to Canadians, can be pursued with dedication, free from upsetting external pressures, only if Canada greatly improves its domestic economic performance and resolves the dilemmas posed both by Quebec nationalist sentiment and, more generally, by the escalating power struggles between Ottawa and the provinces. A prudent and steady course abroad cannot be sustained if there is turmoil at home.

210

Politics

The issues that have dominated Canadian politics for most of our history are likely to change significantly during the next decade. Of course, Ontario's economic power and political clout will not be substantially reduced; Quebec will preserve or enhance its special bargaining power; B.C. and the Prairies will increase their influence, yet will continue to protest against Western alienation and TOM's domination. But changes will result from the way these issues are dealt with, and not from the newness of the issues.

Regional issues will receive more attention. Provincial and local governments are already asserting their views and policies more vigorously, and competition between different levels of government will become more intense. Today, few issues can be decided upon without going through a complex process of federal-provincial (and sometimes municipal) consultations. In the next decade, these consultations will be of paramount importance to Canadian political life, and those provinces who do best economically will also gain in power.

Take Western Canada: The West is no longer heavily rural and "small town," with a low population density. Well over half its population now lives in metropolitan cities. The West, or at least Alberta and B.C., will be two of the fastest growing regions of Canada. Currently western Canada does not have the power to cast the "deciding vote." The last two federal elections showed that a government could remain in power with little or no support in western Canada and that it is exceedingly difficult to achieve power without central Canada—Ontario and Quebec both. Unless there is a nearly even split in central Canada, the West does not even hold the balance of power; and this is one of the major causes of western alienation. However, the West has, and will continue to have, resources, wealth, and economic power. Its ability to influence Canadian politics will be greater than its representation in government. As the West continues to grow and increases its power, more tensions with TOM will develop.

Current rest-of-Canada/Quebec tensions will obviously influence federal-provincial relations. Assuming that Quebec stays within Confederation, Quebec is likely to become a more influential power, but Canadians on the whole, will show some reluctance to let Quebec have its cake and eat it too; and renewed federalism may just lead to a new definition of regional blocs.

In a sense, the Senate might be the instrument that could help attenuate regional tensions. The Senate has largely been pushed out of being a partner in political decisions. It has been reduced to being chiefly a critic and commentator. Canada is unique among federal nations in lacking a federal element in the central government. Although nominally a federal institution, the control of the appointive power by the Prime Minister makes the Senate more or less an instrument of the central government. This has led many reformers to suggest that we adopt the Australian or U.S. system of an elected Senate, either directly by the people or by the provincial legislatures, as was the original U.S. version. This has many costs, as evidenced by the recent Australian constitutional crisis in which a Liberal (i.e. conservative) Senate brought down a Labour government. Nonetheless, the idea of an elected Senate is very attractive in Canada, but will probably bog down in the details of allocation of seats. Obviously we cannot imitate the U.S. and Australian systems of equal representation for each federal unit. For Prince Edward Island to have the same number of seats as Ontario is clearly intolerable. Conversely, an allocation purely on the basis of population is politically impractical. A small proportional Senate with minimum provincial seats would have the effect of over-representing the smaller provinces and cutting down on the representation of our second largest province–Quebec–and would certainly be unacceptable there.

Probably the only practical solution would be along the lines of the historical system of seats in four equal divisions: Maritimes, Quebec, Ontario, West. This was modified slightly by the addition of Newfoundland and territorial seats, but the rule is about the best that can be achieved. However, the present distribution of seats within regions also leaves a lot to be desired and cannot be easily remedied. But, there will be pressures to make the Senate more representative and to increase its say in Canadian politics.

As discussed in the values section, "new values" are emerging which are also likely to influence our political life. In many instances these new values will rival, if not overshadow, the traditional values of our society with members of the new class overpowering the traditional power centres of Canadian politics, such as the traditional economic interests.

"Bread and butter issues" will remain important, but increasingly political discussions will also emphasize the "quality of Canadian life."

The traditional blocs, "labour," "farmers," or "business," will no longer be the only major carriers of policy. These economic blocs will not become meaningless or powerless. The farmer, for example, no longer has the key position he had earlier in this century, but has lost his influence only very slowly. However, such groups are increasingly perceived as representing narrow economic interests as opposed to social, moral, or even aesthetic concerns. In many cases they are seen to be playing an almost negative role as obstacles to policy changes, and are being challenged by members of the new class.

Most observers of the future of the advanced nations believe that the new class will constitute an even more important group in the next century, and it is believed that it might run or at least set the tune for society. Whether or not this is natural, the new class is, and will increasingly be, well organized as a power centre.

On the other hand, while there are as yet no signs of a vigorous neo-conservative intellectual movement emerging in Canada, the movement in the U.S. is likely to have some impact on Canada. More important, short-run neo-conservatism is growing out of indigenous Canadian conditions; it is difficult not to be primarily concerned with fundamental economics and national survival today. But despite a heightened receptivity for discipline and strong leadership, the pendulum is unlikely to swing back to where it was twenty years ago.

Economics will remain a dominant domestic issue, at least for the next five years. But, while most Canadians value economic growth, as they become richer an increasing number of them will be willing to see it slow down or will give it lower priority. Consequently, less emphasis is likely to be put on the pursuit of economic growth than on the distribution and quality of growth.

We can expect political groups on the left to continue complaining about the increasing complexity of our society, in which the individual becomes an anonymous being. The right will complain that the individual is losing control over his destiny and private decision-making. "Alienation" is the new buzz word on both sides.

The Parties

How will this basic context affect the political parties? Any discussion of our political parties is bound to be scrutinized carefully for signs of partisanship. Let us try to assuage skepticism by beginning with what we hope to be a non-political discussion of our political parties. One of the effects of the parliamentary system is the need to maintain the majority in the House of Commons to form a government. This requires strong party discipline and firm leadership. The voter's knowledge that any vote for a party unlikely to be able to form a government is largely wasted tends to reinforce the historical two-party system. Considering this factor, our two national minority parties have done remarkably well, although, to some degree, they have played upon their successes in provincial politics.

Historically, the two major parties have had distinct social bases as well as quite differing outlooks on the most pressing issues facing Canada—nationality and international economic connections. The Progressive Conservatives were the party of the "WASPs," Protestant Canadians almost entirely of British origin. The hard core of the party was of Loyalist stock. In a considerable sense the Tories were the established original backbone of Anglo Canada.

Against the WASPs were arrayed those ethnic groups who were resentful of Anglo dominance—most obviously and most importantly the French, but we must not forget the Irish, the Jews, and other ethnic groups. To a considerable degree, therefore, party affiliation was a form of tribal loyalty. It was difficult for a person brought up as Tory or a Grit to defect to the hereditary enemy. (In fact, this factor is part of the success of the minor parties—one can rebel against what one conceives to be the adverse policies of the traditional party without becoming a "traitor.")

The outlook of the traditional parties on key national issues to some degree was a shadow of these ethnic origins. The Conservatives were the strongest supports for the British connection, the most royalist, pro-English, "loyalist." The Liberals were less enthusiastic about the British connection and tended to look more towards the United States. In international economics, the Tories were pro-imperialist or strongly protectionist while the Liberals supported international free trade (which, of course, in the Canadian context meant trade with the U.S.). In the domestic arena the Progressive Conservatives spoke more for Canadian manufacturing interests, while the Liberals spoke for trading interests and financial.

A large part of our political turmoil today is related to the fact that these traditional alignments are no longer relevant. Tory backbenchers can still become agitated at the latest affront to the monarch, but the idea of British America is nearly dead. Conversely, the Liberals no longer can react against this aspect of Toryism. Nevertheless, the economic distinction between the two parties has not entirely eroded. Manufacturers and some small businessmen still tend to be Conservative, and traders and financiers tend to be Liberal; the Liberals are the pro-American, or the least anti-American, party.

The ethnic aspect of the two parties is also changing. Part of the continued low morale of the Tories, not to mention the society as a whole, is
this loss of the British-American ideal which was so long an organizing
rationale for the polity. The Conservatives have not yet constructed a
substitute for it or found an interest in the society to represent; they have,
in effect, been playing a me-too role vis-à-vis the Liberals, who have
taken the lead in important national issues and maintained the initiative
for over half a century. Worse, the WASPs seem to have been suffering a
general loss of morale, and have been doing a miserable job of defending
their power and dominance over the nation and the other ethnic groups.
Today, the Tories show vigour mainly in the West where they represent a
dynamic version of the traditional developmental capitalist ethic.

The Liberals, on the other hand, are benefitting from these social
changes. The rise of the French, the Jews, and other traditional "out"
groups has benefitted them. However, they have had serious internal tensions over national and international policy. This is caused by a surfeit of
success: the Liberal non-British Canadian policy has triumphed, but there
is now the question of what to do now. Over the past decade, Liberals
have concentrated on appeasing the French interest, and made a major
thrust in a social democratic policy, apparently stimulated by a fear that
the NDP would outflank them on the left. In part, this thrust represents
changes within the Canadian establishment, as the traditional elements
have been challenged by the new class who have tended to support the
Liberals.

The Liberals must gain the allegiance of the educated middle class and the
new class, but at the same time hold the allegiance of the old power
groups, the economic blocs, and the ethnic blocs. The attempt to hold one
could alienate the other. If the Liberals are to break out of the Francophone box, they will have to appeal to Anglo interests in Ontario, the
Maritimes, and the West. However, in so doing they must be careful not
to alienate Quebec. The Quebec-Canada tensions will only make the bargaining more difficult.

There is another danger—that the Liberal Party will cease to be a national party, with its support stemming chiefly and nearly exclusively
from central Canada. Because of current regional tensions, the party will
need broader support. The Liberal Party appears to address itself to the
new realities; its main themes are national unity and economics, but economics linked to quality of life. In one of his major statements, the Prime
Minister and leader of the Liberal Party, in his description of the "New
Society" clearly put "new" values at the centre of his politics. The tensions that this created with the traditional power blocs are all too obvious.

215

In the future the party will try to emphasize consensus politics, as it has done in the past. Thus the Liberals will try to focus on the issue that has served them so well in the past–national unity. Nearly every Liberal Prime Minster, at some time during his career, has run on the platform that only the Liberals could keep the country together.

But there are dangers in the politics of consensus. First of all achieving consensus will be increasingly difficult, given the new power centres. Second, consensus politics restricts the party both in formulating policy and building new alignments. There is a danger of losing the young, the new class, or an increasingly militant class-conscious working class. In its attempt to achieve consensus the Liberal Party may blur its identity, and therein lies the danger of its going the route of the British Liberal Party.

Should Quebec separate, this would certainly have a very negative impact, to say the least, given the party habit of bragging about its record on national unity.

The Progressive Conservative Party has more or less become the permanent opposition, in terms of its traditional standing in the House of Commons. The PC is the "WASP" party; statistically, of course, the WASPs constitute about half the population, but, while it is relatively easy to organize majority support in rural areas, in the cities the WASPs do not see themselves as a coherent group and do not usually vote as such (probably because they do not see themselves as a minority).

In fact there are two scenarios to describe the options available to the PC. Unfortunately the business-as-usual outcome would have the party torn internally by the fight between the adherents of either scenario.

First the "moderate" scenario. In the short run the PC expects to come to power precisely because it is not easy to tell it apart from the government except that it is "out" and therefore not responsible for crises, scandal or whatever. The PC's are able to attract enough protest votes to get into power, but party unity is precarious. (Within the party the moderates are already labelled as "me too" Conservatives or as "Red Tories" by their opponents.)

The moderates can only operate if they control some important power centres–like the Liberal control of Quebec–or some big cities such as Toronto. Specifically, the PC moderates would have to gain control of Ontario's parliamentary representation. To maintain their hold on Ontario, they will probably have to remain "moderates," and could lose some support in Western Canada. This is not to say that Quebec has no room for a conservative party. Quite the contrary, as demonstrated by the erratic success of Social Credit. But historically, the PCs have had a rather dim image in Quebec. A revival of the Social Credit and a Social Credit-PC

216

alliance might just be what the PCs need in Quebec. Then again, if Quebeckers were to cease voting "en bloc," both the PCs and NDP could gain support in the province.

On the other hand, there is a more radical scenario which aims to recreate a populist party "dedicated to principles and traditional values." For this scenario to work requires a candidate who has shown ability for political leadership and enough maturity not to frighten off the moderate wing of his own party. (Though Canada appears ready for more sobriety and seriousness in politics and government, it is difficult to imagine a scenario where Canada goes "crazy right.")

A more populist Conservative Party would be likely to maintain western support, and might make some gains in Quebec and in rural Ontario. If populist, and strongly pro-business, it could even make substantial gains in Ontario.

In both our moderate and populist scenarios, an alignment with the older generation is not unlikely. Also, the Conservatives are more likely to focus on issues related to economics.

The New Democrats are the new class party par excellence. It is not, however, a socialist party *à la* Western Europe. The NDP-labour alliance is not very strong, partly because of the NDP's moderate stand, and partly because of the weakness of labour.

The fact that some provinces have elected NDP governments seems to have paid off only slightly at the federal level. The fact is that the provincial NDP governments are just slightly left of centre, some, in fact, with policies not very difficult from those of the federal Liberals. In fact, the federal Liberals have been said to have recently courted an NDP premier as a potential leader of the party.

The only way the NDP's minority status can change is through social changes which would promote unlikely class-consciousness, permitting its evolution into a true social democratic party allying the working people with new class intellectuals.

We can expect that the old-line Prairie populism, rooted in German and Scandinavian social democracy which found its expression in the CCF, will continue. This type of radicalism, based upon farmers who are by definition very practical people, has been much more level-headed and has had much greater staying power than the socialism of intellectuals and the more enthusiastic trade union leaders elsewhere in Canada. In a considerable sense, the NDP has been two parties, one based on the old CCF of the Prairies and the other on New Canadians in the cities. As the next fifteen years progresses we can expect a blending of that difference, as the intellectual and educated element grows more on the Prairies. To the extent that this happens, the old base of the party will wane, and it is almost certain that the NDP will become less of a force in the Prairies; but this process will certainly be very slow, and the 1990s will almost certainly see the NDP or its successor in power or leading the opposition in the Prairies.

The NDP will have more luck if it succeeds in achieving a "national" image. In fact, putting aside its separatist policy, the PQ is really a provincial version of the NDP. Depending upon the popularity of the PQ, the NDP could make a breakthrough in Quebec, but imagining it taking over Quebec is difficult.

Social Credit's limited, regional appeal makes it difficult to imagine the SC playing a major role in national politics. A PC-SC alliance is possible, but the real benefit would accrue to the PC not the Socreds. Perhaps the best way to view Social Credit is as a mobilization base for potential "populist" sentiment. If, as, and when the major parties forget "the little people," Social Credit strength will grow, and the major parties will at least pretend to respond.

Of course, much of the above is little more than speculation. Much will depend on the personality of the leaders of each of these parties, and this is impossible to predict.

The Future of Confederation

The issue now dominating discussion of the future of Canada is "Will there be a future for Canada?" or more accurately, "Will Quebec separate?", "What if Quebec separates?" or "What will be the new Confederation if Quebec does not separate?" Nearly everyone agrees that important changes will be made in the structure of the Canadian state.

Almost any aspect of the above would be of great concern. For that very reason, we will not attempt at this time to predict the outcome; that would be premature. Nor will many specific political, legal, or economic issues be considered in detail. (The host of such legal issues include the possibility of the federal government reclaiming the Ungava Peninsula, which was not part of any province until it was included in Quebec by an act of the federal Parliament in 1912; the many citizenship problems which could arise; the ability of the Province of Quebec to pass and enforce some of the laws currently under consideration; and the status of the million Anglophones in Quebec. Among the economic issues are capital flows, trade flows, equalization payments, inter-provincial labour mobility, industrial strategy, etc.) Instead, various scenarios will consider a gamut of possible outcomes of the current Quebec situation. In effect, we will outline some of the issues and choices, and some of the consequences which might flow from them.

The principal historical justifications for having and preserving a large nation are:

1. offence or defence, military or cultural;
2. rapid or reliable economic development;
3. undertaking big projects;
4. exerting influence on the world; and
5. the sense of "esprit" that derives from belonging to a bigger unit, one that counts for something in the world.

If these five points are depreciated, it is true that "small is beautiful," "small can be better," and "less can be more." The idea that Canada might break up into small units and these units might flourish, particularly if they co-operated for mutual self-interest, may be an unpopular concept; but it is not necessarily an incorrect one.

Actually, despite the PQ victory, separatist sentiment in Quebec has not increased greatly; rather, both Canada as a whole and Quebec appear to have experienced a waning of Canadian nationalist sentiment, at least up to the last Quebec election. We mean nationalism in its positive aspect of a sense of nationhood, unity, patriotism, and pride in one's country, not economic nationalism or anti-American attitudes. In other words, a factor promoting Quebec nationalism is the weakness of Canadian nationalism, or a paucity of absolute and intense commitment to Canada as a "large" nation. The idea that "small is beautiful," implicit in many recent federal government pronouncements and programs, has reinforced the separatist case.

Nevertheless, if forced to bet on the outcome of the current tension, we would say that the odds are against Quebec achieving outright separation from the rest of Canada during the next generation. Our reasoning is very straightforward. While we do not believe that the average Francophone Quebecois has a strong sense of Canadian nationality, we also doubt that he has a strong aversion to Canada. Since most Quebecois find being part of Canada acceptable and even desirable, they are not willing to bestir themselves to change it; nor passively willing to let others change the situation drastically and then force them to deal with unknown and threatening risks that might result from the changes. This assessment is supported by all poll data, which indicate that support for outright separation has not grown over the years. Furthermore, many in Quebec, both Anglo and French, would oppose separation, independence or even sovereignty fiercely.

Any discussion of this question must go beyond quantitative or qualitative analysis of economic issues. The issue of Quebec is highly emotional and historical: a proud people has a long-held sense of being a minority which has suffered discrimination. They "remember" and, even as they overcame this sense of inferiority, they became determined to strengthen their *sentiment de collectivité* whether or not they remain in Canada.

Many of the PQ supporters describe the conditions they are fighting against in terms which would have been more appropriate some twenty to fifty years ago than to the current situation.** In fact, one of the most

---

* The PQ has, in the past, referred to separation, independence, sovereignty with or without association – and has not precisely defined any of the terms.

** In fact much of their rhetoric is inspired from historical or sociological analyses of colonialism; Albert Memmi and Frantz Fanon are widely read and cited in nationalist intellectual circles.

220

remarkable characteristics of Quebec today is that the basic inferiority complex which many French people felt in dealing with Anglo Canada has now almost completely disappeared. Of course, for these people the mere fact that they are really talking about historical rather than present conditions makes the situation even more emotional, for little can be done in a practical way to change history, except obtain a kind of revenge. This is not intended to deny the many vital current issues and forces associated with the Quebec sovereignty movement. It is just to add that a good deal of the emotion of some of the more intellectual and literate individuals derives from a sense of historical grievance rather than contemporary outrage.

Of course, to a considerable degree, the perceptions of many Anglo-Canadians also feed on historical perspectives—the idea that Francophones do not have a "sense of the bottom line," that they are family and pleasure oriented only, etc.

The response of English Canada may be extremely emotional in part because they can clearly see that progress has been made; some Anglophones are furious that the French should still be making even more demands. In fact we would not be surprised if a strong anti-French backlash emerged as a result of current tensions. This emotion can be a bargaining tactic, whether used consciously or unconsciously, and use of this bargaining tactic may exacerbate the emotionalism. A minority of Anglophones really do feel threatened by "French power," and their reactions derive from deeply ingrained positions, not from bargaining strategies.

The important question is, of course, the existence of a substantial and well-organized elite group in Quebec that is enthusiastically for separation, or "sovereignty" as they now call it. We do not believe that this minority can force its views on the majority but it will certainly try to make the proposal attractive to Quebeckers. This group is well organized, dominates the media, and is influential in schools, universities, and labour unions. Furthermore, it now controls the provincial government.

What it could try to achieve over the next few years is de facto sovereignty by "fabian" or "salami" tactics, bit-by-bit, by enacting various laws (Bill 101 is an example) which increase Quebec's "independence," and "expropriate" jobs or control from *les anglais*. Likewise, Quebec could choose to "expropriate" power from certain companies by regulation and legislation rather than through nationalizations. This could be achieved without having to pass the test of a referendum. Thus Quebec could achieve "sovereignty" while having the costs of its policies borne by the whole country, i.e., unemployment benefits, transfer payments, subsidies, etc., which alleviate the economic impact of Quebec laws. However, at some point the PQ government will very likely be forced to hold a referendum.

The provincial government is committed to a sovereign Quebec, but most of the public are favourable to Canada; the majority of Quebeckers voted for federalist parties in the last provincial election and the majority reject sovereignty in opinion surveys. Nevertheless the result of a referendum cannot be absolutely certain. This uncertainty about the stability of provincial politics is one of the worst situations possible.

In order to achieve power, the PQ ran on a moderate and reformist platform; it put forward no radical programs and had to promise not to separate Quebec without a referendum. It must delay holding that referendum until it feels reasonably certain to win. The race is between the economics of the situation and the hope that people will become used to the idea of sovereignty, or that a backlash against French Canadians will emerge and be so emotional and widespread that Quebeckers will feel unwanted (i.e., let the bastards leave if they want to). But the longer the PQ stalls, the more it will be measured by the voters on the record of its performance as the provincial governing party. In fact, one of the more important results of the election is the "normalizing" of the PQ, i.e., the PQ becomes perceived as just another bunch of politicians.

Political uncertainty scares away new investments, both Canadian and foreign. Investors are timid. About the only thing more timid than a million dollars is ten million dollars. And uncertainty over independence and the social democratic stance of the PQ has already begun to frighten investors,* and therefore injure Quebec's economy, make governance more difficult, and make the federalist position that a sovereign Quebec is an impoverished Quebec more plausible. The provincial government will, of course, try to blame the federal government for Quebec's economic woes, especially since the whole Canadian economy is likely to continue to be uneven during the next few years. In Quebec, the forthcoming debate on decontrolling the Canadian economy will increase the federal government's visibility in the area of economy policy. However, we believe that there is little the Quebec government can do to convince Quebec that the uncertainty caused by the PQ election has not accentuated the underlying economic problems.

Until the issue of separation is settled (if it is settled), we do not expect to see a mass exodus of capital or people in the short-term. Instead, timidity will take the form of a gradual erosion of investment, little or no expansion of existing facilities, measures to increase liquidity, some

*To date, the legislation proposed or enacted by the PQ has done little to reassure investors; the increase and indexing of minimum wages, the remittance of charges laid against union leaders, the increase in family allowances, the automobile insurance scheme, the language law, the anti-scab legislation. Discussions of the possibility of nationalizing certain sectors of the economy or of introducing further protectionist measures in other sectors have also made investors more hesitant.

attrition, and some disinvestment. Of course, many contingency plans are being drawn up today, but business will not write off investments unless it must and will not take big losses unless absolutely necessary.

Nevertheless, Quebec almost certainly must expect slow economic growth, at the very least. This will probably reflect itself in heightening social tensions within the province. Labour is likely to continue to be militant. As a result, the government will have the choice of suppressing it and destroying its potential mass base, or acceding to it, frightening off more capital, instituting more draconic measures, and turning in a more widening gyre. The PQ seems to believe that its views are so reasonable and so widely shared by labour that it can achieve general acceptance of its proposals. However, labour's expectations far exceed what is likely to be economically possible, and tensions will heighten.

The government may be caught in a cleft stick, and may want to deliberately exacerbate conflicts between Quebec and the rest of Canada to hurry the referendum. Alas, the more mischief the government makes, the worse the economic situation will become. The only way for the government to slide through this maze is to pander to business interests on the one side, while exacerbating cultural differences with the central government and Anglophone Canada on the other. This is a very tricky and difficult policy to execute, and we find it difficult to imagine the PQ pulling it off.

With regard to the PQ's social democratic orientation which the PQ claims is based, in part, on the Swedish model, we would argue that it is not practical for Quebec to develop along the lines of Scandinavian social democracy. The labour movement in Quebec has tended towards syndicalism and consequently is not known for its great willingness to co-operate with governments. Already some labour leaders have complained about the "elitist and bourgeois" PQ representatives. Many labour leaders have supported the PQ and have advocated sovereignty only as a vehicle for achieving much broader social and economic reforms, and for acquiring more power. They will support the PQ to the extent that they obtain what they want.

However, the bourgeoisie, whether it is *souverainiste* or not, is firmly entrenched in its position, and is very reluctant to give up any of its prerogatives and powers.

Middle class Quebec is more or less committed to the North American way of life—high standard of living, car, family travels, good education for the children—and will resist giving it up. The population is obviously not consensus-prone.

A more suitable model for Quebec might be inspired by contemporary French technocratic *étatisme* or state capitalism, *viz*, Hydro-Quebec. These remarks apply whether or not Quebec remains a part of Canada.

A referendum will not necessarily settle the issue of Confederation once and for all. There can be many referenda which emphasize a step-by-step approach to sovereignty. Furthermore, in the case of a pro-sovereignty result, the federal government might feel it had to intervene to protect those who desire to remain part of Canada. The PQ could win a referendum and lose the next election; lose a referendum and win the election; or win both or lose both. Much of course will depend on the campaign strategies, the type of question asked, and on the interpretation given to the results.

To illustrate our point, we will consider a few questions ranging from a very ambiguous query to a clear-cut choice on independence.*

"Do you favour a vigorous national life for Quebec?"

If the PQ government thought that it could not win a clear-cut referendum, it could try posing such an open-ended, ambiguous question. The risk, of course, is that such a question would all too easily be made to appear as a trap by opponents of the PQ, and the government would likely be discredited. This type of question is very risky; it would be an error in strategy for the PQ to try this and they are unlikely to do so.

"Are you in favour of serious negotiations to achieve sovereignty-association within the next few years?

It is the most plausible question, especially if the PQ promised not to carry out sovereignty-association without coming back to the people. In all opinion polls, over the years, Quebeckers have rejected proposals for sovereignty-association or even special status. But a majority of Quebeckers support a "renewed federalism," and might be willing to give the provincial government a mandate to negotiate, unless, of course, they could be convinced that the government would not negotiate in good faith. Support for such a question might give the federal government no choice but to hold its own referendum to "clarify" the PQ's mandate.

If the question is decisively defeated and the PQ loses the following election, the issue simmers but is not settled forever. Since the mid-sixties 15 to 20 per cent of Quebeckers have favoured independence, and they will not disappear. But so long as the successor government seems to take some account of the issue, little or no serious difficulties are incurred. If the question is defeated and the government re-elected, emphasis will be on government administration. The PQ government enacts or

*Many groups, including the PQ, are already "testing" questions through opinion polls.

tries to enact many types of legislation, but is limited by public opinion and its own desire to look reasonable. Nothing serious really happens, even though much might be threatened. Anglo Canada might push bilingualism even more.

If the question gained the support of a majority of Quebeckers, yet the next election spelled defeat for the PQ, the next government would have to emphasize constitutional reform. It would be limited, however, by its desire not to look more *souverainiste* than the PQ. Powers could be devolved to all provinces in the areas of immigration, communications, and urban affairs; tax points could be renegotiated; minority language rights could be entrenched in the constitution. Concessions might be made with regard to the appointment of lieutenant-governors, judges, and even Senators; but all of this takes place slowly and generally in a spirit of good will.

Should the PQ win both the referendum and the following election, a compromise scenario becomes more likely. Negotiations would certainly be difficult, since the adversary position of the parties involved would be more serious. However, Ottawa would probably be careful not to "turn off" Quebec.

Let us consider a standard compromise scenario. In this scenario either the federal government's relations with all the provinces change basically, or Quebec achieves "special status." Either way, Canada and the provinces agree to a major constitutional reform relatively quickly. One possibility could allow the provinces to have complete jurisdiction over language, urban affairs, immigration, social welfare policy, communications, and increased power in appointing officials to federal bodies. But monetary and commercial policy remain in the federal sphere as do defence and foreign policy. Alternatively, the "two-nation" concept could be accepted and the powers of Quebec broadened beyond those of the other provinces.

A useful distinction here is between reign and rule or sovereignty and power. Quebec as a semi-autonomous unit could reign but not rule—or it might be the opposite, rule but not reign. Which occurred would depend on how much Quebec was interested in symbols or in the functions of nationhood. Under rule but not reign, the Canadian flag would fly over the *Assemblée Nationale* and school children would sing "O Canada" in French; but, domestically, Quebec would do pretty much as it pleased. Conversely, reign but not rule would mean that Quebec would have all the trappings of a nation-state, but would have a relationship with "Canada" which would severely restrict its real freedom of action.

Either way, in a compromise scenario Quebec stays within Canada, but with a special status; and the rest of Canada operates in a tighter federal system. There are several analogies to this–Sardinia in Italy and Northern Ireland in the United Kingdom. Objections from other provinces to special treatment for Quebec are overborne by common sense: Quebec is a special case in a way that Newfoundland or Alberta are not.

It might even be possible to have quid pro quo arrangements under which every province in effect made its own deal with the federal government. Or one could imagine a federal system with two or three different "statuses," with each province able to choose what suits it best. This is very difficult to achieve, of course. This type of arrangement could also allow different internal political systems to exist in different provinces. Some might adopt a presidential-republican system while others might preserve a parliamentary-monarchical system.

These have the great virtue of preserving the continuity of the federal (or more accurately, "confederal") system and of continuing the basic functions of the federal government in defence and foreign policy and as an arbitrator between the provinces in the "national interest."

Another such scenario, the devolution scenario, sees Canada evolving along current British constitutional lines. The federal covenant would devolve more power to the provinces, but without granting political sovereignty. The probable outcome is a general "federal" Parliament and separate Parliaments in each region. Again the internal political systems can differ. On the whole, the powers of the provinces or regions are broadened. This type of system, combined with a customs union and free trade arrangements, would differ from the current situation only to the extent that "provincial" powers are broadened and the provinces would have more direct "foreign relations" with the outside world. To win such a question, however, the PQ will have to show that it can convince the rest of Canada to negotiate. However, if the rest of Canada agrees to this solution, the likelihood of sovereignty increases. From a sheer bargaining point of view, it is important for Canada to state categorically that this solution is not acceptable, that under no circumstance will it be granted. Anglo Canada views this option as Quebec having its cake and eating it too. Part of this feeling is a genuine emotional reaction; but it is also, without explicitly reconizing it, part of the bargaining process. This may best be described by the phrase "the rationality of irrationality": it is perfectly rational to commit oneself not to do something under any circumstances, but it would be irrational to carry out the commitment when the circumstances arise.*

Canada has a commitment not to grant sovereignty-association. Not permitting that option increases the chances of maintaining the federa-

*If the PQ carried a referendum wherein Quebeckers approved sovereignty-association in principle, but were unable to negotiate, they could very well try to achieve sovereignty unilaterally.

tion. But if the PQ won such a referendum and Ottawa refused to negotiate, Quebec might hold another referendum and convince Quebeckers to support sovereignty. Should separation then occur, it would be irrational not to attempt to make the best of it. This, in effect, depends upon the statesmen and the degree to which Anglo Canada is "locked in." Our current judgement is that the rest of Canada is, in fact, determined not to permit such a solution; and therefore this solution is simply not available because of their emotional commitment. Furthermore, this emotional reaction is likely to be exacerbated by any excessively aggressive tactics by Quebec.

In effect, the PQ is proposing a common market or free trade agreement with the rest of Canada. Sovereignty-association modelled on the relations between Belgium, The Netherlands, and Luxembourg is offered as an example for Canada-Quebec relations, but it certainly is not a perfect or exact one. First of all, Luxembourg plays a role in mitigating confrontation between Belgium and The Netherlands. Secondly, Belgium and Holland are about the same size. Thirdly, we would argue that one of the main reasons for the viability of the Benelux customs union is its broader association with the European Economic Community. If Benelux were on its own, it would have to weave the three economies more closely together, which would mean even closer political co-operation. Furthermore, the EEC itself is pushing for greater political integration.

In the case of Canada, the division would be about 6 million versus 18 million. While a Benelux scenario in which Canada split into larger regional blocs—Western Canada, Central Ontario, Quebec, and the Maritimes—is also conceivable, the additional number of players probably makes the game more difficult.

The loose alliance could include a defence treaty and a great deal of co-ordination on national defence issues. It could, and most certainly would, include monetary union, that is, a common currency. Some type of free trade agreement would be achieved. However, with the U.S. as an important trading partner, "independence" in commercial policy would be constrained by U.S. reaction, as well as by the pattern of world trade and competition in general.

Quebec could negotiate a free trade agreement with the rest of Canada; a partial free trade agreement; or a customs union with rump Canada. A Free Trade Agreement (FTA) would provide for free movement of all goods and some services between Quebec and rump Canada, but Quebec and rump Canada could maintain separate tariffs and import restrictions. This would allow for incremental changes or an evolutionary adjustment of Quebec with the rest of the world.

But to the extent that Quebec's commercial and competition policies

227

differed from those of rump Canada, this approach would require a system of certificates of origin and elaborate value-added criteria to prevent goods from entering Canada cheaply and then ending up in Quebec on a trans-shipment basis. It would also require a set of rules in the FTA agreement governing competition policy to ensure that the benefits of the FTA would not be frustrated by other forms of intervention, except on an agreed basis. This avoidance of "frustration of benefits" is crucial to the continuing viability of any FTA agreement, but obviously it would likely be difficult to negotiate between Quebec and Canada. If Quebec decided to raise the levels of protection for certain industries, it would become vulnerable to retaliation or compensatory measures by other nations. Whether such retaliation or adjustment took place would depend upon how Quebec protected itself.

A partial FTA agreement would involve free trade for some but not all of the trade relations between Quebec and rump Canada. A partial FTA might be acceptable to other nations including the U.S., depending on how it was presented (transitional or permanent), and upon what products were covered. The U.S. has tended to react strongly against partial FTAS, so U.S. commercial policy pressures are to be expected. Moreover, U.S. private interests could seek relief from what they considered to be discrimination against them, by applying counteraction under various provisions of the U.S. Trade Act. This latter threat is probably the most important source of danger to a protective trade policy in Quebec.

A customs union agreement would, in essence, preserve the present trade relationships within Canada; but Quebec would have other forms of economic and political autonomy. A customs union assumes completely free movement of goods and many, but not necessarily all, services. It has a common tariff and level of protection towards the rest of the world. No deviation of external protection is allowed. A customs union would probably not create many frictions with the U.S. or other nations. However, this hybrid type of situation could be quite unstable, and could lead to considerable tensions over the determination of a common tariff and level of protection, "sub-national" and regional aids, subsidies, farm policies, technology policy, monetary policy, etc.

"Do you favour sovereignty association?"

The chances of the PQ winning such a referendum are bleak. If the referendum is lost, the issue is likely to fade away for the next ten years. Separatist sentiment continues, some 10 to 20 per cent of the Quebec population supports separation at least passively, and separation continues to be demanded by an active political organization, but not necessarily the

PQ as presently constituted. Frustrated radicals could revert to violence à *la FLQ*, but this is not widespread.

In the unlikely event that Quebeckers overwhelmingly supported the referendum, the only alternative would probably be "friendly separation." Quebec assumes its fair share of the national debt and federal Crown Corporation property. Francophone minority rights in Canada and Anglophone minority rights in Quebec are carefully protected. Special provisions are made for the Maritimes. As a result of an extraordinary and surprising display of political and economic co-operation, the new arrangement works well, not unlike Scandinavia after Norway separated from Sweden in the early twentieth century. However, the Scandinavian scenario is not an accurate analogy. The relationship of Norway to Sweden and Denmark in the early twentieth century was much more similar to that of Canada to Britain forty years ago than to that of the rest of Canada to Quebec today.

In another version of the same scenario, efforts are made in the same direction; but some bitterness, resentment, and haggling appear. Despite much bad will, the outcome is similar; but no special provisions are made for minority rights or for the Maritimes.

What About Violence?

We have deliberately downplayed more extreme scenarios that describe violent separation.* The reason is not that violence is impossible; the uncertainties are so great and the issues so emotional that even trivial matters could give rise to violence. A situation exists wherein conflicts can be fabricated on practically any subject. But the disutility of violence is also very great, thus making widespread violence much less likely; we feel that violence would have to result from incredibly bad decisions, bad luck or serious emotional over-reaction. We must discuss violent scenarios, however, since they are so often discussed; but we warn the reader that these are what we would call "nightmare scenarios."

In one scenario, a truncation takes place, and those parts of Quebec which choose to stay in Canada do so. In the extreme case, this could be called the Ulster scenario, an extraordinarily elaborate partition whose stability, or even survival, would likely be very tenuous at best.

In both cases, especially in the second version, the Ungava Peninsula might easily be detached. It is not clear whether or not Montreal or part of Ile de Montréal might try to opt out, as very well might some parts of the

---

*We were reluctant to discuss violent scenarios for fear that they would be quoted out of context without the benefit of the caveats mentioned herein. We hope this will not happen.

Eastern Townships, the Ottawa Valley, and Hull. If Quebec goes out, and any significant section of the province wants to stay in Canada and demands the protection of the Canadian government, that government has very little choice but to go along. Irredentism would inevitably flourish in the rump of Quebec.

We must not ignore the possibilities of internal violence within Quebec, prompted by a combination of national and social issues. The Quebec government might push for drastic reforms; and the combination of actual measures for welfare, government ownership, income redistribution, and minimum wages, together with the fear of further such measures, the fear or turmoil because of separation, and the general sense that things may go very badly, causes a gradual erosion of capital investment combined with some flight of capital. Counter-measures by the Quebec government actually exacerbate the problem. The government might even be provoked to some degree by some actions of some other provinces, the Canadian federal government, or even the U.S.; but this is increasingly unlikely in the order given.

In any case, the system becomes almost unviable, and somebody therefore takes action. There could be a counter-democratic movement in which the government is thrown out,* or the current government might try to precipitate the separation issue in order to create a sense of crisis or even violence because of the genuine suffering by the middle class or the workers, particularly if either group becomes very militant, or if they are especially well treated by the provincial government and led to excesses.

An even nastier scenario is a situation wherein independence becomes hopeless, but its supporters have become aroused and turn to violence in desperation. In 1970, Canada had just enough violence to make people sick of it, but not enough to create bitterness. But, here we assume real bitterness as the violence by a tiny minority escalates: English schools resist French teaching or irregular warfare occurs against Canadian transportation (e.g. St. Lawrence Seaway).

One can also imagine an FLQ-type terrorist organization which, even if the PQ government were pushing quite hard for independence, felt that it was just not hard and soon enough or if negotiations were underway, they felt that they were not being conducted "in good faith." Partly to force the PQ's hand and partly to make the situation very uncomfortable, violence could become quite serious. This gang could even emerge from elements now restive within the PQ ranks.

Furthermore, suppose that, for whatever reasons, the PQ movement for constitutional sovereignty fails. The use of force by the federal gov-

---

*A totalitarian government is inconceivable in Quebec. One might have an authoritarian regime, but the pressures for democratic government are likely to prevail.

ernment for whatever reason might be met by force by a small minority of hard core radicals. Conversely, a big danger is that a strong group of French Canadians becomes militantly and violently pro-Confederation. As evidenced by recent events in Uruguay and Ulster, a tiny but devoted and ruthless group with modest acquiescence from a minority of the population can raise hell and destroy liberal government. Such is not entirely beyond the realm of possibility in Quebec, and it is for this reason that neither side in Quebec nor the national government is eager to initiate events which might lead to this outcome.

We have been somewhat cavalier in the above discussion in order to prompt the reader to recognize the different possibilities for Quebec separation. We certainly do not want to overdo the issue of violence. We have focussed on economic and political issues mostly; but in fact one of the great impacts of separation is really not economic or political, but in the realm of the spirit. Most important, a "République du Québec" would be proof that Canada is a failure; the attempt to synthesize two cultures harmoniously over the last two centuries will not have succeeded. Also, the secession of Quebec would be an affront to Canadian national consciousness. Anglophone Canada is already annoyed that an organized and successful political movement in effect says "to hell with your Canada." The secession of Quebec would be a further affront.

We believe that a less important factor, but still worth noticing, is that without Quebec, Canada loses a good part of its distinctive character, especially vis-à-vis the United States. Ironically, most discussions of Confederation have focussed on economic or tangible political costs and advantages. Very little attention has been given to the intrinsic value of belonging to the Canadian nation.

Another cost of Quebec sovereignty is that it almost certainly would mean the rapid destruction of the francophone minorities elsewhere in Canada, except perhaps in the Ottawa Valley and northern New Brunswick. Without Quebec, a bilingualism policy makes no sense, and there is an excellent chance of a sharp backlash against the French language. ("If they want to speak French, let the bastards go to Quebec.") This is a cost that would all too easily be borne by rump Canada.

Perhaps the most interesting question that comes out of a discussion of Quebec is the standard scenario that we consider most likely: a strong majority of Quebeckers opt for staying within Canada. The issue does not disappear altogether but simmers at least for the next decade.

While we do think the standard scenario is the most likely outcome, there is danger that Canadians might give up the "fight" for Canada and Confederation too easily. Complacency might further weaken Canadian nationalist sentiment. Separation could occur by default. Whether or not

Canada is split, Quebec is likely to undergo a period of economic difficulties, partly because of political uncertainty, partly because of labour militancy, partly because of world economic forces. This might reawaken the notion that belonging to a larger unit is better; but then again, unless there is a sense of common purpose or a certain "spirit" of belonging to the large unit, *souverainiste* pressures remain for some time.

The efforts and concessions that will be made to keep Quebec within Canada will probably give French Canadians more status and power. Informal institutions will deal with these issues. The most obvious are the federal-provincial conferences. In effect they give equal representation to the provinces, but also moral leadership to the larger and richer ones. Thus the principles of equal representation yet unequal influences are maintained. Constitutional reform will lead to a "renewed federalism" but we expect this to involve lengthy and rather slow negotiations that could stretch over the better part of the coming decade.

Values

Frequently in this study we have made reference to the fact that, although our individual and national choices are necessarily constrained by objective conditions, what we do and what is done depends largely on what we want to do, which is ultimately derived from what we want as individuals, as a society, and as a nation. In late twentieth-century usage, what we want is conventionally labelled "goals" or "values." Over the past generation, "changing values" has been a major topic of intellectual discourse. The very existence of such a topic is in itself indicative of a culture adrift. Where values are firmly established, they are not the subject of discussion; everybody, or at least everybody who counts, shares them; and the few deviants are ignored or suppressed.

Obviously, such is not the case today. Part of today's internal disputes derive from the co-existence of several differing value systems in the same society, often within the same social class, and occasionally within the same individual. To say the least, this leads to tension.

Most commentators on "changing values" favour them. In effect, they consider it necessary and/or desirable that certain received values be modified or discarded and new values adopted in their place. Advocates of this point of view would hold that the traditional values* of Western culture in general, Canadian civilization in particular, and American civilization most of all are at the very least obsolete and no longer suited to contemporary and emerging conditions. Some would go so far as to maintain that many of the estalished values in our society are fundamentally

---

*By "traditional values" we mean regard for duty, honour, custom, order, restraint, prudence, loyalty to family, church, and nation, and the pursuit of knowledge, technology, and economic growth; by "new values" is meant spontaneity, self-actualization, sensory awareness, equality, concern for self, humanity, and nature, and indifference or opposition to traditional values.

vicious, leading to violence, war, exploitation, racism, sexism, and the pillaging of the natural environment. Conversely, opponents of these "new values" see them as silly, counterproductive, or even depraved. These cultural conservatives, as we must properly call them, since they wish to conserve the established culture, will maintain that it is no accident that a set of values has come down to us and that our civilization cannot function without them.

In this study, we are not going to take sides in this debate. We will merely note some empirical facts and make some forecasts on the basis of past trends and what we believe to be objective social conditions at this time in history. To begin with, it is clear that even when the idea of changing values was most widely discussed in the 1960s, values were not changing so much as was writtten, and were only changing significantly for a relatively thin stratum of the population. The people who experienced these changes tended to associate with others with a similar world view, and they, as do all of us, tended to project their milieu onto the entire population. Yet, most Canadians remained true to the established virtues of patriotism, religion, family, work, deferred gratification, and the like. Most Canadians remained "square."

But we should not exaggerate this squareness or its depth. It is by no means clear how fervently our ancestors believed in these values. The idea of the past as an "age of faith" or of the universal belief in economic man or of general patriotism is a myth. Many, perhaps most, people have always been lukewarm. Only in mythologies of a "golden age" is humanity free of hedonism, selfishness, skepticism, and malingering, both physical and moral. While the "new values" transform many of the previous "vices" into "virtues," these were not invented in the mid-twentieth century, but have always been with us.

We would also argue that it is unchallengeable that contemporary economic and social life *permits* the emergence of new values. An Indian tribe on the verge of starvation in a continuous war against nature could not permit its members to indulge in behaviour that would weaken the organized strength of the community, nor did those objective conditions permit the generation and dissemination of ideas non-functional to those roles. Among primitive peoples, the community is everything and the individual nothing except as part of that community. This situation can be said to have survived up through our colonial period. Only with the Industrial Revolution has the productive power of the economy been sufficient to permit the expansion of individualism in all its forms, positive and negative.

Many writers early in the twentieth century maintained that the increasingly complex social order would require a more collective life and

234

appropriate collective ideologies, such as socialism and fascism. In fact, the converse has been true. Our systems do indeed require a large amount of collective behaviour, but that seems to be accomplished more or less painlessly (although there are strains); and the system functions so well that we can afford much more individualism. Economic activity is almost by definition collective; it consists of co-operative endeavours. Work is what we do for others; fun is what we do for ourselves. As the work week shrinks, more time is devoted to individual pleasure. Similarly, except in the shrinking agricultural sector, the family is no longer a viable economic unit; and its ties seem to be weakening fairly obviously. Whether these changes are good or bad is, of course, a question of values; whether they represent progress or decadence we leave to the reader. But it seems clear that the increased wealth and productive capacity of our systems has permitted the emergence of these new values.

Some empirical evidence to support the association of affluence with progressive values can be seen in this country in this century. Periods of rapid economic advance and great prosperity have seen the emergence of "liberated" values and lifestyles—the 1900s, 1920s and the 1960s; war times and relative hard times—the 1930s and 1970s—see a reinforcement of traditional views that life is tough, competitive, and hard, and that a high degree of social cohesion and subordination of the individual to the group is necessary to survive and to achieve collective and individual goals.

The association of prosperity with new values also gains some support from national comparisons within North America. Canada developed faster than the States during the 1960s, and rapidly became much more progressive in many ways. Similarly, Quebec's breakout from traditionalism occurred in a period of rapid economic advance. The American progressive wave crested much earlier than ours, perhaps because its boom ended earlier. The States began consolidating, economically, socially, culturally, and politically in the late sixties; Canada began to move the same way in the mid seventies when its boom collapsed. This, we believe, is the explanation of why the great expectations for "new values" in the 1960s seem to have come to nought, and that the late 1970s are a period of a widespread conservative mood.

So it seems to us that the short-term projection is conservative; we label it "neo-conservative" and remark that it is by no means distinctively Canadian, but worldwide. The entire world, but especially the bourgeois West, is undergoing one of its occasional periods of consolidation.

The Short-Term Neo-Conservative Trend

We find that the term "neo-conservative" sometimes stirs up misinterpretations. It does not mean that the world is going back to the 1950s or that the reforms and changes of the 1960s will disappear. It does not mean that we are going back to a period of traditional patriotism and laissez-faire economics if we ever had them. Above all, it does not mean that the country will be dominated by conservatives and much less by Conservatives. The importance of the neo-conservative wave is that people who believe themselves to be liberal or progressive are increasingly concerned with what historically have been considered to be conservative issues–order, production, fiscal responsibility, defence of received values and established institutions, the maintenance of privilege and standards, and concern with the very survival of the nation.

If the reader doubts that this is the case, we refer him to movements in the political scene. Intelligent politicians in a democracy respond to the "political market"; and it is obvious that they perceive that the polity is becoming increasingly conservative. One can also look at the media. Journalists pride themselves on their ability to move with or even anticipate short-term trends. The tone of our national press is increasingly conservative; and in some cases one can even see hints of the contempt of those who consider themselves "up-to-date" for "squares" in their attitudes towards people who continue to espouse the fashionable views of the 1960s.

But perhaps the most important evidence of the neo-conservative movement in Canadian society is the reader himself. The educated Canadian of the sort who is likely to read this book is almost certainly more concerned about the traditional issues than he was five or ten years ago. Obviously, the recession and the threats to Confederation have had a powerful effect on his thinking, but we must remember that this trend is not limited to Canada alone.

Another piece of evidence of the neo-conservative trend is found in examination of the political left and cultural radicals. Not only is the left smaller, but it is far less vigorous. It no longer has sanguine expectations of remaking society in the foreseeable future. It remains dissatisfied and restless; it has not lost its urge for fundamental reform of the system, but it doubts that reform will be achieved in its own lifetime. One of the most interesting things going on in the world today is that a good part of the political left has abandoned its hope for social justice through powerful government; leftists are increasingly concerned that big government will necessarily be exploitative of the people. This was the anarchist response to Marxism a century ago; it is continually being rediscovered (as by the

236

"nouveaux philosophes" in France today), and the rediscovery of the potential for exploitation through socialism is one of the stigmata of conservative eras.

The Rediscovery of Economics

The most obvious evidence of the neo-conservative phenomenon is the rediscovery of the most elementary economics: you do not get something for nothing; human desires are insatiable; there is not enough to go around; men and nations must work to live; you cannot live beyond your means; and life is tough and competitive, between nations and individuals. Also, we are rediscovering fundamental economic roles: that the function of labour is working, not striking; that in a capitalistic system, capitalists must make profits; and that government regulation and redistribution presumes somebody else's production to regulate or redistribute. Thus, we have a reaffirmation of the importance of productivity, fiscal responsibility, and the need for capital and investment. Obviously, the most important single factor is the domestic economic situation; but like all of the neo-conservative trend, this is by no means limited to Canada. Indeed, Canada is lagging behind the U.S. and Europe in this regard, but we can already see it here.

Counter-attacks Against Government

Related to this are the counter-attacks which are developing against the expansion of government activity during the past decade. Opposition is building to high taxes, environmental restrictions, other government regulations, "excessive" welfare, and what is increasingly viewed as overweening, bloated, and insensitive government. While we do not believe that these counter-attacks will substantially lessen government (at least in our standard scenario), they indicate an important shift of mood. Even bureaucrats complain about big government. It is hardly possible that the objective performance of government has so much worsened during the last three years; it must be that our perceptions have changed.

The End of the Counterculture

Where have all the flower children gone? To a large degree, the "social" factors that dominated the culture and polity in the 1960s are waning in importance. Partially this is due to the triumph of the "new" progressive/permissive values, but it is also partially due to the fact that some people feel that things have gone too far. Most aspects of the joy/love/new values counterculture have been either selectively absorbed into the mainstream or have trickled away. Canadians are much more informal in their dress, social manners, and public ritual; but the movement towards the

237

new values has certainly slowed, and probably halted, and in a few cases even reversed. Today, it seems incredible that presumably serious people once believed that a new culture was being constructed of marijuana, rock music, long hair, and blue jeans.

Most of the social aspects of the counterculture are "topping out," and some are experiencing a counter-attack. As near as anyone can tell from visible manifestations, open displays of sexual promiscuity seem to have peaked, and the public seems no longer to tolerate the spread of pornography. It is conceivable that no general liberalization of gambling or further liberalization of alcohol laws will take place; indeed, some provinces are now attempting to raise the drinking age. While the current *de facto* legalization of marijuana use may be followed by *de jure* decriminalization, drug use is no longer fashionable, is no longer believed to stimulate creativity, and has probably peaked.

The mini-religious revival is most striking. Never mind the widely publicized conversion of ex-hippies to "the Moonies," Hari Krishna, "Jesus freaks," "Jews for Jesus," and the like–for every one of them a hundred Canadians are more actively participating in traditional orthodox or fundamentalist religious experience, ranging from Quebec's "Mouvement Charismatique" to the million or more regular audience of the radio and T.V. evangelists. Moreover, the mainstream Christian churches, which for a generation have been dominated by elements who saw the church's role as promoting secular redemption ("The NDP at prayer") are rediscovering orthodoxy, and now are placing more emphasis on pastoral service and, yes, even the salvation of souls. The Roman Catholic Church is consolidating the reforms of Vatican II.

Again, Canada is not experiencing a return to the previous moral-cultural-social disposition, nor do we believe that it will; but it is retrenching and selectively reversing some of the reforms of the 1960s and early 1970s. A mild counter-reformation is in progress.

Concern with Security and Order

It is difficult now to recall that scarcely a decade ago it was almost beyond the pale of respectable discussion to hold that the necessary steps against crime were punitive. Today, the situation is reversing. In the same circles, people who deploy clichés about "correcting underlying social conditions" are considered naive. Establishment opinion has shifted markedly, reflecting one aspect of this neo-conservative trend. This, of course, is reflected in the loss of faith in the possibilities of rehabilitating criminals through humane treatment. Related is the recent gun-control legislation

238

which must be interpreted as an internal security more than an anti-crime measure. The resurgence of corporal punishment in the schools is relevant here, as illustrated in the recent debate in Alberta.

Increased Emphasis on International Security

The concern for security is not only internal, but international. The Western world is coming out of what is viewed as an over-reaction to the Vietnam War, and is becoming increasingly concerned with the real or potential threat implied by expansion of the quantity and quality of Soviet armed forces. In 1976-77, for the first time in this decade, defence spending increased in real dollars. This, we project, is just the beginning. It would be certainly implausible to expect a return to the spending level of the 1950s (in real dollars or in percentage of GNP), but the expansion will be significant. Also, the U.S. is going to invest substantially in new weapons systems over the next decade, some of which will spill over to Canadian manufacturing.

A Reaffirmation of Standards

A central part of what Herman Kahn has called the "counter-reformation" is a reaction against some of the presumed excesses of the 1960s. As we recall, that was a period in which the dominant concerns were for liberating people from artificial and stifling requirements, so that they would be able to develop their full personal potential. It is today believed that the performance of those liberated people has been disappointing, to say the least. Take, for example, the presumption that students would perform better doing what they wanted to do. This reasoning was behind the widespread curtailment of required courses and the expansion of electives in schools. Of course, many were skeptical of this approach, and now their position is becoming dominant. Today, it is increasingly felt that performance is best achieved through the possession of formal skills which can only be achieved through discipline applied externally and hopefully adopted internally. Hence, the present "back-to-basics" movement in the schools.

The Re-establishment of Authority

This is more subtle and more questionable than many of the above, but it seems to us that a strong case can be made that there is at least the beginnings of an effort to re-establish authority for traditional values and institutions. By this we mean that critical attitudes towards Canadian values and institutions are becoming muted and discredited, while positive approaches are being pushed forward.* In the 1960s, it was almost an article of faith in enlightened circles to point out our shortcomings; today, many people are having second thoughts, and seem to be saying that things are not as bad as all that, despite considerable problems.

Renewed Emphasis on Class Interests

One of the subtler aspects of the neo-conservative wave is one which we have not seen discussed in print and have some difficulty in formulating carefully. It seems to us that, as a reaction to levelling and some of the more grotesque manifestations of egalitarianism, some Canadians are beginning to get their backs up, and are becoming more agreeable to programs and attitudes which are very definitely and explicitly in their narrow self-interest. The most obvious manifestation of this tendency may sound odd to the reader: it is the "limits-to-growth" movement as expressed in what we have earlier called localism—for some, a useful ideological justification for the haves keeping out the have nots.

One must not disregard what seems to us to be an increased awareness of class, a rejection of equal opportunity, and a resurgence of the belief that, yes, indeed, there are some people (i.e. "us") who are more valuable to the society than are others. One aspect of this is the revival of hereditarian ideas, discredited since the defeat of their pathological version in National Socialism. Which is the "correct" side in the I.Q. argument is, we believe, less important than the fact that it has appeared. Related to this is the resurgence of theories justifying punitive rather than rehabilitative measures for dealing with crime. Also relevant is the loss of vigour of ideas of "community control" and "participation" in favour of traditional forms of representative government and decision making by presumably trained and enlightened experts.

After the Neo-Conservative Period

The reader has certainly already noticed more than a little discrepancy between the long-term trends mentioned earlier and the short-term trends going on at the present time, and has concluded that an obvious area of attention is the potential for movement from the present neo-conservative consolidation back to the long-term trend. How will that be achieved and when? Before going too far into that subject, let us consider

*An idea that is constantly recurring in the national unity debate is that Canada has not put enough emphasis on traditional values such as patriotism, and attached too little importance to official symbols and institutions. There is likely to be less tolerance for those who question these symbols in the future and less acceptance of disruptive minority groups.

briefly the possibility that these current manifestations of the conservative mood are the harbinger of a fundamental change in many of the long-term trends. It is intellectually conceivable that the long progressive period of the last two hundred years has crested, and that we are moving into a new phase of long-term consolidation of western industrial civilization. We think this view is untenable on several grounds. First, this sort of thing has happened before. Second, if we are entering a new period it is incredibly odd that we have no new ideas to embody a new world-view. We think a fair assessment of the thought of the leading thinkers of today is that it is a sometimes interesting and sometimes thoughtful rehash of some very old ideas. We are drinking very old wine in some not-so-new bottles.

Furthermore, the present situation seems to us to be extremely shallow and unstable. There have been no distinguished neo-conservative or conservative political leaders or even a political movement. Most of our politicians are turning carefully to the right, probably behind the nation, just as they moved too slowly to the left a decade ago. The present period has very few positive moral or morale aspects. There is a widespread grumbling and surliness in the system, a sense that the country and the world is treading water. All manner of groups seem to be exhausted by the exertions of the 1960s, which is all the more disturbing because those exertions and disturbances were trivial and one would not think that they would tire a healthy culture.

The current quiescence and conformity of youth has little beneficial content. The campus atmosphere does not so much reflect any positive value on the part of the students as a whining and careerist withdrawal into cynicism and self-interest, what the journalist Tom Wolfe called "the ME generation." If the representative student of the 1960s was the campus radical, today perhaps it is the aspiring medical student who sabotages his competitors' chemistry experiments.

So we suggest that Canada will experience a shift, perhaps a very rapid, almost revolutionary shift out of this period back onto the long-term trend. In other words, there is a possibility of a replay of the 1960s, but perhaps even more vigorous and violent. Today, there is a loosely organized but active, radical-left, potentially revolutionary opposition eager to move. Worse, examples from throughout the world have shown how effective, at least from the point of view of "the symbolism of the act," terrorism can be.

But perhaps most interesting is that, by the late 1980s, the "veterans" of the 1960s will be moving towards positions of operational authority in Canada. They will then be in their mid forties, not in the positions that make decisions, but in the middle levels which are necessary to supply

241

information to the powerful and to see that the decisions are carried out effectively. To a large degree they were influenced by the experience of the 1960s; and although they have matured, many of them will have felt that they have to some degree sold out and, in any event, will almost certainly find it difficult to consider young people espousing views similar to their own as dangerous enemies of society who need to be crushed. (There is nothing especially sinister in this attitude. Most groups in history have been a little soft on extremists who appear to be on their side—witness the attitudes of conservative German nationalist bureaucrats and professors towards the young "idealistic" Nazis during Weimar Germany—but its effects may be extremely dangerous.) The middle managers of the 1960s were veterans of the Second World War, products of quite a different milieu. Look how ineffectively they dealt with dissidents; what can be expected of ex-radical sympathizers?

But what is certain to appear at some time before the end of this century is a return to a reformist period which will bring up again "new values" which seemed central to the culture, society, polity in the 1960s: justice rather than efficiency, freedom rather than order, peace rather than defence, self-actualization rather than duty, and the like. We are not prepared to put a date on when this will occur nor would it be plausible to try to determine how one could judge whether it has appeared; but it seems to us that when the present neo-conservative period of consolidation ends and the new reformist wave appears depends largely on the progress of the period of consolidation. We presume that the re-emergence of new values is "scenario-dependent," i.e., it depends on the rate of economic recovery. Everyone agrees that this has to be worldwide, and must be led by the United States. And herein lies a threat to Canada: The U.S. has been economically out of phase with Canada for a decade, and culturally out of phase as well. Only now are the American neo-conservative ideas spilling over the border. What if the Americans get very far ahead of us economically? One of the most dangerous things that could happen to Canada is that the U.S. comes out of the recession faster than we do, begins to move back towards the new values in accordance with its new prosperity, and we track with it even though we lack the prosperous economic base to underpin it. The U.S. is so large and rich that it can tolerate very many economic, social, and cultural inefficiencies. We cannot. We must live closer to the bone to remain competitive. Paradoxically, if we are to live as well as Americans, we cannot think like them.

But on the other hand, we are a much more deferential and tolerant people. Canada can absorb and channel change more easily. Sometime soon in historical terms—possibly the mid 1980s—Canada will move back towards the new values of personal liberation and the rejection of tribal and economic man; and we will take another halting step towards earthly paradise, or pandemonium.

As in so many other subjects, perhaps John Maynard Keynes said it best:*

> I see us free, therefore, to return to some of the most sure and certain principles of religion and traditional virtue – that avarice is a vice, that the exaction of usury is a misdemeanour, and the love of money is detestable, that those walk most truly in the paths of virtue and sane wisdom who take least thought for the morrow. We shall once more value ends above means and prefer the good to the useful. We shall honour those who can teach us how to pluck the hour and the day virtuously and well, the delightful people who are capable of taking direct enjoyment in things, the lilies of the field who toil not, neither do they spin.
>
> But beware! The time for all this is not yet. For at least another hundred years we must pretend to ourselves and to every one that fair is foul and foul fair; for foul is useful and fair is not. Avarice and usury and precaution must be our gods for a little longer still. For only they can lead us out of the tunnel of economic necessity into daylight.

"Not yet," according to Lord Keynes. "Not ever," according to the traditionalists. But certainly *not now*!

*"Economic Possibilities for Our Grandchildren." (1930)

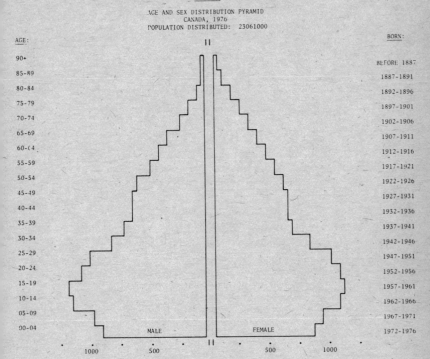

Chart 1

AGE AND SEX DISTRIBUTION PYRAMID
CANADA, 1976
POPULATION DISTRIBUTED: 23061000

AGE:		BORN:
90+		BEFORE 1887
85-89		1887-1891
80-84		1892-1896
75-79		1897-1901
70-74		1902-1906
65-69		1907-1911
60-64		1912-1916
55-59		1917-1921
50-54		1922-1926
45-49		1927-1931
40-44		1932-1936
35-39		1937-1941
30-34		1942-1946
25-29		1947-1951
20-24		1952-1956
15-19		1957-1961
10-14		1962-1966
05-09		1967-1971
00-04		1972-1976

MALE   FEMALE

1000   500   500   1000

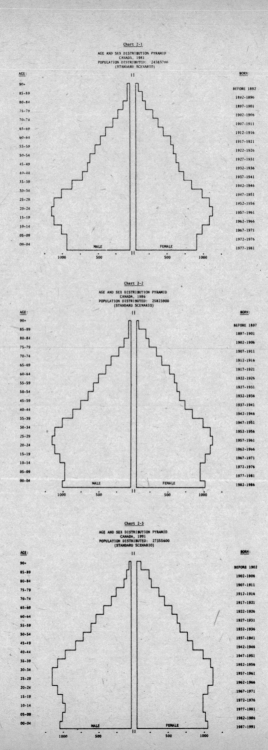

Chart 2-1

AGE AND SEX DISTRIBUTION PYRAMID
CANADA, 1981
POPULATION DISTRIBUTED: 24583700
(STANDARD SCENARIO)

AGE:		BORN:
90+		
85-89		BEFORE 1892
80-84		1892-1896
75-79		1897-1901
70-74		1902-1906
65-69		1907-1911
60-64		1912-1916
55-59		1917-1921
50-54		1922-1926
45-49		1927-1931
40-44		1932-1936
35-39		1937-1941
30-34		1942-1946
25-29		1947-1951
20-24		1952-1956
15-19		1957-1961
10-14		1962-1966
05-09		1967-1971
00-04		1972-1976
	MALE FEMALE	1977-1981

1000   500   500   1000

Chart 2-2

AGE AND SEX DISTRIBUTION PYRAMID
CANADA, 1986
POPULATION DISTRIBUTED: 25823900
(STANDARD SCENARIO)

AGE:		BORN:
90+		
85-89		BEFORE 1897
80-84		1897-1901
75-79		1902-1906
70-74		1907-1911
65-69		1912-1916
60-64		1917-1921
55-59		1922-1926
50-54		1927-1931
45-49		1932-1936
40-44		1937-1941
35-39		1942-1946
30-34		1947-1951
25-29		1952-1956
20-24		1957-1961
15-19		1962-1966
10-14		1967-1971
05-09		1972-1976
00-04		1977-1981
	MALE FEMALE	1982-1986

1000   500   500   1000

Chart 2-3

AGE AND SEX DISTRIBUTION PYRAMID
CANADA, 1991
POPULATION DISTRIBUTED: 27355600
(STANDARD SCENARIO)

AGE:		BORN:
90+		
85-89		BEFORE 1902
80-84		1902-1906
75-79		1907-1911
70-74		1912-1916
65-69		1917-1921
60-64		1922-1926
55-59		1927-1931
50-54		1932-1936
45-49		1937-1941
40-44		1942-1946
35-39		1947-1951
30-34		1952-1956
25-29		1957-1961
20-24		1962-1966
15-19		1967-1971
10-14		1972-1976
05-09		1977-1981
00-04		1982-1986
	MALE FEMALE	1987-1991

1000   500   500   1000

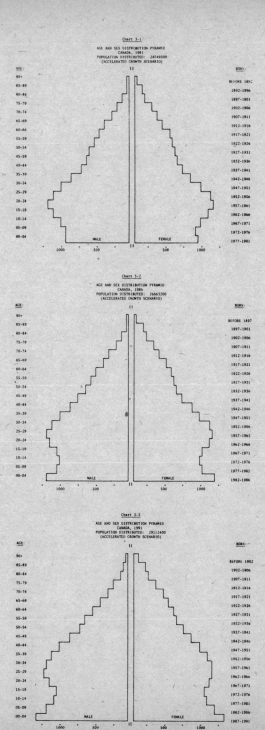

Chart 3-1

AGE AND SEX DISTRIBUTION PYRAMID
CANADA, 1981
POPULATION DISTRIBUTED: 24549300
(ACCELERATED GROWTH SCENARIO)

AGE: BORN:

90+   BEFORE 1892
85-89   1892-1896
80-84   1897-1901
75-79   1902-1906
70-74   1907-1911
65-69   1912-1916
60-64   1917-1921
55-59   1922-1926
50-54   1927-1931
45-49   1932-1936
40-44   1937-1941
35-39   1942-1946
30-34   1947-1951
25-29   1952-1956
20-24   1957-1961
15-19   1962-1966
10-14   1967-1971
05-09   1972-1976
00-04   1977-1981
              MALE   FEMALE
     1000   500   500   1000

Chart 3-2

AGE AND SEX DISTRIBUTION PYRAMID
CANADA, 1986
POPULATION DISTRIBUTED: 26663200
(ACCELERATED GROWTH SCENARIO)

AGE: BORN:

90+   BEFORE 1897
85-89   1897-1901
80-84   1902-1906
75-79   1907-1911
70-74   1912-1916
65-69   1917-1921
60-64   1922-1926
55-59   1927-1931
50-54   1932-1936
45-49   1937-1941
40-44   1942-1946
35-39   1947-1951
30-34   1952-1956
25-29   1957-1961
20-24   1962-1966
15-19   1967-1971
10-14   1972-1976
05-09   1977-1981
00-04   1982-1986
              MALE   FEMALE
     1000   500   500   1000

Chart 3-3

AGE AND SEX DISTRIBUTION PYRAMID
CANADA, 1991
POPULATION DISTRIBUTED: 29112400
(ACCELERATED GROWTH SCENARIO)

AGE: BORN:

90+   BEFORE 1902
85-89   1902-1906
80-84   1907-1911
75-79   1912-1916
70-74   1917-1921
65-69   1922-1926
60-64   1927-1931
55-59   1932-1936
50-54   1937-1941
45-49   1942-1946
40-44   1947-1951
35-39   1952-1956
30-34   1957-1961
25-29   1962-1966
20-24   1967-1971
15-19   1972-1976
10-14   1977-1981
05-09   1982-1986
00-04   1987-1991
              MALE   FEMALE
     1000   500   500   1000

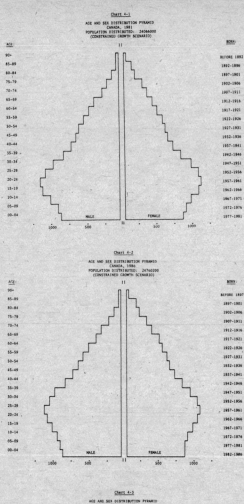

Chart 4-1

AGE AND SEX DISTRIBUTION PYRAMID
CANADA, 1981
POPULATION DISTRIBUTED: 24066000
(CONSTRAINED GROWTH SCENARIO)

AGE:

90+	BEFORE 1892
85-89	1892-1896
80-84	1897-1901
75-79	1902-1906
70-74	1907-1911
65-69	1912-1916
60-64	1917-1921
55-59	1922-1926
50-54	1927-1931
45-49	1932-1936
40-44	1937-1941
35-39	1942-1946
30-34	1947-1951
25-29	1952-1956
20-24	1957-1961
15-19	1962-1966
10-14	1967-1971
05-09	1972-1976
00-04	1977-1981

MALE   FEMALE

1000   500   500   1000

BORN:

Chart 4-2

AGE AND SEX DISTRIBUTION PYRAMID
CANADA, 1986
POPULATION DISTRIBUTED: 24760200
(CONSTRAINED GROWTH SCENARIO)

AGE:

90+	BEFORE 1897
85-89	1897-1901
80-84	1902-1906
75-79	1907-1911
70-74	1912-1916
65-69	1917-1921
60-64	1922-1926
55-59	1927-1931
50-54	1932-1936
45-49	1937-1941
40-44	1942-1946
35-39	1947-1951
30-34	1952-1956
25-29	1957-1961
20-24	1962-1966
15-19	1967-1971
10-14	1972-1976
05-09	1977-1981
00-04	1982-1986

MALE   FEMALE

1000   500   500   1000

BORN:

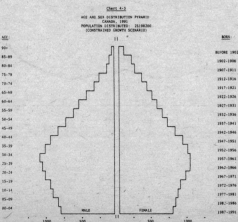

Chart 4-3

AGE AND SEX DISTRIBUTION PYRAMID
CANADA, 1991
POPULATION DISTRIBUTED: 25198200
(CONSTRAINED GROWTH SCENARIO)

AGE:

90+	BEFORE 1902
85-89	1902-1906
80-84	1907-1911
75-79	1912-1916
70-74	1917-1921
65-69	1922-1926
60-64	1927-1931
55-59	1932-1936
50-54	1937-1941
45-49	1942-1946
40-44	1947-1951
35-39	1952-1956
30-34	1957-1961
25-29	1962-1966
20-24	1967-1971
15-19	1972-1976
10-14	1977-1981
05-09	1982-1986
00-04	1987-1991

MALE   FEMALE

1000   500   500   1000

BORN:

Chart 5

INDICATORS OF PRESSURE ON CAPACITY

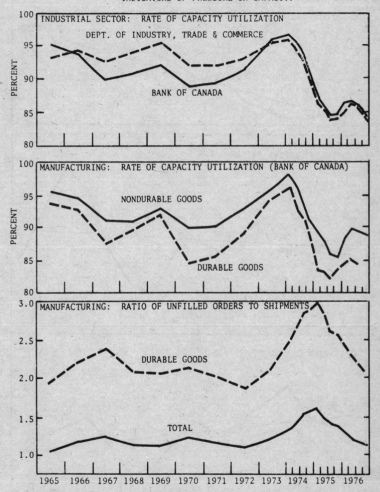

SOURCE: BANK OF CANADA MONTHLY REVIEWS; INDUSTRY, TRADE AND COMMERCE
          CAPACITY INDEX; STATISTICS CANADA.

Chart 6

LABOUR INCOME AND PROFITS
(PERCENT OF GNP)

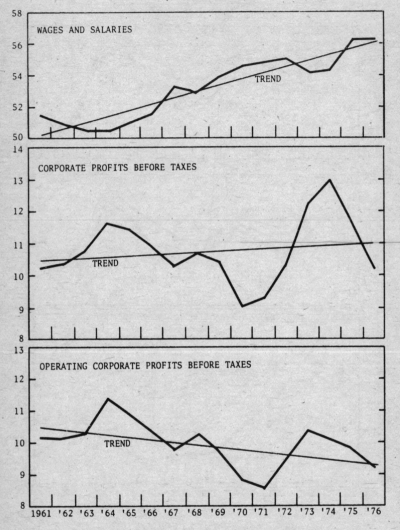

SOURCE: STATISTICS CANADA.

250

Chart 7

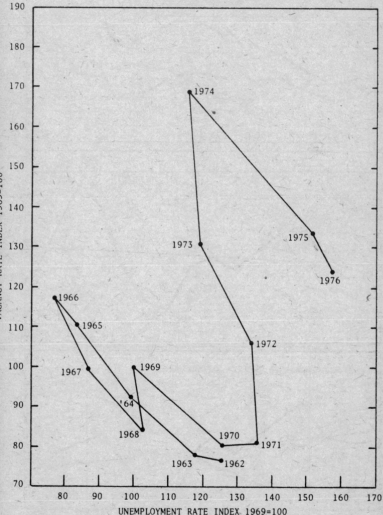

RELATIONSHIP BETWEEN
THE UNEMPLOYMENT AND VACANCY RATES

SOURCE: DEPARTMENT OF FINANCE.

251

Chart 8

UNEMPLOYMENT

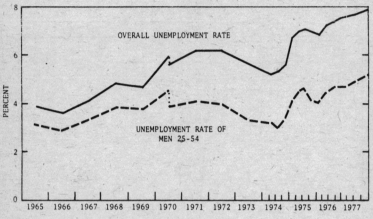

SOURCE: BASED ON DATA FROM STATISTICS CANADA.

Chart 10

TREND IN TOTAL GOVERNMENT
TRANSFERS TO PERSONS
IN 1961 DOLLARS

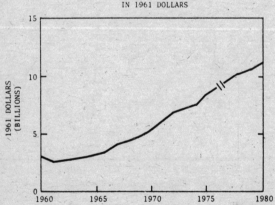

Chart 9

TOTAL GOVERNMENT TRANSFERS TO PERSONS SINCE 1960
CANADA: TREND AND PROJECTIONS

NOTES: 1960-1970 FIGURES FOR A, AND PROJECTIONS FOR B
AND C ARE DERIVED FROM ECONOMIC COUNCIL OF CANADA,
NINTH ANNUAL REVIEW, APPENDIX A, PP. 294, 299,
319. PROJECTION B'S ASSUMPTIONS INCLUDED AVERAGE
ANNUAL INFLATION, 1973-1980 OF 4% AND ROUGHLY 4%
UNEMPLOYMENT. PROJECTION C ASSUMED ABOUT 3%
INFLATION AND A RISE IN UNEMPLOYMENT TO 6% (1976=
5.6%).

1971-1973 FIGURES ARE DERIVED FROM ECC, ELEVENTH
ANNUAL REVIEW, P. 32. ESTIMATES FOR 1974-1976
ARE DERIVED FROM FEDERAL DATA IN BUDGET PAPERS,
MAY 25, 1976. THE PROVINCIAL-MUNICIPAL SHARE OF
TRANSFERS IS ASSUMED TO DECLINE TO 38% BY 1976
(FROM 47% IN 1972 AND 41% IN 1973). IF THE DECLINE
IS GREATER, THE TOTALS SHOWN ON THE GRAPH ARE TOO
HIGH. ON THE OTHER HAND, THE FEDERAL FIGURE FOR
1976 WAS A FORECAST AND MAY BE EXPECTED TO HAVE
UNDERSTATED UNEMPLOYMENT PAYMENTS.

THE EXTENSION OF A IS BASED ON A SIMPLE ASSUMPTION
OF A 13% INCREASE IN 1977 AND 09% ANNUAL INCREASES
THEREAFTER. SINCE MOST TRANSFER PAYMENTS ARE
INDEXED TO PRICES OR WAGES, THESE ASSUMPTIONS
SUGGEST INFLATION IN THE 5-6% RANGE, OR PROGRAM
MODIFICATIONS WITH COUNTERBALANCING EFFECT.

COMPONENTS OF THE TRANSFERS TO PERSONS CATEGORY
ARE DISCUSSED IN ECC, TENTH ANNUAL REVIEW, P. 32.
MEDICAL CARE AND OTHER "IN KIND" BENEFITS ARE
NOT INCLUDED.

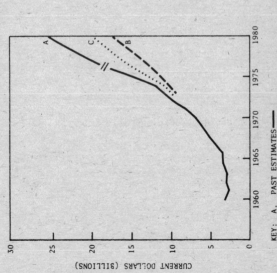

KEY: A.   PAST ESTIMATES
      B.   ECC "CHAPTER 4" PROJECTIONS
      C.   ECC "HIGH TRANSFER PAYMENTS"
            PROJECTION

Table I

NATIONAL POPULATION

(thousands)

	A	B	C
1976	23061	23061	23061
1981	24549	24384	24066
1986	26663	25824	24760
1991	29113	27355	25195
1996	31642	28824	25358

A - Accelerated growth scenario

B - Standard scenario

C - Constrained growth scenario

Table 2

POPULATION PROJECTIONS - ATLANTIC PROVINCES

	A	B	C
NFLD	**(1976 - 553,000)**		
1981	582,000	580,000	570,000
1986	623,000	608,000	579,000
1991	672,000	638,000	581,000
1996	720,000	665,000	577,000
P.E.I.	**(1976 - 120,000)**		
1981	118,000	120,000	116,000
1986	118,000	119,000	109,000
1991	117,000	118,000	102,000
1996	115,000	113,000	92,000
N.S.	**(1976 - 830,000)**		
1981	829,000	837,000	812,000
1986	840,000	843,000	779,000
1991	852,000	847,000	736,000
1996	854,000	843,000	683,000
N.B.	**(1976 - 692,000)**		
1981	734,000	729,000	719,000
1986	794,000	770,000	737,000
1991	864,000	814,000	747,000
1996	935,000	855,000	749,000
TOTAL ATLANTIC	**(1976 - 2,195,000)**		
1981	2,263,000	2,266,000	2,217,000
1986	2,375,000	2,340,000	2,204,000
1991	2,505,000	2,417,000	2,166,000
1996	2,624,000	2,479,000	2,101,000

Table 3

QUE.　(1976 - 6,229,000)

	A	B	C
1981	6,517,000	6,479,000	6,382,000
1986	6,955,000	6,748,000	6,444,000
1991	7,459,000	7,028,000	6,434,000
1996	7,981,000	7,279,000	6,351,000

Table 4

ONT.　(1976 - 8,327,000)

	A	B	C
1981	8,982,000	8,927,000	8,799,000
1986	9,883,000	9,584,000	9,164,000
1991	10,930,000	10,290,000	9,439,000
1996	12,030,000	10,986,000	9,614,000

· Table 5

POPULATION PROJECTIONS - WESTERN PROVINCES

	A	B	C
MANITOBA (1976 - 1,021,000)			
1981	1,012,000	1,005,000	1,001,000
1986	1,039,000	1,003,000	984,000
1991	1,053,000	1,008,000	968,000
1996	1,071,000	994,000	924,000
SASKATCHEWAN (1976 - 922,000)			
1981	874,000	868,000	856,000
1986	832,000	803,000	796,000
1991	781,000	734,000	718,000
1996	710,000	647,000	599,000
ALBERTA (1976 - 1,838,000)			
1981	2,107,000	2,008,000	1,978,000
1986	2,381,000	2,170,000	2,099,000
1991	2,721,000	2,406,000	2,198,000
1996	3,039,000	2,592,000	2,305,000
BRITISH COLUMBIA (1976 - 2,468,000)			
1981	2,727,000	2,764,000	2,767,000
1986	3,120,000	3,101,000	2,996,000
1991	3,574,000	3,389,000	3,196,000
1996	4,101,000	3,754,000	3,382,000
TOTAL WEST (1976 - 6,250,000)			
1981	6,720,000	6,645,000	6,602,000
1986	7,373,000	7,077,000	6,875,000
1991	8,129,000	7,537,000	7,080,000
1996	8,921,000	7,987,000	7,210,000

Table 6

POPULATION PROJECTIONS - TERRITORIES
(1976 EST. - 60,000)

	A	B	C
1981	68,000	67,000	67,000
1986	78,000	75,000	73,000
1991	91,000	83,000	78,000
1996	104,000	92,000	83,000

Table 7

REGIONAL POPULATION PROJECTIONS
(THOUSANDS)

	ATLANTIC	QUEBEC	ONTARIO	WEST	CANADA
ACCELERATED GROWTH SCENARIO					
1976	2,195 (10%)	6,229 (27%)	8,327 (36%)	6,250 (27%)	23,061
1981	2,263 (9%)	6,517 (27%)	8,982 (37%)	6,720 (27%)	24,549
1986	2,375 (9%)	6,955 (26%)	9,883 (37%)	7,373 (28%)	26,663
1991	2,505 (9%)	7,459 (26%)	10,930 (38%)	8,129 (28%)	29,113
1996	2,624 (8%)	7,961 (25%)	12,030 (38%)	8,921 (28%)	31,642
STANDARD SCENARIO					
1976	2,195 (10%)	6,229 (27%)	8,327 (36%)	6,250 (27%)	23,061
1981	2,266 (9%)	6,479 (27%)	8,927 (37%)	6,645 (27%)	24,384
1986	2,340 (9%)	6,748 (26%)	9,584 (37%)	7,077 (27%)	25,824
1991	2,417 (9%)	7,028 (26%)	10,290 (38%)	7,537 (28%)	27,355
1996	2,479 (9%)	7,279 (25%)	10,986 (38%)	7,987 (28%)	28,824
CONSTRAINED GROWTH SCENARIO					
1976	2,195 (10%)	6,229 (27%)	8,327 (36%)	6,250 (27%)	23,061
1981	2,217 (9%)	6,382 (27%)	8,799 (37%)	6,602 (27%)	24,066
1986	2,204 (9%)	6,444 (26%)	9,164 (37%)	6,875 (28%)	24,760
1991	2,166 (9%)	6,434 (26%)	9,439 (37%)	7,080 (28%)	25,195
1996	2,101 (8%)	6,351 (25%)	9,614 (38%)	7,210 (28%)	25,358

Table 8

TORONTO METRO POPULATION
(1976 EST. - 2,831,000)

	A	B	C
1981	3,160,000	3,169,000	3,121,000
1986	3,486,000	3,438,000	3,283,000
1991	3,868,000	3,725,000	3,411,000

Table 9

HAMILTON METRO POPULATION
(1976 EST. - 530, 000)

	A	B	C
1981	570,000	572,000	563,000
1986	612,000	603,000	576,000
1991	660,000	636,000	582,000

Table 10

KITCHENER METRO POPULATION
(1976 EST. - 261,000)

	A	B	C
1981	298,000	299,000	295,000
1986	343,000	338,000	323,000
1991	396,000	382,000	349,000

Table 11

ST. CATHARINES METRO POPULATION
(1976 EST. - 322,000)

	A	B	C
1981	342,000	343,000	338,000
1986	366,000	361,000	345,000
1991	396,000	381,000	349,000

Table 12

MONTREAL METRO POPULATION
(1976 EST. - 2,821,000)

	A	B	C
1981	2,884,000	2,865,000	2,826,000
1986	3,110,000	3,008,000	2,878,000
1991	3,367,000	3,156,000	2,896,000

Table 13

VANCOUVER METRO POPULATION
(1976 EST. - 1,156,000)

	A	B	C
1981	1,319,000	1,292,000	1,270,000
1986	1,475,000	1,391,000	1,325,000
1991	1,647,000	1,495,000	1,364,000

Table 14

VICTORIA METRO POPULATION
(1976 EST. - 216,000)

	A	B	C
1981	241,000	236,000	232,000
1986	269,000	254,000	242,000
1991	299,000	271,000	248,000

Table 15

OTTAWA METRO POPULATION
(1976 EST. - 662,000)

	A	B	C
1981	730,000	725,000	716,000
1986	814,000	788,000	756,000
1991	910,000	855,000	787,000

Table 16

CALGARY METRO POPULATION
(1976 EST. - 446,000)

	A	B	C
1981	580,000	553,000	541,000
1986	696,000	627,000	589,000
1991	827,000	705,000	631,000

Table 17

EDMONTON METRO POPULATION
(1976 EST. - 553,000)

	A	B	C
1981	689,000	638,000	624,000
1986	785,000	707,000	665,000
1991	915,000	780,000	698,000

Table 18

REGINA METRO POPULATION
(1976 EST. - 151,000)

	A	B	C
1981	159,000	159,000	159,000
1986	163,000	160,000	158,000
1991	163,000	157,000	153,000

Table 19

QUEBEC CITY METRO POPULATION
(1976 EST. - 522,000)

	A	B	C
1981	552,000	548,000	541,000
1986	620,000	600,000	574,000
1991	699,000	655,000	601,000

Table 20

HALIFAX METRO POPULATION
(1976 EST. - 236,000)

	A	B	C
1981	241,000	240,000	242,000
1986	251,000	243,000	245,000
1991	261,000	245,000	245,000

Table 21

METRO AREA RANKING

1976	1991

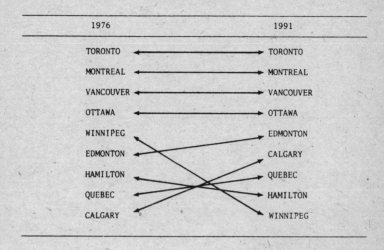

1976	1991
TORONTO	TORONTO
MONTREAL	MONTREAL
VANCOUVER	VANCOUVER
OTTAWA	OTTAWA
WINNIPEG	EDMONTON
EDMONTON	CALGARY
HAMILTON	QUEBEC
QUEBEC	HAMILTON
CALGARY	WINNIPEG

Table 22

MAIN AGGREGATES - STANDARD SCENARIO

	ACTUAL (pre-stagflation)		PROJECTED	
	1964-72	1976-80	1981-85	1986-90
	(average annual percentage change)			
REAL GNP	5.0	4.0-4.5	3.5-4.0	2.0-3.0
OUTPUT PER PERSON EMPLOYED	2.3	2.6	2.3	2.0
CONSUMER EXPENDITURES	4.7	5.3	5.3	5.3
RESIDENTIAL CONSTRUCTION	5.4	3.6	3.7	3.3
PLANT AND EQUIPMENT OUTLAYS	3.7	6.0	5.9	5.8
GOVERNMENT EXPENDITURES ON GOODS AND SERVICES	5.9	4.8	4.7	4.7
EXPORTS	9.2	5.8	5.8	5.8
IMPORTS	8.1	6.0	6.0	6.0
REAL PERSONAL DISPOSABLE INCOME PER CAPITA	3.6	3.9	3.8	3.8
EMPLOYMENT	2.8	2.5	2.2	2.0
LABOUR FORCE	3.1	2.25	1.9	1.8
GNE DEFLATOR	4.0	5.0	3.0-4.0	2.0-3.0

Table 23

ENERGY CAPITAL SPENDING IN RELATION TO TOTAL CAPITAL SPENDING
(Annual averages, Billions 1975 $)

ENERGY	1961-65	1966-70	1971-75	1976-80	1981-85	1986-90
	$	$	$	$	$	$
ELECTRIC POWER	1.20	2.13	3.21	4.34	6.50	7.40
PIPELINES	0.22	0.33	0.42	1.14	3.84	0.60
PETROLEUM						
EXPLORATION AND DEVELOPMENT	0.80	1.00	1.47	2.12	3.10	2.84
REFINING AND MARKETING	0.17	0.35	0.56	0.78	0.82	0.96
OIL SANDS	0.00	0.00	N.A.	0.60	0.82	0.96
COAL	0.02				0.46	0.06
TOTAL ENERGY	2.49	3.90	5.79	9.14	15.02	12.04
NON-ENERGY CAPITAL SPENDING (excluding residential con-struction)	12.58	16.96	20.44	26.34	33.14	41.00
TOTAL	15.07	20.86	26.23	35.48	48.16	53.04
% ENERGY OF TOTAL	17%	19%	22%	26%	31%	23%
AVERAGE COMPOUND GROWTH RATE		6.7%	4.7%	6.2%	6.3%	2.0%

SOURCE: BURNS FRY LTD., JANUARY 1977

Table 24

ACTUAL AND PROJECTED INVESTMENT AS A PERCENT OF GNP

	TOTAL	PERSONAL SAVING	GOVERNMENT $ SAVING	CORPORATE SAVING	FOREIGN SAVING
1951-55	23	8.9	3.8	9.1	1.2
1956-60	25	7.0	2.7	11.3	4.0
1961-65	23	7.1	3.2	10.4	1.5
1966-70	23	7.2	5.0	10.8	0.4
1971-75	23	8.5	4.3	9.0	1.2
1976-80	24	8.7	4.1	8.7	2.4
1981-85	25	9.4	4.6	8.6	2.3
1986-90	25	9.7	4.7	8.6	2.0

Table 25

RELATIVE SHARE OF NET NEW ISSUES

	CORPORATE DEBT %	CORPORATE EQUITY %	ALL GOVERNMENTS %
1956-60	25.5	19.5	54.8
1961-65	25.9	9.5	64.6
1966-70	20.4	12.0	67.6
1971-76	20.5	7.4	72.0
1974	16.3	6.7	87.0
1975	19.8	7.5	72.7

Table 26

PROPORTION OF FINANCING DONE ABROAD

	CORPORATE %	FEDERAL GOVT. %	PROVINCIAL %	MUNICIPAL %	TOTAL %
1956-1960	28.3	-19.2	23.8	34.0	14.7
1961-1965	36.1	+ 5.3	23.4	8.8	19.5
1966-1970	41.9	0.0	33.8	17.7	22.9
1971-1975	11.3	-1.5	34.6	30.7	16.8
1974	10.1	-1.1	39.5	28.9	17.0
1975	15.9	-1.0	49.0	43.6	22.2
1976	45.7	---	60.8	71.2	28.1

Table 27

ACTUAL & PROJECTED LABOUR FORCE PARTICIPATION RATES

		1951	1976	1990
15-19	M	58.6	52.7	54.2
	F	37.8	47.0	53.9
20-24	M	92.4	85.1	81.0
	F	46.9	67.3	79.9
25-34	M	96.4	95.5	95.1
	F	24.4	53.9	70.9
35-44	M	96.7	96.0	96.0
	F	21.8	53.3	71.9
45-54	M	94.5	92.5	91.5
	F	20.4	48.5	64.6
55-64	M	85.7	76.7	71.7
	F	14.5	32.1	42.7
65 +	M	38.6	16.0	3.4
	F	5.1	4.1	3.5

266

Table 28

LABOUR FORCE PROJECTIONS (thousands)
BUSINESS-AS-USUAL SCENARIO

YEAR	15-19	20-24	25-34	35-44	45-54	55-64	65+	TOTAL
				AGE				
1976	1159	1663	2737	1982	1726	1025	185	10477
1981	1128	1793	3275	2432	1837	1133	165	11764
1986	1078	1776	3643	2971	2078	1223	137	12905
1990	1075	1734	3822	3463	2446	1339	100	13979
BREAKDOWN BY SEX								
1981 M	596	981	2032	1514	1161	747	--	--
F	532	812	1243	918	676	386	--	--
1986 M	558	939	2187	1776	1263	774	--	--
F	520	837	1457	1195	815	449	--	--
1990 M	544	883	2218	1995	1430	813	--	--
F	531	851	1604	1468	1016	526	--	--

Table 29

LABOUR FORCE PROJECTIONS (thousands)
ACCELERATED GROWTH SCENARIO

				AGE				
YEAR	15-19	20-24	25-34	35-44	45-54	55-64	65+	TOTAL
1976	1159	1663	2737	1982	1726	1025	185	10477
1981	1133	1810	3302	2440	1839	1134	165	11824
1986	1094	1818	3728	3008	2089	1228	137	13101
1990	1132	1819	3989	3552	2477	1351	101	14419
				BREAKDOWN BY SEX				
1981 M	599	990	2050	1520	1162	748	--	--
F	534	820	1252	920	677	386	--	--
1986 M	566	962	2240	1799	1270	776	--	--
F	528	856	1488	1209	819	452	--	--
1990 M	573	927	2120	2048	1448	819	--	--
F	559	892	1669	1504	1029	532	--	--

Table 30

LABOUR FORCE PROJECTIONS (thousands)
CONSTRAINED GROWTH SCENARIO

				AGE				
YEAR	15-19	20-24	25-34	35-44	45-54	55-64	65+	TOTAL
1976	1159	1663	2737	1982	1726	1025	185	10477
1981	1119	1758	3216	2413	1831	1129	165	11631
1986	1048	1690	3468	2895	2054	1212	136	12503
1990	1000	1586	3503	3286	2384	1316	99	13175
				BREAKDOWN BY SEX				
1981 M	592	961	1993	1502	1158	745	--	--
F	527	767	1223	911	673	384	--	--
1986 M	543	892	2075	1728	1250	769	--	--
F	505	798	1393	1167	804	443	--	--
1990 M	506	806	2023	1887	1394	802	--	--
F	494	780	1498	1399	990	514	--	--

Table 31

INDUSTRIAL GROWTH PATTERNS
STANDARD SCENARIO

	ACTUAL (PRE-STAGFLATION)		PROJECTED	
	1964-72	1976-80	1981-85	1986-90
	(AVERAGE ANNUAL PERCENTAGE CHANGE IN OUTPUT)			
AGRICULTURE	1.6	4.0	3.8	3.8
FORESTRY	1.0	5.0	4.8	4.6
FISHING	-0.3	1.1	1.0	0.9
MINING, OIL, GAS	5.8	5.2	4.7	4.7
MANUFACTURING	4.9	5.2	4.9	5.0
CONSTRUCTION	3.8	5.2	5.2	4.7
UTILITIES	8.4	6.4	6.4	6.3
TRANSPORTATION, STORAGE, COMMUNICATIONS	6.2	5.2	5.2	5.0
TRADE	4.9	5.0	5.0	4.9
FINANCE	5.6	5.3	5.2	5.2
SERVICES	6.0	4.8	4.9	5.0
PUBLIC ADMINISTRATION	3.3	3.9	3.9	3.9

SOURCE: ECONOMIC COUNCIL OF CANADA; HUDSON CANADA PROJECTION

Table 32

UNEMPLOYMENT IN FAMILY UNITS, BY POSITION IN FAMILY, ANNUAL AVERAGES
1961-74*

| | | FAMILY UNIT | | | UNATTACHED INDIVIDUALS | TOTAL UNEMPLOYED |
	HEAD	SINGLE SONS OR DAUGHTERS	OTHER MEMBERS	TOTAL		
	%	%	%	%	%	%
1961	46	34	11	91	9	100
1966	41	37	14	92	8	100
1971	37	37	16	90	10	100
1974	33	38	17	88	12	100

SOURCE: ECONOMIC COUNCIL OF CANADA, WORK AND JOBS, OTTAWA, 1976.

Table 33

UNEMPLOYMENT IN FAMILY UNITS, BY NUMBER EMPLOYED IN FAMILY, ANNUAL AVERAGES
1961-74*

| | | | | NUMBER EMPLOYED IN FAMILY | | |
	TOTAL	ALL MEMBERS UNEMPLOYED	SOME UNEMPLOYED	ONE	TWO	THREE OR MORE
	%	%	%	%	%	%
1961	100	45	55	33	15	7
1966	100	38	62	36	17	8
1971	100	36	64	39	16	8
1974	100	33	67	41	17	9

SOURCE: IBID.

Table 34

LONG-TERM UNEMPLOYMENT RATE,* SELECTED AGE-SEX GROUPS, 1966-74

AGE-SEX GROUP

	14-24 YEARS			25-44 YEARS			45 YEARS AND OVER		
	MALES	FEMALES	TOTAL	MALES	FEMALES	TOTAL	MALES	FEMALES	TOTAL
	%	%	%	%	%	%	%	%	%
1966	1.3	0.8	1.1	0.6	0.5	0.6	1.3	**	1.1
1967	1.5	0.9	1.3	0.8	0.4	0.7	1.4	**	1.1
1968	2.3	1.3	1.9	1.2	0.5	1.0	1.7	0.7	1.4
1969	2.5	1.3	2.0	1.1	0.8	1.0	1.9	0.8	1.6
1970	3.6	1.9	2.8	1.7	1.0	1.5	2.3	1.1	1.9
1971	4.8	2.9	4.0	2.1	1.5	1.9	2.7	1.3	2.3
1972	4.2	2.5	3.5	2.0	1.6	1.9	2.4	1.3	2.1
1973	3.4	2.4	2.9	1.7	1.5	1.6	1.9	**	1.8
1974	3.2	2.1	2.7	1.4	1.2	1.3	1.8	**	1.6

* UNEMPLOYED FOR FOUR MONTHS OR MORE.

** BASED ON SAMPLES TOO SMALL TO BE RELIABLE.

SOURCE: ECONOMIC COUNCIL OF CANADA, OP CIT.

Table 35

RELATIVE GROWTH OF GNP AND RELATIVE ENERGY DEMAND IN THREE SCENARIOS (1975-2000)

		1975	1980	1985	1990	2000
ACCELERATED GROWTH	GNP	1.0 (5.5%) *	1.3070 (5.0%)	1.668 (4.0%)	2.0294 (3.5%)	2.863
	ENERGY DEMAND **	1.0 (4.5%)	1.2462 (3.0%)	1.4447 (2.2%)	1.6108 (1.7%)	1.906
STANDARD (B.A.U.)	GNP	1.0 (4.5%)	1.2462 (4.0%)	1.5162 (3.0%)	1.7577 (2.5%)	2.250
	ENERGY DEMAND	1.0 (4.0%)	1.2167 (3.5%)	1.4451 (2.5%)	1.6350 (2.2%)	2.032
CONSTRAINED GROWTH	GNP	1.0 (4.0%)	1.2167 (2.5%)	1.3766 (2.3%)	1.5424 (2.0%)	1.880
	ENERGY DEMAND	1.0 (3.0%)	1.1593 (1.5%)	1.2489 (1.4%)	1.3388 (1.2%)	1.508

* PARENTHESES SHOW THE AVERAGE GROWTH RATES DURING THE INTERVALS SHOWN.

** THE BASIC 1975 BREAKDOWN OF 7.867 TRILLION BTUs OF ENERGY DEMAND IS GIVEN BY MEMR (IN ENERGY STRATEGY FOR CANADA) AS FOLLOWS:

    OIL   45.7% OR 3,595 TRILLION BTU (ABOUT .62 BILLION BBLS)

    GAS   19.4% OR 1,526 TRILLION BTU (ABOUT 1.5 TRILLION CUBIC FEET)

    COAL   8.8% OR   692 TRILLION BTU (ABOUT 30 MILLION METRIC TONS)

    ELECTRIC 26.1% OR 2,053 TRILLION BTU (BASED ON FOSSIL FUEL EQUIVALENT OF 10,000 BTU/KWH)

NOTE: THE ACCUMULATED ENERGY DEMANDS TO THE YEAR 2000 FOR THESE 3 CASES ARE:

    ACCELERATED GROWTH: 298.5 QUADRILLION BTU

    STANDARD (B.A.U.) :   303.8 QUADRILLION BTU

    CONSTRAINED GROWTH: 254.5 QUADRILLION BTU

Table 36

OIL PROPHECIES AND REALITIES

DATE	U.S. OIL PRODUCTION RATE (BILLION BBLS/YR)	PROPHECY	REALITY
1866	0.005	SYNTHETICS AVAILABLE IF OIL PRODUCTION SHOULD END (U.S. REVENUE COMMISSION)	IN NEXT 82 YEARS THE U.S. PRODUCED 37 BILLION BBLS. WITH NO NEED FOR SYNTHETICS
1885	0.02	LITTLE OR NO CHANCE FOR OIL IN CALIFORNIA (U.S. GEOLOGICAL SURVEY)	8 BILLION BBLS. PRODUCED IN CALIFORNIA SINCE THAT DATE WITH IMPORTANT NEW FINDINGS IN 1948
1891	0.05	LITTLE OR NO CHANCE FOR OIL IN KANSAS OR TEXAS (&.S. GEOLOGICAL SURVEY)	14 BILLION BBLS. PRODUCED IN THESE TWO STATES SINCE 1891
1908	0.18	MAXIMUM FUTURE SUPPLY OF 22.5 BILLION BBLS. (OFFICIALS OF GEOLOGICAL SURVEY)	35 BILLION BBLS. PRODUCED SINCE 1908, WITH 26.8 BILLION RESERVE PROVEN AND AVAILABLE ON JANUARY 1, 1949
1914	0.27	TOTAL FUTURE PRODUCTION ONLY 5.7 BILLION BBLS. (OFFICIAL OF U.S. BUREAU OF MINES)	34 BILLION BBLS. PRODUCED SINCE 1914, OR SIX TIMES THIS PREDICTION
1920	0.45	U.S. NEEDS FOREIGN OIL AND SYNTHETICS: PEAK DOMESTIC PRODUCTION ALMOST REACHED (DIRECTOR OF U.S. GEOLOGICAL SURVEY)	1948 U.S. PRODUCTION IN EXCESS OF U.S. COSUMPTION AND MORE THAN FOUR TIMES 1920 OUTPUT
1931	0.85	MUST IMPORT AS MUCH FOREIGN OIL AS POSSIBLE TO SAVE DOMESTIC SUPPLY (SECRETARY OF THE INTERIOR)	DURING NEXT 8 YEARS IMPORTS WERE DISCOURAGED AND 14 BILLION BBLS. WERE FOUND IN THE U.S.
1939	1.3	U.S. OIL SUPPLIES WILL LAST ONLY 13 YEARS (RADIO BROADCASTS BY INTERIOR DEPARTMENT)	NEW OIL FOUND SINCE 1939 EXCEEDS THE 13 YEARS' SUPPLY KNOWN AT THAT TIME
1947	1.9	SUFFICIENT OIL CANNOT BE FOUND IN UNITED STATES (CHIEF OF PETROLEUM DIVISION, STATE DEPARTMENT)	4.3 BILLION BBLS. FOUND IN 1948, THE LARGEST VOLUME IN HISTORY AND TWICE U.S. CONSUMPTION
1949	2.0	END OF U.S. OIL SUPPLY ALMOST IN SIGHT (SECRETARY OF THE INTERIOR)	PETROLEUM INDUSTRY DEMONSTRATED ABILITY TO INCREASE U.S. PRODUCTION BY MORE THAN A MILLION BBLS. DAILY IN THE NEXT 5 YEARS

SOURCE: PRESIDENTIAL ENERGY PROGRAM, HEARINGS BEFORE THE SUBCOMMITTEE ON ENERGY AND POWER OF THE COMMITTEE ON INTERSTATE AND FOREIGN COMMERCE, HOUSE OF REPRESENTATIVES. FIRST SESSION ON THE IMPLICATIONS OF THE PRESIDENT'S PROPOSALS IN THE ENERGY INDEPENDENCE ACT OF 1975. SERIAL NO. 94-20, P. 643. FEBRUARY 17, 18, 20, and 21, 1975. WASHINGTON, D.C.: U.S. GOVERNMENT PRINTING OFFICE.

Table 37

SOME IMPORTANT MINERALS AND THEIR PRINCIPAL SUBSTITUTES

MATERIAL	PRINCIPAL SUBSTITUTES
ALUMINUM	COPPER, STEEL, WOOD, PLASTICS, TITANIUM
BAUXITE	ALUNITE, ANORTHOSITE, DAWSONITE, NEPHELINE, KAOLITE
CHROMIUM	NICKEL, MOLYBDENUM, VANADIUM
COBALT	NICKEL
COPPER	ALUMINUM, PLASTICS
LEAD	RUBBER, COPPER, PLASTIC, TILE, TITANIUM, ZINC
MOLYBDENUM	TUNGSTEN, VANADIUM
TIN	ALUMINUM, PLASTICS
TUNGSTEN	MOLYBDENUM
ZINC	ALUMINUM, PLASTICS

Table 38

RELATIVE CONSUMPTION OF IMPORTANT
INDUSTRIAL METALS (1968)

CLEARLY INEXHAUSTIBLE	WORLD
IRON	89.93%
ALUMINUM	4.47
SILICON	.71
MAGNESIUM	.09
TITANIUM	.01
SUB TOTAL	95.11%

PROBABLY INEXHAUSTIBLE	
COPPER	1.35
ZINC	.97
MANGANESE	1.76
CHROMIUM	.45
LEAD	.20
NICKEL	.09
TIN	.03
SUB TOTAL	4.85%
TOTAL	99.96%

SOURCE: GOELLER AND WEINBERT (1975) DERIVED THIS DATA
FROM MINERAL FACTS AND PROBLEMS, 1970, U.S.
BUREAU OF MINES, BULLETIN 650. WASHINGTON, D.C.
GOVERNMENT PRINTING OFFICE, 1970.

Table 39

HOW "KNOWN WORLD RESERVES" ALTER

ORE	KNOWN RESERVES IN 1950 (1,000 METRIC TONS)	KNOWN RESERVES IN 1970 (1,000 METRIC TONS)	PERCENTANGE INCREASE
IRON	19,000,000	251,000,000	1,321
MANGANESE	500,000	635,000	27
CHROMITE	100,000	775,000	675
TUNGSTEN*	1,903	1,328	-30
COPPER	100,000	279,000	179
LEAD	40,000	86,000	115
ZINC	70,000	113,000	61
TIN	6,000	6,600	10
BAUXITE	1,400,000	5,300,000	279
POTASH	5,000,000	118,000,000	2,360
PHOSPHATES	26,000,000	1,178,000,000	4,430
OIL	75,000,000	455,000,000	507

*PRESUMABLY, "KNOWN" TUNGSTEN RESERVES ARE DOWN BECAUSE THE MAJOR SOURCE IN 1950 WAS MAINLAND CHINA.

SOURCE: SPECIAL REPORT, CRITICAL IMPORTED MATERIALS, COUNCIL ON INTERNATIONAL ECONOMIC POLICY, EXECUTIVE OFFICE OF THE PRESIDENT, DECEMBER, 1974 (PAGE 14). WASHINGTON, D.C.: U.S. GOVERNMENT PRINTING OFFICE.

Table 40

PRICE OF MINERALS RELATIVE TO AVERAGE COST OF LABOUR

	1900	1920	1940	1950	1960	1970
COPPER	785	226	121	99	82	100
IRON	620	287	144	112	120	100
ZINC	794	400	272	256	126	100
ALUMINUM	3,150	859	287	166	134	100
CRUDE PETROLEUM	1,034	726	198	213	135	100

BASE: 1970 = 100

SOURCE: W.D. NORDHAUS, "RESOURCES AS A CONSTRAINT ON GROWTH,"
AMERICAN ECONOMIC REVIEW, MAY 1974. (THESE ARE U.S.
FIGURES; CANADIAN RELATIONSHIPS ARE ROUGHLY THE SAME.)

Table 41

METAL PRICES
(¢/lb)

YEAR	ALUMINUM		COPPER		LEAD	
	CURRENT PRICES	CONSTANT $ PRICES	CURRENT PRICES	CONSTANT $ PRICES	CURRENT PRICES	CONSTANT $ PRICES
1946	14.0	14.0	13.8	13.8	8.1	8.1
1948	14.7	11.9	22.0	17.8	18.0	14.6
1950	16.7	13.5	21.2	17.2	13.3	10.8
1952	18.4	13.5	24.2	17.8	16.5	12.1
1954	20.2	14.5	29.7	21.3	14.0	10.0
1956	24.0	17.2	41.8	30.0	16.0	11.5
1958	24.8	16.8	25.8	17.4	12.1	8.2
1960	26.0	17.1	32.0	21.1	12.0	7.9
1962	23.9	15.4	30.6	19.8	9.6	6.2
1964	23.7	14.9	32.0	20.2	13.6	8.6
1966	24.5	14.7	36.2	21.8	15.1	9.1
1968	25.6	14.4	41.8	23.5	13.2	7.4
1970	28.7	14.4	57.7	29.0	15.6	7.8
1972	26.4	12.0	50.6	23.0	15.0	6.9
1974 (MAY)	31.5	13.0	130.0	53.5	32.5	13.4
1975 (OCT)	40.0	14.6	56.0	20.5	20.0	7.3

BASE DATE FOR CONSTANT PRICES IS 1946.

SOURCE: METAL STATISTICS (FRANKFURT-ON-MAIN. METALLGESELLSCHAFT
AKTIENGESELLSCHAFT, 1973), FOR CURRENT PRICE DATA THROUGH
1972; THE NEW YORK TIMES FOR 1974 AND 1975 CURRENT PRICE
DATA.

Table 42

SOME COMPARATIVE LAND AND SEA RESOURCES
(TONS)

	LAND [A]	OCEAN NODULES [B]	SEA WATER [C]	EARTH CRUST [D]
ALUMINUM [F]	5.0 BILLION	-	18 BILLION	80,000 TRILLION
CHROMIUM	5.6 BILLION	-	80 MILLION	110 TRILLION
COBALT	20 MILLION	3 BILLION	800 MILLION	25 TRILLION
COPPER	1.1 BILLION	3 BILLION	6 BILLION	63 TRILLION
GOLD	140,000	-	8 MILLION	3.5 BILLION
IRON	≫ 860 BILLION	130 BILLION	18 BILLION	58,000 TRILLION
LEAD	.5 BILLION	1 BILLION	60 MILLION	12 TRILLION
MANGANESE	19 BILLION	160 BILLION	4 BILLION	1,300 TRILLION
MERCURY	1 MILLION	-	60 MILLION	9 BILLION
URANIUM	29 MILLION [E]	-	6 BILLION	180 BILLION

[A] IDENTIFIED, HYPOTHETICAL, SPECULATIVE, AND CONDITIONAL RESOURCES. CALCULATED FROM DATA FOUND IN U.S. MINERAL RESOURCES, 1973.

[B] ASSUMES 1 TRILLION TONS RECOVERABLE ORE. UNCERTAINTIES ARE LARGE. BUT J. MERO ESTIMATES 1.6 TRILLION TONS IN THE PACIFIC OCEAN ALONE. [JOHN L. MERO, "POTENTIAL ECONOMIC VALUE OF OCEAN-FLOOR MANGANESE NODULE DEPOSITS," IN DAVID R. HORN (ED.), A CONFERENCE ON FERROMANGANESE DEPOSITS ON THE OCEAN FLOOR (WASHINGTON, D.C.: THE OFFICE FOR THE INTERNATIONAL DECADE OF OCEAN EXPLORATION, NATIONAL SCIENCE FOUNDATION, JANUARY 1972), P. 191.]

[C] NATIONAL RESEARCH COUNCIL, RESOURCES AND MAN (SAN FRANCISCO: W.H. FREEMAN, 1969).

[D] UPPER LAYER ONLY: 1 MILLION TRILLION TONS--ABOUT 4 PERCENT OF TOTAL. FROM U.S. MINERAL RESOURCES, 1973.

[E] HIGH ESTIMATE OF U.S. RESOURCES AT COSTS UP TO $100/LB.

[F] FROM BAUXITE ONLY. OTHER ALUMINUM-BEARING ORES ARE ESSENTIALLY INEXHAUSTIBLE, BUT MORE COSTLY TO PROCESS.

Table 43

SOME STATISTICS ON NON-FUEL MINERALS

	RELATIVE VALUE OF NON-FUEL MINERAL EXPORTS (1973)	1970 DOMESTIC CONSUMPTION (% OF PRODUCTION)	1970 RESERVES AT 3.5% GROWTH RATE	PROSPECTS FOR NEW RESERVES
COPPER	23%	35.4	28 YEARS	EXCELLENT
NICKEL	16%	3.9	27 YEARS	EXCELLENT
IRON ORE	12%	23.8	50 YEARS	EXCELLENT
ZINC	13%	8.5	21 YEARS	EXCELLENT
ASBESTOS	5%	5.0	95 YEARS	AVERAGE
POTASH	3%	6.0	181 YEARS	EXCELLENT

SOURCE: EMR, TOWARDS A MINERAL POLICY FOR CANADA, 1974.

Table 44

WORLD NICKEL-SULFIDE IDENTIFIED RESOURCES

AREA	TONS OF ORE	Ni (PERCENT)
UNITED STATES:		
CALIFORNIA	100,000	1.5
COLORADO	70,000	0.8
MONTANA (STILLWATER)[1]	150,000,000	0.25
MISSOURI	10,000,000	0.5
NEVADA	30,000	0.3
PENNSYLVANIA (GAP)	800,000	0.7
WASHINGTON	100,000	0.9
MINNESOTA (ELY)[2]	6,500,000,000	0.21
ALASKA, BRADY GLACIER	200,000,000	0.25
YAKOBI ISLAND	20,000,000	0.3
FUNTER BAY	600,000	0.35
MAINE	10,000,000	1.00
TOTAL (0.21 PERCENT Ni AVG.)	6,900,000,000	
CANADA:		
THOMPSON DISTRICT:		
THOMPSON MINE	150,000,000	3.0
MYSTERY LAKE DEPOSIT	200,000,000	0.45
MOAK LAKE DEPOSIT	400,000,000	0.7
OTHERS	250,000,000	1.0
TOTAL (1.0 PERCENT Ni AVG.)	1,000,000,000	
SUDBURY DISTRICT	400,000,000	1.5
OTHER CANADIAN	100,000,000	1.5
OTHER CANADIAN	200,000,000	0.2
SOUTH AFRICA	200,000,000	1.0
NORWAY	2,000,000	1.0
BURMA	25,000,000	0.3
AUSTRALIA	300,000,000	0.6
AUSTRALIA	100,000,000	1.5
U.S.S.R.	100,000,000	0.6

1. ALSO CONTAINS 0.25 PERCENT CU.
2. ALSO CONTAINS 0.64 PERCENT CU.

NOTE: [IDENTIFIED RESOURCES ARE SPECIFIC, IDENTIFIED MINERAL
       DEPOSITS THAT MAY OR MAY NOT BE EVALUATED AS TO EXTENT AND
       GRADE, AND WHOSE CONTAINED MINERALS MAY OR MAY NOT BE
       PROFITABLY RECOVERABLE WITH EXISTING TECHNOLOGY AND
       ECONOMIC CONDITIONS.]

SOURCE: DONALD A. BROBST AND WALDEN P. PRATT, EDS., UNITED STATES
        MINERAL RESOURCES, GEOLOGICAL SURVEY PROFESSIONAL PAPER
        820, U.S. GOVERNMENT PRINTING OFFICE, WASHINGTON, D.C.,
        1973, P. 440.

Table 45.

WORLD NICKEL-LATERITE IDENTIFIED RESOURCES

AREA	TONS OF ORE	Ni (PERCENT)
PHILIPPINE ISLANDS	1,000,000,000	0.8
INDONESIA	500,000,000	0.9
AUSTRALIA	100,000,000	1.2
SOLOMON ISLANDS	100,000,000	1.2
NEW CALEDONIA	500,000,000	1.8
MALAGASY	2,000,000	2.0
CUBA	2,000,000,000	1.0
DOMINICAN REPUBLIC	70,000,000	1.5
GUATEMALA	100,000,000	1.5
VENEZUELA (LOMA HIERRO)	60,000,000	1.6
COLOMBIA (CERRO MATOSO)	40,000,000	2.5
BRAZIL	20,000,000	2.0
PUERTO RICO	100,000,000	0.9
GREECE	2,000,000	1.7
U.S.S.R.	100,000,000	1.5
YUGOSLAVIA	20,000,000	1.0
UNITED STATES:		
NICKEL MOUNTAIN (RIDDLE), OREGON	10,000,000	1.5
NORTHERN CALIFORNIA AND REST OF OREGON	55,000,000	0.75
WASHINGTON (CLE ELUM, BLEWETT)	30,000,000	0.5
NORTH CAROLINA	5,000,000	1.0

NOTE: IDENTIFIED RESOURCES ARE SPECIFIC, IDENTIFIED MINERAL DEPOSITS THAT MAY OR MAY NOT BE EVALUATED AS TO EXTENT AND GRADE, AND WHOSE CONTAINED MINERALS MAY OR MAY NOT BE PROFITABLY RECOVERABLE WITH EXISTING TECHNOLOGY AND ECONOMIC CONDITIONS.

SOURCE: DONALD A. BROBST AND WALDEN P. PRATT, EDS., UNITED STATES MINERAL RESOURCES, GEOLOGICAL SURVEY PROFESSIONAL PAPER 820, U.S. GOVERNMENT PRINTING OFFICE, WASHINGTON, D.C., 1973, P. 441.

Table 46

ATTITUDES ON GOVERNMENT OUTLAYS, 1974

	CANADA	REGIONAL EXTREMES
EXISTING GUARANTEED ANNUAL INCOME:		
STRONGLY APPROVE	52%	QUE. 61%; ONT. 44%
DISAPPROVE	9	PR/ONT. 11-12%; QUE. 4%
UNEMPLOYMENT BENEFITS: FAVOUR		
DECREASE FOR YOUNG WORKERS	39%	ONT. 45%; ATL. 25%
DECREASE FOR WORKING WIVES	44	ONT. 50%; ATL. 25%
IMPROVE CONTROL	26	--
BEST WAY FOR GOV'T TO HELP		
UNEMPLOYED: JOB CREATION	92%	--
--FINANCIAL HELP	4	--
--BOTH	3	--
OLD AGE PENSIONS NOT HIGH ENOUGH	69%	B.C. 81%; ATL./QUE./PR. 63-4%
SHOULD LOWER PENSION ELIGIBILITY		
TO AGE 60	78%	QUE. 85%; PR. 70%
PRO GOV'T ALLOWANCES FOR MOTHERS		
WHO STAY HOME WITH CHILDREN	72%	QUE. 80%; PR. 66%
% OF FAMILY ALLOWANCE RECIPS.		
WHO SAY COULD DO WITHOUT	30%	PR/BC 39-40%; QUE. 17%
FAVOUR GOV'T DAY-CARE CENTRES	60%	QUE. 69%; PR. 49%
FAVOUR FREE DENTAL CARE	54%	QUE. 71%; ONT. 42%
FAVOUR GOV'T CONTROL OF		
HOUSING PRICES	70	ATL. 77%; PR. 55%
RENTS	62	QUE. 73%; PR. 46%
PREFERENCE FOR LOW-INCOME		
HOUSING POLICY		
--CONSTRUCT MORE UNITS	65%	--
--SHELTER ALLOWANCES	25	--
EDUCATION SYSTEM IS "BAD" OR "VERY		
BAD" IN PREPARING PEOPLE FOR		
LABOUR FORCE	42%	B.C. 58%; ATL. 19%
DID NOT HAVE ENOUGH EDUCATION		
ONESELF	61%	QUE. 69%; B.C. 54%

KEY: ATL. = ATLANTIC PROVINCES; QUE. = QUEBEC; ONT. = ONTARIO;
      PR. = PRAIRIE PROVINCES; B.C. = BRITISH COLUMBIA

SOURCE: J. LAFRAMBOISE, A QUESTION OF NEEDS, SURVEY CONDUCTED FOR
         CANADIAN COUNCIL ON SOCIAL DEVELOPMENT IN SUMMER 1974,
         PUBLISHED SEPTEMBER 1975.

Hudson Institute of Canada Inc.

The Hudson Institute of Canada is a non-profit policy research institute. The Institute does not represent any "official" position and is dedicated solely to intellectual quality and to making a valid contribution to our national debate.

The Board of Directors of the Institute is as follows:

Chairman of the Board:
Arnold C. Smith

Members of the Board:
Pierre Dansereau, ecologist
Marie-Josée Drouin, economist, also Executive Director
Roy Faibish, member CRTC
Claude Frenette, businessman
Douglas Fullerton, economist, urban development specialist
Ralph Gillan, businessman
Herman Kahn, founding director, Hudson Institute (U.S.A.)
Angus MacNaughton, businessman
Rudy L. Ruggles, Jr., President, Hudson Institute (U.S.A.)
Jean-Louis Servan-Schreiber, writer, publisher
Michel Vennat, lawyer